Jurists: Profiles in Legal Theory

General Editor:
William Twining

Lon L. Fuller

Robert S. Summers

STANFORD UNIVERSITY PRESS
Stanford, California 1984

Stanford University Press
Stanford, California

Printed in the United States of America
ISBN 0-8047-1210-7
LC 83-42834

Contents

Preface

If this introductory book on the legal theory of Lon L. Fuller were to have a dedication page, it would read as follows: "For Lon L. Fuller of Harvard and H. L. A. Hart of Oxford, who jointly and severally rejuvenated the subject of legal theory in our time." In the English-speaking world, most branches of this subject had come to a standstill by 1940. Through their books and articles, and especially their published exchanges with each other, Fuller and Hart not only advanced the subject, but stimulated the interest of thousands. It was my own special privilege to sit at the feet of both in my student days. A book on Hart has already appeared in this series, ably authored by Neil MacCormick of the University of Edinburgh. It is fitting that one on Fuller follow soon after, and I am pleased to offer it.

The contents of this book may come as a surprise to some, for it is a decidedly sympathetic account, one that diverges from my own early writing on Fuller. In the late 1970's I re-read the whole of his writings and came to two conclusions. Some of us who had earlier studied his works had, for one reason or another, missed a good deal in them. Partly because of this, Fuller had by no means received his just due when he died in 1978. I put myself in print to this effect not long before his death and take consolation in the fact that this evidently pleased him.

Fuller is one of the truly important legal theorists of this century, and I have sought, in this book, to pay him tribute. That task is made the easier in a sense, for an introduction to the work of a leading legal theorist should accentuate the positive anyway. Accordingly, I here provide a sympathetic general account of Fuller's thought, with little by way of criticism. On some topics, I have found it necessary to offer my own reconstruction of his views. Fuller did not always develop his views systematically, and he did not always see how to get the most theoretical mileage out of his insights. It is partly because of this that the full merits of his works are not yet adequately appreciated today in some quarters.

I wish to thank Debra Kearl Minnock of the Cornell Law School secretarial staff for excellent work on the final draft of the manuscript; and

Brent Gordon Summers, Class of 1982, University of Oregon School of Law, Peter J. Grossman and Steven Clymer, Class of 1983, Cornell Law School, and Erik M. Jensen, Class of 1979, Cornell Law School, for various forms of assistance. Professors Alan Gunn, Dale R. Oesterle, and Russell K. Osgood of the Cornell Law School kindly commented on various chapters. I would also like to thank Professor R. Kent Greenawalt of Columbia University for comments on an early draft.

I owe a profound debt of gratitude to Professor Fuller's literary executor, Kenneth I. Winston, professor of philosophy at Wheaton College, for extended commentary on the entire manuscript and for many other kinds of valuable assistance. I also wish to thank Professor David Cavers and Dean Erwin Griswold for reviewing the biographical sketch in Chapter One and making valuable suggestions.

Geoffrey Marshall, Fellow and Tutor of Queens College, Oxford, provided a good deal of helpful commentary during my sabbatical year there in 1981–82. Stanley Paulson of Washington University in St. Louis commented in detail on the entire manuscript, and I am deeply indebted to him for this and for extensive discussions of Fuller in Berlin and Oxford during the spring of 1982. Patrick Atiyah, professor of English law at Oxford University, also provided numerous detailed comments, and I am very grateful indeed to him for this help, and for moral support. Neil MacCormick of the University of Edinburgh kindly read Chapters Two, Three, Four, and Five, and made a number of useful suggestions for which I am most grateful. John Lucas, Fellow and Tutor of Merton College, cast much light, particularly on adjudication, during our walks around The Meadow in 1981–82, and I thank him too.

In the final stages, Rod Macdonald of McGill University read the entire manuscript and made many helpful suggestions. Melvin Eisenberg of the University of California at Berkeley also kindly read three chapters and made many useful comments. I am very grateful to both.

I am also grateful to Erika Chadbourn of the Harvard Law School Library for her generous assistance with the Fuller collection.

Barbara Mnookin of Stanford University Press served as copy editor of the manuscript. I greatly appreciate her generous efforts to help make this a better book.

William Twining, General Editor of the series, read two early drafts of the manuscript and made valuable suggestions. I thank him for this, and for his sustained encouragement in this venture.

I read parts of Chapters Three and Four to the Social Philosophy Discussion Group at All Souls College, Oxford, on February 16, 1982, and I am indebted to the participants (including H. L. A. Hart) for their reactions, some of which have influenced several pages of the final version.

I wish to thank Dean Peter Martin of the Cornell Law School for research support, and Louis E. Martin, head of the Cornell University Libraries, for many forms of assistance, including a faculty study in the central library. I also wish to thank my research assistants, Patricia Ceruzzi and Michael Hingerty, Cornell Law School Class of 1984, for assisting me with the proofs and index.

My wife, Dorothy Kopp Summers, typed the penultimate draft of the manuscript during our sabbatical year in Oxford. For this, as well as all the customary things, and much beyond, words will not do.

Finally, I did most of the work on this book in 1981–82 as a Visiting Research Fellow at Merton College, Oxford University. I wish to record my unbounded appreciation to the Warden and Fellows of Merton College for electing me to the Fellowship and for many kindnesses.

Robert S. Summers
Ithaca, N.Y., May 1983

Works by Lon L. Fuller

Books

The Law in Quest of Itself. Evanston, Ill.: Northwestern University Press, 1940; Boston, Mass.: Beacon Press, 1966.

Basic Contract Law. St. Paul, Minn.: West Publishing Company, 1947; 2d ed., with Robert Braucher, 1964; 3d ed., with Melvin Aron Eisenberg, 1972; 4th ed., with Melvin Aron Eisenberg, 1981.

The Problems of Jurisprudence. Temporary ed., Mineola, N.Y.: Foundation Press, 1949.

The Morality of Law. New Haven, Conn.: Yale University Press, 1964; rev. ed., 1969.

Legal Fictions. Stanford, Calif.: Stanford University Press, 1967.

Anatomy of the Law. Chicago: Britannica Perspectives, 1968; Harmondsworth, Eng.: Penguin Books Ltd., 1968; New York: Praeger, 1968; New York: New American Library, 1969; Westport, Conn.: Greenwood Press, 1976.

The Principles of Social Order (posthumous). Durham, N.C.: Duke University Press, 1981.

Articles

"Adverse Possession—Occupancy of Another's Land Under Mistake as to Location of a Boundary," 7 *Oregon Law Review* 329 (1928).

"Legal Fictions," 25 *Illinois Law Review* 363, 513, 877 (1930–31). (Reprinted as *Legal Fictions*, Stanford University Press, 1967.)

"The Legal Mind," 152 *Atlantic Monthly* 85 (1933).

"What Motives Give Rise to the Historical Legal Fiction?," 2 *Recueil d'études en l'honneur de François Gény* 157 (1934).

"American Legal Realism," 82 *University of Pennsylvania Law Review* 429 (1934).

"Special Nature of the Wage-Earner's Life Insurance Problem" (symposium), 2 *Law and Contemporary Problems* 10 (1935); also "Foreword" 1–2.

"The Reliance Interest in Contract Damages" (with William R. Perdue, Jr.), 46 *Yale Law Journal* 52, 373 (1936–37).

"Williston on Contracts," 18 *North Carolina Law Review* 1 (1939).

"My Philosophy of Law." In *My Philosophy of Law: Credos of Sixteen American Scholars*. Boston: Boston Book Co., 1941.
"Consideration and Form," 41 *Columbia Law Review* 799 (1941).
"Reason and Fiat in Case Law," 59 *Harvard Law Review* 376 (1946).
"Objectives of Legal Education," 2 *Record of New York City Bar Association* 120 (1947).
"What the Law Schools Can Contribute to the Making of Lawyers" (conference), 1 *Journal of Legal Education* 189 (1948).
"The Place and Uses of Jurisprudence in the Law School Curriculum," 1 *Journal of Legal Education* 495 (1948).
"Introduction" to *The Jurisprudence of Interests*, ed. M. Magdalena Schoch, 20th-Century Legal Philosophy Series, vol. 2. Cambridge, Mass.: Harvard University Press, 1948.
"The Case of the Speluncean Explorers," 62 *Harvard Law Review* 616 (1949).
"Pashukanis and Vyshinsky: A Study in the Development of Marxian Legal Theory," 47 *Michigan Law Review* 1157 (1949).
"On Teaching Law," 3 *Stanford Law Review* 616 (1949).
"What Is the Bar Examination Intended to Test?," 20 *Bar Examiner* 111 (1951).
"Legal Education and Admissions to the Bar in Pennsylvania," 25 *Temple Law Quarterly* 249 (1952).
"American Legal Philosophy at Mid-Century," 6 *Journal of Legal Education* 457 (1954).
"Some Reflections on Legal and Economic Freedoms—A Review of Robert L. Hale's 'Freedom Through Law,'" 54 *Columbia Law Review* 70 (1954).
"Role of the Lawyer in Labor Relations," 41 *American Bar Association Journal* 342 (1955).
"The Philosophy of Codes of Ethics," 74 *Electrical Engineering* 916 (1955).
"Freedom—A Suggested Analysis," 68 *Harvard Law Review* 1302 (1955).
[A memorandum on the teaching of law]. In *On the Teaching of Law in the Liberal Arts Curriculum*, ed. Harold J. Berman. Mineola, N.Y.: Foundation Press, 1956.
"Human Purpose and Natural Law," 53 *Journal of Philosophy* 68 (1958).
"A Rejoinder to Professor Nagel," 3 *Natural Law Forum* 83 (1958).
"Positivism and Fidelity to Law—A Reply to Professor Hart," 71 *Harvard Law Review* 630 (1958).
"Professional Responsibility: Report of the Joint Conference" (with John D. Randall), 44 *American Bar Association Journal* 1159, 1216 (1958).
"Governmental Secrecy and the Forms of Social Order." In *Community, Nomos II*, ed. C. J. Friedrich. New York: Liberal Arts Press, 1959.

"Adjudication and the Rule of Law," 54 *American Society for International Law Proceedings* 1 (1960).
"The Academic Lawyer's 'House of Intellect,'" 14 *Journal of Legal Education* 153 (1961).
"The Adversary System." In *Talks on American Law*, ed. Harold J. Berman. New York: Vintage Books, 1961.
"Collective Bargaining and the Arbitrator," *Wisconsin Law Review* 3 (1963).
"Christopher Columbus Langdell." In 13 *Encyclopaedia Britannica* 689 (14th ed. 1963).
"La Philosophie du droit aux États-Unis," *Les Études Philosophiques* 559 (1964).
"Irrigation and Tyranny," 17 *Stanford Law Review* 1021 (1965).
"Jurisprudence." In 13 *Encyclopaedia Britannica* 149 (14th ed. 1965).
"A Reply to Professors Cohen and Dworkin," 10 *Villanova Law Review* 655 (1965).
"Afterword: Science and the Judicial Process," 79 *Harvard Law Review* 1604 (1966). (Reprinted in *Social Science Approaches to the Judicial Process*. New York: Da Capo Press, 1971.)
"Oliver Wendell Holmes, Jr.: The Path of the Law." Edited with commentary in *An American Primer*, ed. Daniel Boorstin. Chicago: University of Chicago Press, 1966.
"Freedom as a Problem of Allocating Choice," 112 *Proceedings of the American Philosophical Society* 101 (1968).
"Some Observations on the Course in Contracts," 20 *Journal of Legal Education* 482 (1968).
"Some Unexplored Social Dimensions of the Law." In *Path of the Law from 1967*, ed. Arthur E. Sutherland. Cambridge, Mass.: Harvard University Press, 1968.
"Two Principles of Human Association." In *Voluntary Associations, Nomos XI*, ed. J. Roland Pennock and John Chapman. New York: Atherton Press, 1969.
"The Law's Precarious Hold on Life," 3 *Georgia Law Review* 530 (1969).
"Human Interaction and the Law," 14 *American Journal of Jurisprudence* 1 (1969).
"Mediation—Its Forms and Functions," 44 *Southern California Law Review* 305 (1971).
"The Justification of Legal Decisions," *Archiv für Rechts- und Sozialphilosophie*, 7 Beiheft Neue Folge (1972).
"Law as an Instrument of Social Control and Law as a Facilitation of Human Interaction," *Archiv für Rechts- und Sozialphilosophie*, 8 Beilage Neue Folge (1974).
"Some Presuppositions Shaping the Concept of 'Socialization.'" In *Law, Justice and the Individual in Society*, ed. June L. Tapp and Felice J. Levine. New York: Holt, Rinehart & Winston, 1977.

"The Forms and Limits of Adjudication," 92 *Harvard Law Review* 353 (1978).

Book reviews

Kaden, Bibliographie der rechtsvergleichenden Literatur (1930), 26 *Illinois Law Review* 481 (1931).

Friedman, Die Bereicherungschaftung im angloamerikanischen Rechtskreis in Vergleichung mit dem deutschen bürgerlichen Recht (1930), 26 *Illinois Law Review* 481 (1931).

Ogden, Bentham's Theory of Fictions (1932), 47 *Harvard Law Review* 367 (1933).

Llewellyn, Präjudizientrecht und Rechtsprechung in Amerika (1933), 82 *University of Pennsylvania Law Review* 551 (1934).

Rheinstein, Die Struktur des vertraglichen Schuldverhältnisses im angloamerikanischen Recht (1932), 35 *Columbia Law Review* 140 (1935).

Hall, Readings in Jurisprudence (1938), 87 *University of Pennsylvania Law Review* 625 (1939).

Pound, The Formative Era of American Law (1938), 34 *Illinois Law Review* 372 (1939).

Bodenheimer, Jurisprudence (1940), 41 *Columbia Law Review* 965 (1941).

Jones, Historical Introduction to the Theory of Law (1940), 55 *Harvard Law Review* 160 (1941).

Adler, A Dialectic of Morals: Toward the Foundations of Political Philosophy (1941), 9 *University of Chicago Law Review* 759 (1942).

Buckland, Some Reflections on Jurisprudence (1945), 59 *Harvard Law Review* 826 (1946).

Paton, A Textbook of Jurisprudence (1946), 61 *Harvard Law Review* 383 (1948).

Brown, Lawyers, Law Schools and the Public Service (1948), 62 *Harvard Law Review* 155 (1948).

Reuschlein, Jurisprudence—Its American Prophets (1951), 12 *Louisiana Law Review* 531 (1952).

Viehweg, Topik und Jurisprudenz (2d ed., 1963), 10 *Natural Law Forum* 236 (1965).

Schwartz and Skolnick, eds., Society and the Legal Order (1970), 85 *Harvard Law Review* 523 (1971).

Translation

H. Mankewicz, "German Law of Alimony Before and Under National Socialism," 6 *Law and Contemporary Problems* 301 (1939).

1

Introduction

Lon Luvois Fuller was one of the four most important American legal theorists of the last hundred years. Of the others, Oliver Wendell Holmes Jr., Roscoe Pound, and Karl N. Llewellyn, only Llewellyn was truly a contemporary of Fuller's, and he was a decade older. Books on the others have already appeared, but this is the first one on Fuller (in English). It is offered as a sympathetic general introduction, not as a definitive assessment. (It is too early to attempt such an assessment anyway.)

Between 1926 and 1939 Fuller was a professor of law at the universities of Oregon and Illinois, and at Duke University. From 1939 until 1972, when he retired, he was a professor of law at Harvard Law School. In 1948 he succeeded to Pound's chair at that institution: the Carter Professorship of General Jurisprudence.

The importance of Fuller

Fuller addressed the moral facets of law and the role of value and reason in law. He, more than any thinker before him, stressed law's essential purposiveness and the necessary "direction-giving quality" of the purposes of specific forms of law. He showed that notions of value—of what "ought to be"—figure in the very existence of rules and other legal precepts, and that law therefore must be value-laden. He demonstrated that it is impossible to draw sharp lines between law and morals. He also originated the now well-known view that there can be no general "master test" by which judges can determine whether any given rule is a valid law of the system. Certainly it is far too simple to say that valid law is whatever is laid down by officials. The validity of law depends on the quality of its content, not just the authoritativeness of its source. Criteria of content cannot be captured in a master test.

In his time Fuller was the leading standard-bearer of secular "natural law" theory in the English-speaking world. His stress on reason in law, on its purposes, on its content rather than just its sources, and on the internal morality of certain legal processes qualified him as a robust yet distinctive participant in the secular natural law tradition.

Fuller also developed an enlarged and original conception of law, one that embraced legal processes, including customary interaction, contractual ordering, mediation, adjudication, legislation, and managerial direction. He is the first major theorist to make the notion of "a legal process" a more fundamental unit of jurisprudential analysis than either the notion of "a legal rule" or the notion of "the legal system." He explored the "internal demands" of various legal processes more fully than any predecessor, and demonstrated that much of our law emerges from essentially private processes of interaction without the intervention of officials. Fuller's writings on legal processes, together with his work on the procedural aspects of the rule of law, qualify him as the greatest proceduralist in the history of legal theory.

We may also characterize Fuller as one of the leading "means-end" theorists in modern social thought. In distinctive ways, he combined an emphasis on law's processes and modes of implementation with an emphasis on its internal and external ends. And he developed an important new body of ideas about the relations and interactions between the law's means and ends.

Fuller wrote with much insight on what legal educators call legal method, a loose amalgam of topics that includes statutory interpretation and the theory of precedent. That prize of the American law-school curriculum, the first-year course in contracts, fell to Fuller early in his career. Although he used the course largely to teach legal method, he made major contributions to the substance of contract law before he was forty years old.

Fuller was a keen critic as well, a role he took with special seriousness. His three main targets were (1) British and European legal positivism, the dominant legal theory in England and on the Continent during most of this century, (2) formalistic legal method, a general approach mainly to the interpretation and application of law, which was influential in the United States in the early decades of this century, but which does not qualify as a general theory of law, and (3) what I call pragmatic instrumentalism, a synthesis of pragmatism, sociological jurisprudence, and certain tenets of legal realism that became the dominant legal theory in the United States during the middle decades of this century.

Fuller is also important today for the continuing influence of his thought, a matter to which I will return at the conclusion of the biographical survey that follows. This survey is based largely on a study I made of the Fuller Papers in the Harvard Law School Library.[1] Even this brief and necessarily highly selective account of Fuller's "life and times" casts a good deal of light on his thought, the full illumination of which will not be evident until one reads through later chapters. In the survey, I will introduce and date all of Fuller's major intellectual concerns. The survey follows the chronology of Fuller's life and is rather more "life" than "times." A systematic study in which events in Fuller's life and his own evolving views are related to the full social context, including the intellectual climate of twentieth-century America, is beyond the scope of an introductory book.

Early life and first academic post

Lon Luvois Fuller was born on June 15, 1902, in Hereford, Texas, into a family of modest means. His father, Francis Bartow Fuller, was a rancher and also a bank employee; his mother, Mary Salome Moore Fuller, pursued literary interests that extended to the French novel. But Fuller can more properly be called a Californian, for in 1906, when he was still a toddler, the family moved to the Imperial Valley, in the southern part of the state, where his father eventually became president of the El Centro National Bank.

Mrs. Fuller died soon after the move to California, and the young Fuller was brought up by his father and stepmother. He attended the University of California at Berkeley in 1919–20, then transferred to Stanford University, where he majored in economics. After his graduation in 1924, he stayed at Stanford to earn a Doctor of Jurisprudence degree in 1926. His father had encouraged him to study law and become a practicing lawyer, but though Fuller fell in love with the law and finished first in his class, he disappointed his father, and immediately sought an academic career.

In the year of his graduation from law school, Fuller married Florence Gail Thompson, also a Stanford graduate (A.B. 1926). She was to be wife, mother of his two children,[2] and intellectual companion for many years. (After her death in 1960 following several years of hospitalization, he was married a second time, to Marjorie D. Chapple.)

Only a few months out of law school, Fuller began his academic career at the age of twenty-four at the University of Oregon School of Law in Eugene. (He seems to have been one of the first of several well-known legal academics who spent their early years at that institution: Dean Bernard Gavit of Indiana University; Vernon X. Miller of Catholic University, a onetime president of the Association of American Law Schools; Fowler Harper of Yale; Sam Bass Warner of Harvard; Senator Wayne L. Morse, who was dean of the law school; and Justices Kenneth J. O'Connell and Hans A. Linde of the Oregon Supreme Court.) Fuller's earliest teaching assignments were partly in the property field. He authored his first published work as an Oregon faculty member, a brief comment on the law of adverse possession.[3]

The Illinois and Duke years

From Oregon Fuller moved first to the University of Illinois, where he taught from 1928 to 1931, and then to Duke University, where he remained until 1939. Early in this period, he had attracted widespread attention with the publication, in 1930–31, of three articles on legal fictions in the *Illinois Law Review*.[4] The legal community was curious. Who was this twenty-eight-year-old man who had read so widely in philosophy and linguistics, and who was so conversant with legal literature in French and German? Fuller received complimentary letters about the articles from both Justice Louis D. Brandeis and Justice Oliver Wendell Holmes Jr. (through Holmes's secretary).

At the time Fuller began to make a name for himself, a new general theory of law and its use was revolutionizing American legal thought. This theory, pragmatic instrumentalism, was resolutely anti-formalist; it conceived law as essentially an instrument made by man to serve practical ends, rather than as a "deduction from axioms" or a "brooding omnipresence in the sky." Pre-existing legal concepts do not dictate judicial decisions as a matter of logical necessity, contrary to what many formalists had assumed. Moreover, judges (as well as legislators) are free to make law and in fact often do so.[5] Oliver Wendell Holmes Jr., Roscoe Pound, John Dewey, and John Chipman Gray were the leading progenitors of this new instrumentalist approach to law and legal decision-making, but in the 1930's it was pushed most vigorously by the so-called realists, led by Karl N. Llewellyn, Joseph Walter Bingham, Jerome Frank, and Walter Wheeler Cook.

Still, there were some who stood fast against the instrumentalist revolution. A good many legal educators viewed the Harvard Law School (despite the presence of Roscoe Pound, Felix Frankfurter, and Thomas Reed Powell) as the citadel of formalistic legal thinking. Historically, there was much to this charge, for such influential members of the faculty as Dean Christopher Columbus Langdell, Samuel Williston, and Joseph Henry Beale had long and consistently taught that judges extract decisions from the "logic" of pre-existing legal concepts and rarely make any law themselves. The Yale and Columbia law schools, on the other hand, were considered centers of anti-formalism.

The controversey over formalism dominated American legal theory well into the 1930's.[6] There is no question where Fuller stood: he was on the side of the instrumentalists. However, though he was as much an anti-formalist as most realists, he did not belong to the realist wing of American pragmatic instrumentalism. Fuller himself saw his own legal method as closer to that of the French theorist Robert Pothier than to that of Llewellyn or Cook.[7] He repudiated the realist views that the law is to be found in the behavioral patterns of judges, and that legal theory may be reduced to an empirical science. His struggle against scientism in law became a lifelong affair. Fuller also rejected such extreme positions of certain realists as their disregard of the reasons judges actually give, their conceptual nihilism, and their moral skepticism. While on the Duke faculty he wrote an impressive essay critical of certain realists, for which he received the Phillips Prize of the American Philosophical Society in 1935.[8]

This work was followed a few years later by his monumental contribution to the law of contracts, an essay in the *Yale Law Journal* entitled "The Reliance Interest in Contract Damages," co-authored with William R. Perdue, a Duke Law School student.[9] Fuller was only thirty-five when the article appeared, and his renown as a legal theorist stems partly from it.

In 1938 Fuller spent six months in Europe, mainly in Paris, studying legal theory and the comparative law of contracts. Before leaving, he wrote to Roscoe Pound, then the foremost legal theorist in the United States, requesting introductions to European scholars, including the great Austrian jurist Hans Kelsen. Pound was glad to accommodate a colleague he regarded as "the coming man in jurisprudence in this country."[10]

By this time (according to his friend David Cavers) Fuller had become somewhat skeptical of the increasing governmental intervention in American life associated with President Franklin D. Roosevelt's New Deal policies. He probably did not take an unqualifiedly positive view of the heavy involvement of certain Duke colleagues in various New Deal programs. He was, however, a member of the Democratic Party, and stayed in the party despite his growing disenchantment with the administration.

The Harvard appointment and 'The Law in Quest of Itself'

During the academic year 1939–40 Fuller was a visiting professor of law at Harvard. His office was next to that of Samuel Williston, then age seventy-nine. Williston was indisputably the *doyen* of American contracts scholars. He had edited a leading contracts casebook, had served as the Chief Reporter of the American Law Institute's Restatement of Contracts, was author of the definitive treatise on the common law of contract, and had drafted the Uniform Sales Act.[11] Fuller, who had published a critical review of Williston's contracts treatise earlier that year, was pleased to find the old professor "most cordial . . . in spite of my use of Corbin's book and my review of his."[12] Before the year was out, Fuller accepted a permanent appointment at Harvard, his home for the next thirty-odd years.

Fuller had little difficulty in deciding to leave Duke. He seems to have been much taken with Harvard, and with virtually all aspects of his reception there. A few days before he accepted the appointment, he wrote to a colleague at Duke:

> Through curiosity the other day I looked through the seven copies of volume 46 [of the *Yale Law Journal*]. Imagine my surprise and pleasure to discover that "The Reliance Interest in Contract Damages" showed signs in each of

> these volumes of having been read a good many times. Whatever the librarian might say about it, the thumb prints, marks, interlineations, and tears on those sheets looked good to me. I may be revealing a rather naive egotism in referring to a trifling matter of this sort, but after all, one writes for the purpose of being read, and an attentive audience of 250 bright young men is not something to be sneezed at.[13]

Not least of the attractions Harvard held for Fuller was the thought that he might be able to make a truly distinctive contribution. For one thing, he found that formalism was by no means dead at Harvard, even as late as 1940. He wrote to another Duke colleague: "I have never taught in any school where I was more free from the fear that I might lead the students too far down the paths of realism and juristic nihilism. There is not much on the other end of the scales here, and I can throw my own little counters on my end and listen to them ring with unadulterated joy."[14] A month later he wrote to Karl Llewellyn in a similar vein: it seemed to him he had "a role here in serving as a sort of counterpoise to the excessively legalistic and conceptualistic approach of some of my colleagues."[15]

The spring of 1940 saw another important milestone in Fuller's life. Before his tour as a visiting professor, he had agreed to deliver the prestigious Rosenthal Lectures at Northwestern University. He worked hard on this project during the fall and winter of his visiting year, gratefully acknowledging to his friend David Cavers at Duke that his Harvard colleague (and future close friend) Henry M. Hart had been most helpful in this effort.[16] In these lectures, entitled "The Law in Quest of Itself" (and published under that title the same year), Fuller attacked the positivistic views of Holmes, Gray, various realists, and certain European predecessors and contemporaries, including Hans Kelsen, for holding (as it seemed to him) that law is merely something laid down or acted upon by officials, a "mere purposeless datum" essentially devoid of all notions of what ought to be.[17] Many of his listeners were probably thunderstruck when he argued that, on the contrary, law consists not merely of what is, but also of what ought to be, and that values figure no less in the reality of rules than their derivation from authoritative sources. At the same time, he showed that law cannot be sharply distinguished from non-law.

To Fuller's startled amazement, *The Law in Quest of Itself* was reviewed in numerous periodicals. He later wrote to Llewellyn that before the lectures his work was "neither cited nor discussed," but after them, he was "widely praised and condemned." He guessed that "if one wants to be heard above the tumult one must . . . shout a little."[18] But he had shown no desire to be heard above the tumult in an earlier letter to Llewellyn, written right after the Rosenthal Lectures: "I plan from now on to devote myself chiefly to contracts. My book represents a kind of farewell to jurisprudence."[19] He could not have been more wrong.

The war and early postwar years

Well before Pearl Harbor, Fuller was a vigorous advocate of U.S. intervention in the war in Europe. He was an early member of the American Defense League–Harvard Group; and in August 1940 he wrote Charles A. Lindbergh a long letter, urging him to abandon his widely published advocacy of the German cause. Highly sympathetic to the plight of European intellectuals who were fleeing from the Nazis, he undertook to help several find jobs, including Edgar Bodenheimer and the famous Hans Kelsen himself. Much of the writing Fuller was later to do on the ideal of the rule of law was stimulated by the Nazi example.

As the United States began to prepare for war, Harvard Law School scaled down its operations, and in April 1942 Fuller joined the Boston firm of Ropes and Gray, working largely in the labor relations field. During this period, his first extended experience in law practice, he negotiated collective bargaining agreements, participated in arbitrations, appeared before various boards and commissions, and argued a case before the War Labor Board. He also continued to teach one course (contracts) at Harvard two days a week. This period of active law practice appears to have been an extraordinarily stimulating one for Fuller. His interest in developing a general theory dealing with the nature, functions, and limits of various processes of socio-legal ordering—contract, mediation, legislation, adjudication, managerial direction, and so forth—arose mainly out of his experiences at Ropes and Gray. These experiences also significantly shaped the influential thinking and writing about legal education he did just after the war.

During these years, Fuller published a landmark piece on the doctrine of consideration and the rationales that inform it.[20] Written in 1941, this was his second—and as it turned out—last major article on contract law. Another outstanding article, "Reason and Fiat in Case Law," appeared in 1946, the outgrowth of the Cardozo Lecture he gave before the Association of the Bar of the City of New York in October 1942.[21]

In 1945 Fuller resumed his post at Harvard. Yet he did not make a clean break with the world of law practice. Shortly after he left Ropes and Gray, he embarked on what was to be a twenty-year career in the labor relations field, mainly as a private arbitrator of grievances under collective bargaining agreements. From all appearances, he spent some considerable time in this role, which probably helps explain why he did not publish more than he did.[22] For example, he served for a time as permanent arbitrator of grievances arising in the drafting department of Bethlehem Steel (shipbuilding division), and for several years was an arbitrator of grievances involving the laboratory technicians at the Massachusetts Institute of Technology. For many of these years, he was also an arbitrator by appointment of the American Arbitration Association.

These experiences, like those at Ropes and Gray, appear to have enriched Fuller's teaching in various ways. He drew on them in his jurisprudence class to compare and contrast such legal processes as negotiation, adjudication, and mediation. In his contracts course he often stressed that a judge (or lawyer) is not well qualified to interpret contracts unless he has participated in drafting them, a truth that may apply with special force to labor agreements. He also brought to his contracts classroom a keen sense of realism about how negotiated contracts come into being. In 1947 he published a casebook in contracts that included problems on drafting and planning. This book was, and (in later editions) still is, widely used.

Fuller's experiences in practice and as an arbitrator also appear to have influenced his ideas about the ends and means of legal education. At Ropes and Gray, he was called on to plan, to draft, and to negotiate. Later, as an arbitrator, he was called on to adjudicate and even to mediate. In his writings on legal education, he came to stress the need for reforms that would provide education in such important activities. In his view, law teachers dwelled far too much on the appellate case.

The war years at Ropes and Gray and the experiences as an arbitrator influenced Fuller in still another way. They appear to have stimulated what was to become his deepest and most continuous research interest for the rest of his life, namely "eunomics"—the study of basic processes of social ordering and their corresponding forms of law. It is largely his pursuit of this interest that justifies the claim that he was this country's first great proceduralist. (His later interest in the requirements of the rule of law is also broadly procedural.) His first extended work along these lines appeared as the final chapter of his *Problems of Jurisprudence*, published in a temporary (but, as it turned out, final) edition in 1949. When Fuller coined the term eunomics in 1954 to refer to his new "science of social ordering," he entered a vigorous plea to other scholars to join in an extended study of the nature, functions, and limits of legal processes.

In this period Fuller also published what many consider a literary classic: "The Case of the Speluncean Explorers," a not-so-hypothetical case in which a court is called on to decide what to do about some starving explorers trapped in a cave who devoured one of their number and were thereafter charged with murder.[23] Fuller designed the various opinions of the judges to represent different approaches to the law. He received admiring letters from many people, including the mystery writer Erle Stanley Gardner and the novelist James Gould Cozzens.

In the early 1950's Fuller began offering a seminar on the role of law in a planned economy, in addition to his regular courses in contracts and jurisprudence. He continued this seminar for many years, and some of his thought on "managerial direction" as a distinctive process of social order originated here.

For all this activity, it is interesting to note that Fuller found the time to pursue several hobbies. He much enjoyed music, especially opera. He frequently read for pleasure, particularly in German. At various times he enjoyed the art of cooking (primarily Chinese). Carpentry, gardening, and photography were also interests.

The "polemical" years

Lon Fuller seems always to have had a penchant for polemics. But in the mid to late 1950's he engaged in debate with two philosophers, Columbia's Ernest Nagel and Oxford's H. L. A. Hart, with rather more than the usual intensity. Only his "Reply to Critics," published in 1969, again rose to this level.[24]

Two theoretical interests occupied Fuller most during this period: the relations between law and morals and the various basic processes of social ordering. His polemics, however, were confined to the first. An exchange of letters with the Harvard philosopher W. V. Quine in 1953 turned out to be a kind of preliminary to the debate with Nagel. Fuller wrote a long letter to Quine in which he condemned the empiricists' traditional rejection of "purpose" even as a "principle of interpretation." To this Quine replied that scientists had indeed unduly neglected purpose as a category for "systematizing experience," but that he could not "agree that recognition of purpose militates against a distinction between the descriptive and the normative. Organizations as purposive would still invite description even in point of purpose; there would remain as much of a distinction as ever between what one's purposes descriptively are and what they normatively should be."[25]

Fuller's debate with Nagel, published in the *Journal of Philosophy* in 1956 and the *Natural Law Forum* in 1958–59, centered on the nature of what legal theorists often call the "is-ought" distinction in law.[26] Fuller returned to the argument of the 1940 Rosenthal Lectures, insisting that forms of law cannot be understood without reference to the purposes of those who brought them into being—notions of what "ought to be"—and that all forms of law are in consequence necessarily value-laden.

The other man with whom Fuller tangled in this period, H. L. A. Hart, was a professor of jurisprudence at Oxford University, a lawyer and also, unlike the self-taught Fuller, a fully trained philosopher. In 1956–57 Hart served as a visiting professor in both the law school and the philosophy department at Harvard, where he gave the Holmes Lecture in the fall of 1956. In that famous lecture, "Positivism and the Separation of Law and Morals" (which Fuller, other faculty, and many students including myself attended), Hart set out important criticisms of Fuller's views. The editors of the *Harvard Law Review* undertook to publish Hart's paper and invited Fuller to prepare a response. This he did with zeal; as he wrote to a colleague at the time, he viewed his upcoming published debate with Hart as a "kind of showdown on legal positivism."[27] The result was perhaps the most interesting and illuminating exchange of views on basic issues of legal theory to appear in English in this century. Shortly after the debate was published,[28] Fuller received a letter from the distinguished political theorist Leo Strauss of the University of Chicago congratulating him on his reply: "Your argument is superior to his."[29]

It is worth remarking that the extraordinary system of student-edited legal periodicals (recently termed "incredible" by the economist Paul Samuelson) nearly deprived us all of the Hart-Fuller debate. The student editors of the *Harvard Law Review* substantially rewrote Hart's article, and on seeing the revised copy, he declined to have it published in that form. He eventually got his way, and it was his original text that was published. Fuller wrote to Hart at the time: "I am sorry for what they did though I have to confess that this sort of thing comes close to standard practice with articles written by American authors. Being near at hand I could save my baby from mayhem. Had I dreamed they would take such liberties with your text, I would have stood over them."[30]

During the middle and late 1950's Fuller worked on drafts of his most important single essay dealing with the processes of social ordering—"The Forms and Limits of Adjudication." He presented parts of the essay at a meeting of Harvard faculty and at a Jurisprudence Roundtable during the annual meeting of the Association of American Law Schools in 1957. He also distributed it to his classes in jurisprudence; and mimeographed copies circulated widely among American law professors. But he apparently thought it needed further polishing, and this work was not published in his lifetime; the *Harvard Law Review* carried it as part of a memorial issue devoted to him.[31]

In 1954 Fuller gave a lecture at the University of Chicago called "Freedom—A Suggested Analysis," which was published in the *Harvard Law Review*.[32] He also gave the Edward Douglas White Lectures at Louisiana State University in 1958, again on freedom. Although he thought a great deal about problems of freedom throughout his life, he never found time to write his projected book on the subject.[33]

In the late 1950's Fuller and another Harvard professor, Carl J. Friedrich of the government department, founded the American Society of Political and Legal Philosophy. Fuller took considerable pride in this organization, which today meets annually and publishes a well-known yearbook, *Nomos*. Fuller himself contributed two essays to the yearbook (one in 1959 and one in 1969).

The 1960's, retirement, and last years

Between 1960 and the early 1970's Fuller published several pieces in the field of his primary interest, the processes of legal ordering. One was on collective bargaining and the arbitrator, one mainly on customary law, one on mediation, and one on managerial direction. In addition, he devoted parts of two books to this subject.[34] However, he never completed his projected treatise. In part, this appears to have been a matter of his reluctance to work systematically on a project of such proportions. But it is also true that he was diverted from time to time, and not merely by his extensive activities as a private arbitrator (which lasted well into this period). He had planned to write his treatise during his sabbatical in 1960, remaining in Cambridge for that purpose. Instead, Fuller, a lifelong Democrat, became heavily involved in the presidential campaign of the Republican candidate, Richard M. Nixon, one of his students at Duke. By September, as he told E. V. Rostow of Yale, he was "up to [his] ears" in the campaign.[35] Immediately after Nixon's defeat by the narrowest of margins, he wrote to Fuller: "I would not want this day to pass without taking the opportunity to tell you again how deeply gratified I am for all that you did for our cause."[36]

Fuller's service as chairman of the Scholars for Nixon Committee was not an isolated excursion away from the study. He may even have been a bit more inclined to organizational life than most law-school academics. During his career he joined and was active in many groups. He was a member of the presidium of the International Association for Philosophy of Law and Social Philosophy. He was president of the American Society of Political and Legal Philosophy, the body he co-founded, and served on the Executive Committee of the Association of American Law Schools. He was an active member of the association's Editorial Committee on publication of translations of European scholarship. He was a member of the Board of Editors of the *American Journal of Jurisprudence* (originally the *Natural Law Forum*). For many years he served as Directing Editor of the Board of Editors of The Foundation Press, Inc. He also served for lengthy periods as a consultant to various organizations, including the Rockefeller Foundation. Inside Harvard Law School, he held numerous assignments, including the chairmanship of the graduate program for a lengthy period.

In the spring of 1961 Fuller visited Warsaw, Krakow, and Poznan, and later circulated a rather elaborate "unsolicited report" on this trip, in which he set forth facts, impressions, and reflections.[37] One question that interested him was whether Poland could "be brought over to our side (i.e. democracy)." For the time being, at least, he was pessimistic—"not for twenty years or more," he thought.

In 1963 Fuller gave the well-known Storrs Lectures at Yale, which issued in a book entitled *The Morality of Law*, published in 1964. Though rich with insight into the requirements of the rule of law, the book was not well argued in some of its essentials and was frequently misinterpreted. As a result, it drew a number of unsympathetic reviews. This seems to have pained Fuller; indeed, from his correspondence it is safe to say he felt somewhat embattled. John Jay Osborne (author of *The Paper Chase* and a student of Fuller's) records that he met him one day in this period in front of Langdell Hall: "I asked him what he was working on—he was holding a sheaf of papers. 'They've attacked my book, *The Morality of Law*,' he said. 'Another attack?' I said, as angry at the thought as he was. 'Another,' he answered, 'and it shall not go unnoticed.' We shook hands. He strode fiercely up the steps of Langdell."[38]

Fuller again took a research leave during the 1964–65 academic year, and devoted much of it to reading widely in sociology, anthropology, and social psychology.

In the mid-1960's the editor of the *Encyclopaedia Britannica* induced him to write a book on law, supposedly for lay readers. The result was *Anatomy of the Law*, a truly superb effort that appeared in 1968 and was immediately well received. The book includes much of great interest to legal theorists. Perhaps most important is the distinction between "made law" (statutes and the like) and "implicit law" (customary law and the like). Fuller worked this distinction out with remarkable insight, illuminatingly treating "implicit elements in made law" and "made elements in implicit law."[39]

In 1967 Fuller spent some weeks visiting Oxford University. He was well known by reputation there, mainly as H. L. A. Hart's intellectual adversary. His views had in fact become a part of the university's regular examination in jurisprudence. One observer (Patrick Atiyah) reports that Fuller's legal theory had even been well received in some Oxford quarters as a refreshing alternative to the traditional positivism. In any event, Fuller was warmly received by Hart during his visit and seems to have enjoyed his stay immensely.

In 1968 Fuller's former student Richard M. Nixon was elected President. This time Fuller had not been active in the campaign. Nor did he go off to Washington to join the administration, as so many of his colleagues had done when John F. Kennedy took office. Part of the explanation for his decision to remain aloof from the campaign is revealed in a letter he had written to Nixon in 1965:

> I suppose my decision to keep away from politics from now on out is chiefly the result of my observations of colleagues who went to Washington with the Kennedy administration. It is no reflection on them to say that most of them have compromised themselves for future works of scholarship simply because they have been a part of the events they might have occasion later to appraise.[40]

In 1969 Fuller brought out a revised edition of *The Morality of Law*, which included, as a new fifth chapter, his "Reply to Critics." Much of this chapter is devoted to the views of four critics: H. L. A. Hart, Ronald M. Dworkin, Marshall Cohen, and myself. But the chapter also includes valuable insights into "managerial direction" and customary law as distinct processes for ordering human relations. By this time Fuller's interests had turned more broadly to the sociology of law, and he taught several seminars on branches of this subject, two with the Harvard sociologist Talcott Parsons.

Fuller's contracts casebook continued to be widely used in American law schools during these years. He had asked his colleague Robert Braucher to co-author the second edition, published in 1964. When Braucher resigned from Harvard to become a Massachusetts supreme court justice, Fuller invited Melvin A. Eisenberg of the University of California at Berkeley to serve as co-author of the third edition. Eisenberg accepted and a most fruitful collaboration ensued, with Fuller spending the summer session of 1971 at Berkeley, where the two worked on the book together. That edition was published in 1972 and included (in Chapter Two) his last general account of basic social ordering processes.

Fuller retired from Harvard on July 1, 1972, at the age of seventy. Still active, he spent much of that month accompanying, at President Nixon's request, a delegation to the USSR. It was this delegation that in fact worked out the first major sale of American wheat to the Soviets, but Fuller seems to have played no role in this. In the six years he was to live beyond retirement, Fuller did not write his projected book on legal processes. His interests seem to have shifted still further toward the sociology of law and legal anthropology. (It fell to his literary executor, Kenneth I. Winston, to bring most of Fuller's major published writings and some unpublished papers on processes together in a volume called *The Principles of Social Order*, published only in 1981.) He continued to read widely, and was especially concerned to learn more about structural functionalism, symbolic interactionalism, customary law, and the "tacit dimension" in social life generally. One of his last published pieces had to do with the concept of socialization.[41]

Those who met Fuller for the first time in his last few years met a man in ill health who had failed badly. He died on April 8, 1978. He left among his papers plans and parts of manuscripts for several books, including the one on the principles of social order, one on freedom, and one on democracy. He also left outlines and notes for articles on many other topics, including Oliver Wendell Holmes Jr., legal rights, traditions of justice among Western peoples, purpose and intent in contract law, the clarification of legal terms, legal method, and social religion.

Many today acknowledge that Fuller was a man of remarkably creative intellect. Those who believe (and many profess to do so) that creativity is somehow incompatible with wide reading, particularly in one's field, will have to explain away Fuller's example. When his literary executor examined his private library, he found that Fuller had read and made notes on hundreds of books, many on the law, many not. Indeed, it seems quite clear that throughout his active academic career he regularly devoted large parts of every working week to reading, far and near.

Fuller's continuing influence

Fuller's influence through former colleagues and former students continues to be extensive. One set of teaching materials on legal processes used at Harvard and other American law schools for more than twenty years now draws significantly on Fuller.[42] Its authors, Henry M. Hart and Albert M. Sacks, were Fuller's colleagues at Harvard, and Hart was a particularly close friend. Another widely used set of teaching materials, his own contracts casebook, lives on through the continuing editorship of a former student, Professor Melvin A. Eisenberg of Berkeley. Several other contracts casebooks, in the United States and in Canada, are modeled importantly on Fuller's.

Fuller is also having increasing influence directly through his four books and his other writings on legal theory. To cite only a single significant example, one of today's leading Anglo-American legal theorists is Ronald M. Dworkin, an American who occupies the chair of jurisprudence at Oxford University. Dworkin is himself a stimulating, original, and often brilliant thinker.[43] Yet he would acknowledge that some of his root ideas are to be found in Fuller, particularly in *The Law in Quest of Itself* and in the 1958 essay "Positivism and Fidelity to Law—A Reply to Professor Hart." Dworkin's celebrated view that there can be no "master test" by which all putative law can be identified as valid can be found in Fuller. So, too, can Dworkin's related view that the content as well as the source of putative law is relevant to its validity.

Fuller's writings on legal processes ("eunomics") are today inspiring further research and reflection. This is particularly true of his work on the limits of adjudication, but his general theory of process has attracted attention, not least at the new School of Jurisprudence and Social Policy at the University of California at Berkeley, where Philip Selznick, a long-time admirer of Fuller's "process" jurisprudence, is a principal figure.[44] On the subject of legal method—statutory interpretation, the application of precedent, and the like—one encounters many articles in legal periodicals today that include references to Fuller. The second Restatement of Contracts, published in 1981, clearly reflects his influence.[45] The leading contract scholar of our day, Patrick Atiyah of Oxford, has acknowledged a major indebtedness.[46]

During the past ten or fifteen years in the United States, there has been a striking increase in the number of social scientists, historians, and philosophers who have discovered the role of law in society as a subject that merits study. Much of this work is addressed to issues that deeply interested Fuller, and it is certain that his example has been an inspiration to some of these scholars. Fuller himself drew widely on social theory, moral philosophy, and the humanistic disciplines to illuminate the law. His work is also less technical and generally more accessible to non-lawyers than is usually true of a legal theorist. And some of his central views are not uncongenial to scholars from other disciplines. Certainly he rejected any theory to the effect that society is merely clay in the hands of the law.

In matters of law-school curriculum design, Fuller was, and continues to be, influential in important ways. He quickly became one of the most influential intellectual leaders of the newly rejuvenated Harvard faculty that assembled after the war. With the concurrence of his colleague David Cavers, Fuller formally recommended, in 1946, the establishment of a program at Harvard in International Legal Studies, a proposal that led to a program that is now the most elaborate in the Western world. He chaired Harvard Law School's Special Committee on Legal Education, whose "Preliminary Report" in 1947 (labeled confidential), drafted largely by Fuller, continues to circulate today. Dean Albert Sacks later wrote of Fuller's committee that it "stressed the importance of reducing concern with problems at the appellate level and focusing on the many perspectives of the lawyer—e.g., trial, counseling, negotiating, drafting, and the like. . . . [L]aw school classes were too concerned with the breakdowns in ordering and not enough with the planning that successfully avoided those breakdowns." Sacks also remarked that the committee's reforms "were among the most successful in recent times."[47] Not surprisingly, given Harvard's role, these reforms influenced American legal education generally and continue to do so in the 1980's.

The curricular reforms of the Fuller committee provided for required "perspective courses" at the second-year level. The object of these courses, on jurisprudence, comparative law, legal process, and legal history, was to take "the student outside the legal system and [give] him some view of it as a whole, so that he might be led to reflect on the more general aims of law and government and the conditions that conduce to realization of those aims."[48] Fuller himself taught the course in jurisprudence. As "one of the great law teachers" of his day, in the words of Erwin N. Griswold, dean of the Harvard Law School during most of Fuller's years there, Lon Fuller in his jurisprudence course "reached more American law students and stimulated more speculative thought about the law than any other American law teacher."[49]

2

The purposive and value-laden nature of law

One of Fuller's leading ideas was that law, both in general and in its various forms, is essentially purposive.[1] He was thus a participant in a long tradition of teleological thought about law dating back to Aristotle and Aquinas, and carried on, in our own time, by such instrumentalists as Oliver Wendell Holmes Jr., Roscoe Pound, and John Dewey. Fuller developed the concept of law's purposiveness more widely than any of his predecessors, thereby advancing our understanding of the general nature of law itself.

In order for a rule of law to exist, it must embody or reflect an intelligible purpose and incorporate a minimally sufficient means to that purpose. These substantive and instrumental purposes are notions of what ought to be, at least in the eyes of those who bring the law into being. Hence they are notions of value (though not necessarily of goodness). Such notions are for Fuller part of the very "existence conditions" of legal precepts. Thus we can say that for him law is value-laden, though he himself did not usually adopt this terminology except in his 1940 work, *The Law in Quest of Itself*.[2] As we will see, Fuller extended his thesis about law's value-laden character beyond legal precepts to the legal system as a whole and to legal processes as well.

Fuller also linked law's purposiveness and its value-laden character to other staples of jurisprudence—the relationships between law and moral values, and between law and reason, topics to be treated in Chapters Three–Five. In Chapters Six–Eight, we will see how, through the analysis of purposes, Fuller developed criteria for differentiating among basic legal processes and also cast light on means-end relations in the law generally. Fuller's stress on law's purposiveness and its value-laden nature will also be evident in the further chapters of this book dealing with applied jurisprudence.

Before presenting Fuller's own affirmative general view of law as essentially purposive and value-laden, I will introduce a fundamentally different view of law—one to which he was in part reacting. A look at this view as Fuller conceived it will help us to understand why this general issue was such a live one for him, and why his own theory cannot be dismissed as platitudinous.

Law as essentially non-purposive and non-value-laden

The term "law" is often used in various senses to refer to particular rules and other legal precepts; to the legal system as a whole; and to legal processes such as adjudication or legislative activity. Now, it is possible to view the reality of law in any of the foregoing senses in ways that take no explicit account of its purposes or the values it embodies. For example, the reality of law may be viewed as consisting essentially of words in certain authoritative texts, or of the behavior patterns of officials, or of the emanations of state power, or of some combination of these.

On such views, a form of law is not essentially purposive or value-laden. Rather, it is more like a datum of nature such as a pebble or a piece of soil, which may be analyzed, classified, described, or otherwise studied scientifically. Not surprisingly, during the great advances in natural science between 1750 and 1950, many legal theorists called positivists came to approach the law in just this way. If the scientific positivists, by their study of natural data, were making such great progress in discerning the laws of the universe, why should not legal theorists similarly undertake the scientific study of the data of law as posited by humans?

The kinds of questions about law that interested legal positivists were quite varied. Who makes law? What are the sources from which law is made? By what criterion is the law of a society to be identified? That is, how can we tell what is truly law within a society rather than, say, merely a form of morality? What is the nature of a legal rule? How should fundamental legal concepts such as "right" and "duty" be analyzed? What is the hierarchical structure of law? What is a legal sanction? How far can law be reduced to the behavior patterns of officials? What are the relations between law and coercion? What are the social effects of law? What law ought we to have, and how ought it to be made?

In treating all but the last of these questions, a legal theorist might well ignore the purposes and values of the forms of law under study. To determine the authoritativeness of the source of a rule of law, for example, one need not inquire into its purpose. It is possible to analyze the concept of a rule without reference to the purposes and values that may figure in rules. To determine the effects of a law, it is not necessary to go into its purposes or the values it embodies. And so on. Thus the very nature of nearly all of the questions that interested most legal positivists seemed to make a concern with purposes and values of forms of law irrelevant or at least not so pressing. Small wonder that so many of them did not think of law as essentially purposive or value-laden.

Fuller would have admitted that such utilitarian positivists as Jeremy

Bentham (1748–1832) and John Austin (1790–1859) and their modern-day followers did and do stress that laws ought to serve utilitarian purposes and values. But this broad normative question about the kinds of purposes and values laws ought to have is one of the very few questions on the agenda of most positivists that directly invites inquiry into the purposes and values of law. Moreover, to say that law ought to be utilitarian is not to say that law (in its particular forms or in the large) is essentially purposive and value-laden, the very point that Fuller insisted on the most, as we will see. Indeed, most utilitarian positivists actually seem to have differed with Fuller on this point. That is, they did not hold that "L is a law" implies that "L has a purpose," or that "L is value-laden." Rather, it only implies that "L was made by some human beings."

Fuller claimed that a general scientific ethos influenced many legal positivists to adopt and transmit a general theory of law as non-purposive and non-value-laden, a theory highly susceptible of influence other than as mere "scientific truth." He identified several distinct features of this ethos.[3] First, many thinkers of a modern scientific and anti-metaphorical temper were disinclined to characterize particular varieties of law as essentially purposive and value-laden. On their view, to say that particular rules of law are essentially purposive or value-laden is to adopt a manifest fiction. Only human beings, not laws, can have purposes or pursue values. Accordingly, any notion that the legal system as a whole is essentially purposive and value-laden is simply manifest fiction writ large. Indeed, it suggests that the spirit of Hegel rides again. True scientists do not go in for fiction, and anything that smacks of the Hegelian spirit must surely be metaphysical nonsense.

Second, Fuller attributed a behavioristic scientism to some positivists, particularly certain American realists. On their view, purposes and values cannot be the object of true scientific study, for they cannot be observed. The behavior of officials, however, can be observed. It therefore qualifies as an object of genuine scientific study and constitutes the primary subject matter of legal theory.

Third, Fuller seems to have attributed to many positivists the view that a truly scientific account of any phenomenon must be mechanistic. In the natural sciences, we do not observe events and describe them in terms of purposes or the pursuit of values. Thus, for instance, "no one would think of explaining the fall of a stone by saying that it is moved by an impulse to join its mother, Earth."[4] In human affairs, of which law is a part, scientific truth is much the same. Thus, whatever the legal positivist or other scientific theorist truly needs to say about law can be said without resort to purposes. (Fuller did not make clear to which legal positivists he actually attributed a mechanistic view; it is not a view attributable to very many of them.)

Fourth, science requires that the object of study and the procedures of study be kept free of all "contaminating influences." True science must be value-free. Purpose always reflects at least some individual's notion of what ought to be, either prudentially or ultimately. Any purposes or values in law, or reflected in legal action, are thus best kept out of the scientific study of law, whether that study be primarily analytical or primarily sociological.

Fuller rejected all of the above. He did not think it fictional or merely metaphorical to say that forms of law have purposes or embody values. He did not think that the actual purposes or values of lawmakers were merely mental and therefore unobservable or otherwise indeterminable (though he did admit that the goals of particular forms of law might be difficult to determine). And even when not, in some sense, observable, the relevant purposes and values were, in Fuller's view, at least something that could be the subject of rational attribution. Fuller also repudiated the mechanistic doctrine of natural science as applied to legal activity. And he thought it not only unsound but impossible to keep purpose and value out of the law in the name of some misguided scientific ideal of value-free inquiry.

Fuller did not hold that legal theorists in the positivist or any other tradition should never study questions about law that require no inquiry into its purposes and values. Rather, he believed that many legal positivists tended to adopt general theories and orientations toward law that could not be confined in their bearing to questions of a kind that require no inquiry into purpose or value. Thus, if at the most general level these thinkers left purpose and value out of law, they would also tend, for example, to neglect purpose and value in defining the conditions under which a rule of law may be said to exist, or in describing (or prescribing) interpretational practice. As we will see, Fuller held that purpose and value figure in the very conditions for the existence of a legal rule, and figure in sound precepts of interpretational practice. He therefore thought it important not only to try to demonstrate the essentially purposive and value-laden nature of law, but also to combat the positivists' views, and especially what he saw as their tendency to import a scientific ethos into legal theory.

But were there any leading positivists who truly neglected law's purposive and value-laden nature? The most influential legal positivist of this century, the Austrian Hans Kelsen (1881–1973), set forth what he called a "pure theory of law." He sometimes wrote as if his theory were purified of all "wish law," a phrase he used to refer to the foreign matter of purpose and value.[5] For Kelsen, this purified law was normative in character. On his view, a legal system itself is a unified system of norms. These norms tell officials what they are to do if private citizens act or fail to act in certain ways. These norms are also to be sharply differentiated from morality, and they derive their validity as law from the fact that they may be traced back to a single basic norm at the very foundation of the system.

H. L. A. Hart of Oxford, since the 1950's the most influential legal positivist in the English-speaking world, developed a general theory of law in which he stresses that a legal system consists of a "union of primary and secondary rules."[6] Primary rules impose duties. Secondary rules confer powers. Such rules may be identified as rules of a given legal system because they satisfy criteria of validity captured in a "rule of recognition" accepted within the society. In Hart's explicit general theory of law, purpose and value play little role (with one major exception).

Both Kelsen and Hart, despite some important differences between them, qualify as leading positivists in the analytical tradition, as opposed to the American Karl N. Llewellyn (1893–1962), a positivist of a more sociological bent. In his early work, Llewellyn (unlike Kelsen and Hart) laid great stress on law in the form of official behavior patterns, and he was keen to have empirical studies done to identify those patterns.[7] In doing these studies, the researcher was to focus not on purposes or values, but on the brute facts of official behavior. (When Fuller came on the scene, only Llewellyn's early work had been done.)

Although at the highest levels of theory about law in the sense of legal system, legal positivists appear to have neglected purposes and values, can it be said that in their treatment of particular rules and other precepts of law, these thinkers stressed law's purposiveness and its value-laden nature? For example, when specifying the conditions for the existence of a rule of law did these thinkers require that the rule be sufficiently well designed minimally to serve its purpose? Generally the answer is "no." In regard to statutory interpretation, for example, did the positivists all adopt a purposive approach? Again, the answer is "no." Of the thinkers just named, only Llewellyn appears to have adopted a purposive theory of interpretation, and he rarely insisted on it in his early work. Kelsen said little about interpretation. And Hart's theory about the interpretation of the core meaning of written law is, at bottom, non-purposive, rooted as it is in a doctrine drawn from the philosophy of language.[8]

We may conclude, then, that although Fuller may have unfairly attributed some specific features of the scientific ethos to certain legal positivists (Hart, for example, has seldom been guilty of scientism), the influence of that general ethos nonetheless probably does help to explain the neglect of purpose and value in much legal theorizing of a positivistic character.

Still, it seemed to some of Fuller's contemporaries that he was, in the end, really only jousting at windmills when, in the 1930's and early 1940's, he attacked the positivistic viewpoint. In the United States, at least, a view of law as purposive and value-laden had for some time been accepted in many quarters (despite the behavioristic turn of legal realism). This view reflected the successes of the general instrumentalist revolution in American legal thought led by Holmes, Pound, and Dewey between 1880 and 1940.[9] Fuller's own preferred approach to law had therefore already received a more congenial reception in the United States than in Britain and the countries influenced by Kelsenism, where no similar instrumentalist revolution had ever taken place, or had taken place but did not hold.

So much for what Fuller was reacting to. Let us now turn to his affirmative case for the purposiveness and value-laden character of law, in the various basic senses of that word. In each instance, we will begin first with law's purposiveness and then turn to its value-laden character.

Legal precepts

Fuller distinguished between "implicit law" and "made law."[10] "Implicit law" includes custom and certain other forms of human interaction having normative significance, though these may not in fact be reduced to words, let alone to authoritative textual statement. "Made law" consists of explicitly stated rules and other prescriptions, and includes statutes and explicit contract terms. Only officials may make statutes and the like. Both officials and private parties may create law in the form of contract terms. Officials and private parties alike may bring custom and other forms of implicit law into being. So, too, with constitutions. But much law originates privately, and unlike most positivists, Fuller was far from preoccupied with "state law"—law brought into being solely by officials. Both implicit law and made law are purposive: "the essential meaning of a legal rule lies in a purpose, or, more commonly, in a congeries of purposes."[11]

Even in regard to made law, Fuller stressed that words standing alone or even together in a phrase or sentence cannot alone give a precept meaning. The purposes to be served affect its meaning too. If a rule says that "no vehicles shall be taken into the park," and a defendant is prosecuted for bringing a World War II jeep (in good working order) into the park and placing it on a pedestal as a war memorial, the meaning of this law cannot be determined merely by looking at the words and interpreting them as one would plain English in a non-legal context. Of course, on such a literalist approach, the law might easily be said to be violated. After all, the jeep is a "vehicle," and the defendant has "taken" it into the park. But let us assume the city council records reveal the purpose of the law to be making the park safe and quiet. We would then see that the meaning of the law does not justify the prosecution of the defendant.[12]

One cannot tell what a legal precept (statutory, customary, judicial, or other) means, and therefore cannot tell what it is, without determining what it is for. Fuller often put this point in a way that was confusing to some. He said that "the law as it is" cannot be divorced from "the law as it ought to be." What he meant was that some conception of what the law is for must inform the meaning of the words in which the law is expressed. In the case of statutes, for example, this purposive conception must be justifiably attributable to the legislature. Not just anyone's purposes will do.

Fuller did not contend that the purposive conception that appropriately infuses the precept with meaning is necessarily good or right. Those who make the law might have bad or wrong aims. Rather, his essential point was that somebody's notions of purpose—of the ends the precept ought to serve—must figure in the very meaning of the precept. To adapt one of his metaphors, if we leave what the law is for out of our concept of what it is, we are left with something like a wheelbarrow, and an empty one at that; it can easily be pushed in almost any direction and has no real power to go anywhere on its own.[13]

Fuller's purposive account is far from banal. In the case of much customary and still other forms of implicit law, the relevant purposes are not typically stated in so many words. They have to be derived from context, and if this is not done with sensitivity, the normative significance of the implicit law involved will be lost or distorted. In the case of made law, legal rules are commonly formulated without any robustly explicit incorporation of purpose. Legal educators who teach even the ablest law students can testify that many students fail to inquire into or lose sight of the purposes in or behind legal precepts. Moreover, it certainly cannot be said that judges and official interpreters and administrators of legal precepts always understand them as purposive. The "plain-meaning" interpretation of statutes and the "wooden" reading of judicial opinions are not at all uncommon. Fuller's message becomes even more important if one subscribes to the Kantian philosopher Hans Vaihinger's principle of "the preponderance of means over ends." According to one version of this principle, legal personnel easily become submerged in the often thick verbiage and other implementive reality of law, and thus tend to ignore or lose sight of the purposes law is supposed to serve.

Nor has law's purposiveness been obvious and straightforward in the history of legal theory. As we have already noted, many adherents of one major tradition of legal theory—positivism—have tended to neglect law's purposiveness. Consider, for instance, one central question that has attracted the sustained interest of nearly all of them, namely, that of specifying the criteria for identifying what precepts count as valid law. Almost all of these theorists specified conditions for the existence of legal precepts that require no inquiry whatsoever into the specific ends they are designed to accomplish. According to Austin, for example, a precept exists as law if an authorized official has laid it down. According to Holmes, the law consists of a prediction of the future use of state force. According to certain realists, law consists of the behavior patterns of officials. According to Kelsen, a legal precept exists if it may be traced to some basic constitutional norm. These positivistic theories have one major feature in common: they omit all reference to purpose.[14] Such theories can be highly influential. As Fuller put it, they exalt authoritative form over substantive content and thus invite a formalistic approach to law. (In the case of Holmes and the realists, this is peculiarly paradoxical, for they were anti-formalist.) Similarly, Fuller attributed the excessively literal approach to interpretation of British judges partly to a desire to "conform their practice to the pattern [positivist] legal theory has been ascribing to it for more than a century."[15] He believed that "the dispute of the schools centers on the problem of interpretation."[16] As he said in 1960, in a letter to a philosopher:

> In many discussions with non-lawyers (most of them philosophers and social scientists) I find that where they generally go wrong (in my opinion) on the issue of positivism is in not appreciating the problem of interpretation. They seem usually to assume that lawyers have some highly developed technical language that is capable of phrasing injunctions in such a way that no reference to purpose or to extra legal norms is necessary. This just isn't so. The fact is that for its *meaning* any rule of law is tragically dependent upon an understanding of the purpose pursued and this in turn usually requires a feeling for the extra legal community and its problems. . . . Even in the more technical areas, interpretation cannot proceed without an examination, and often, a reformulation of purpose.[17]

Fuller thought that positivism fosters formalistic legal method. Judges, for example, are more likely to interpret precedents in a wooden fashion or interpret statutes literally because the positivistic philosophy influencing them does not encourage them to dig out and hold in view the purposes of the law they are applying. A purposive theory, on the other hand, requires just this, and accordingly provides direction and guidance. It also invites more reasoned argument over the law's ends and means, and this allows a much larger role for critically reasoned judgment in determining the existing law. The positivist theory does not stress the purposive content of the precept as such, yet it is here where the scope for meaningful argumentation over substance lies. Further, the critical evaluation of a form of law is inevitably sharpened if purpose is taken into account. Indeed, it is often impossible to evaluate a precept without knowing what it is for.

Fuller devoted special attention to the purposiveness of constitutional law. He believed that true constitutional law has its own distinct purposes, namely, to embody and implement the basic organizational principles required for representative, orderly, and decent government.[18] Democratic precepts, basic protections against the abuse of majority rule, the principles defining the rule of law, and various requirements of due process are all examples of forms of law that embody and implement genuine constitutional purposes. This kind of law makes law itself possible. It also limits the purposes that may be pursued through law.

Fuller was at pains to emphasize that in the most healthy legal order, the public and especially the legal profession will have a lively sense of genuine constitutional purpose and an understanding of at least the basic rules of constitutional law. What is more, all this will be "vitalized by an appreciation of the reasons why such rules are necessary."[19] People will see, for instance, why it is necessary to have basic rules about how law is to be made if there is to be a true system of law at all. They will see that the nature of the legal enterprise implies at the very least the constraints of such rules. Thus if just anything can count as legislation, then nothing can. Observed rules about who can make such law, and by what steps, are essential to the very existence and intelligibility of the system. To grasp such things is to understand a purposive framework of means-end relationships.

Yet even in a healthy legal order there is always a serious risk that the public and the legal profession will lose sight of genuine constitutional purposes or fail to understand what those purposes require by way of law. For one thing, such purposes are very general, and people do not always have the imagination to grasp their bearing in particular cases. For another, there is a tendency to confuse constitutional matters with legal matters of a lower order so that the priorities of the two tend to become skewed. Then, too, and especially for officials, there are the temptations of expediency.

Although a written constitution has its advantages, Fuller warned of a profound disadvantage, too:

> In a country where the constitution is unwritten, it is necessary to ask whether a departure from established practice comports with the demands of decent and orderly government as a whole. *The absence of an authoritative formulation keeps alive a sense of purpose*. . . . Where doubtful procedures emerge, [Americans] tend to inquire into their legality, not into their effects. Instead of engaging in an effort to articulate the restraints that must be accepted to insure orderly, fair, and decent government, American lawyers are likely to compete with one another in predicting what the Supreme Court will do. (Emphasis supplied.)[20]

These, then, are Fuller's arguments for the essentially purposive nature of legal precepts. Let us now consider how he argued for their essentially value-laden character. Indeed, just what was this thesis as applied to legal precepts? As we will see, Fuller's thesis tends to reinforce his views on law's purposive character.

Fuller distinguished between mere things and artifacts. Pebbles along a stream and pieces of soil are mere things. They are not human inventions informed by anyone's conceptions about what ought to be. They are not "infused with human purpose." Also, their existence can be ascertained entirely without reference to the extent that they may be suitable for some human purpose—someone's notions of what ought to be.

Artifacts are quite a different matter. To use one of Fuller's examples, assume that we have before us an assemblage of wheels, gears, and pistons, and that the question is whether this assemblage *is* a steam engine. This question cannot be answered without regard to another question: whether the assemblage can make steam and make moving parts move by steam pressure, a notion of what ought to be. The assemblage will count as a steam engine if the assemblage (the "is") at least minimally serves the creator's purpose of making steam (the "ought"). Thus a steam engine, and any artifact, is an "is-ought complex" (my terminology). The question of what it is cannot be separated from the question of what it ought to be. Thus it cannot be said to exist independently of whether it has a purpose and is suitably designed for that purpose. A dubious assemblage of wheels, gears, and pistons, for example, might well not qualify as an existing steam engine. It might simply be insufficiently suited to making steam, to fulfilling such a purpose—such an "ought."

Fuller's most general thesis was this: "In the field of purposive human activity, which includes both steam engines and the law, value and being are not two different things, but two aspects of an integral reality."[21] Thus the question, "Is this assemblage a steam engine?," overlaps mightily with the question, "Is this a good steam engine?" Contrary to what common sense and what some positivists suggest, such questions *are* to a considerable extent inseparable. The "is" and the "ought" are two aspects of an "integral reality."

When we turn to rules and other forms of law, Fuller says, we can discern similar elements implicit in any judgment that such a rule exists. Again, contrary to what is commonly assumed, the question, "Is this a rule of law?," overlaps mightily with the question, "Is this rule what it ought to be (at least in certain respects)?" For example, not just anything that falls from the collective lips of legislators, however solemnly pronounced and however procedurally correct, can qualify as statutory law. To begin with, it must have a substantive purpose or purposes. A putative statute not informed by some such authoritative conception of what ought to be, would not be a rule of law. But it would also not qualify as a rule of law if it were so poorly designed as to lack minimally sufficient efficacy. It might be so unclear that it could not be reliably applied, for example. Or it might incorporate a totally false hypothesis about the means required to serve an end. Conceptions of means as well as ends therefore necessarily figure in true precepts. Thus a precept is an "is-ought" complex in two senses of "ought."[22] It embodies or reflects a substantive purpose that ought to be served (by the lights of some appropriate entity) and also embodies or reflects notions of *how* the purpose ought to be served. It is therefore much more than a thing that merely is the case (e.g., some appropriate words on paper duly laid down).

My reconstruction of Fuller's view, then, is this: a rule of law is an "is-ought" complex, a unity of "being" and "value"—an aggregate (1) of what is the case (e.g., appropriate words on paper duly laid down), (2) of an intelligible substantive purpose (or purposes) that ought to be served (by the lights of some appropriate entity), and (3) of minimally sufficient instrumental means. On this view, it follows that a rule of law is value-laden. Contrary to what Fuller took to be the positivist view, a true legal precept is not "an ought-free datum of pure fact." There is no such thing as a "pure fact of law existing independently of its purposes." In Fuller's terminology, the "value" that here joins with "being" in an "integral reality" is dual: it includes both substantive and instrumental conceptions of what ought to be.

Once a putative rule qualifies on the foregoing Fullerian grounds as a rule of law, it does not follow that the rule does so robustly or in "full flower," so to speak. Some rules barely meet the requirements. Others go far beyond them and embody fully articulated substantive purposes and thoroughly well-designed means-end hypotheses. Observe that the purposive and instrumental requirements that Fuller lays down for the existence of a rule of law are universally applicable. These criteria do not depend for their applicability on the nature and content of the law of any particular system.

What if those who try to create law fail? That is, what if the putative rule fails to qualify as law either because it lacks a sufficiently intelligible substantive purpose or because it is not sufficiently well designed to serve its purpose, or both? Judges, administrative officials, and private parties might still purport to act in its name, and many might actually be affected, for good or for ill. Indeed, let us suppose that in a particular instance, a judge or an official so acted, for good. Would Fuller sound any alarm? He certainly would. He would stress that such "law" cannot serve as a justification for the decision (as in "accord with the law"), cannot provide guidance either in the case at hand or in future cases, cannot serve as a safeguard against arbitrariness or other abuse of power, cannot provide a meaningful basis on which to found any duty of obedience, cannot provide a test against which the soundness of the decision at hand as a member of a class of cases can be judged, and more. At the very least, the values associated with the rule of law would not be fulfilled. (Whether these values have any moral significance as such is something to which we shall return.)

What if the law that comes into being qualifies both as sufficiently purposive and sufficiently instrumental? Fuller did not hold that these notions of what ought to be necessarily translate into values that are morally sound. As he once put the matter in a letter to Llewellyn, "You say that there are obviously bad rules which exist. I don't deny that."[23] But Fuller stressed that even bad "oughts" can have a powerful shaping role, and that legal rules must be seen for what they are—phenomena that necessarily embody notions of value, good or bad. Likewise, instrumental notions about how the purpose of a rule ought to be realized have no essential connection with good morals. Means might be highly effective yet morally bad. In sum, to say that a rule of law is an "is-ought" complex is not to say that the operative notions of what ought to be done through law and of how this ought to be achieved are morally good notions. To say that a legal rule exists is not, on Fuller's analysis, to say that it is a good rule (except, perhaps, for the point that if well designed it will not unduly waste resources).

Fuller's affirmative thesis about the law's value-laden character was not conceived in a vacuum. For one thing, it conflicted with a common-sense view that law is not intrinsically a matter of value and evaluation, but merely a matter of authoritative promulgation. Equally important to Fuller, he thought his thesis conflicted with the spirit of much sophisticated legal positivist thinking in which law was conceived, in Fuller's terms, as an "ought-free datum of pure fact." The influential English jurist John Austin had proclaimed: "The existence of law is one thing, its merit or demerit is another."[24] John Chipman Gray, a leading American positivist, asserted: "The law of a state . . . is not an ideal, but something which actually exists. . . . It is not that which ought to be, but that which is."[25] Hans Kelsen, the leading continental positivist, held that the existence of law is a matter of "objective imputation" divorced from all forms of "wish law."[26] The philosopher-lawyer H. L. A. Hart of Oxford (with whom Fuller clashed several times) argued in the positivist spirit that there is no necessary connection between law "as it is" and law as it "ought to be."[27] Ernest Nagel, an American philosopher, held forth in the same vein.[28]

It is not really necessary to interpret any of these positivists as denying Fuller's thesis about the value-laden nature of law. They can be read, instead, as merely insisting that all law is subject to criticism. But many of them did often write as if all notions of what the law ought to be are utterly irrelevant, *in every sense*, to what it actually is and to whether it exists. And these views Fuller emphatically repudiated.

The legal system

Fuller formulated a general theory that a legal system is the purposive human "enterprise of subjecting human conduct to the guidance and control of general rules."[29] This is in itself to attribute a broad general purpose to law in the sense of "legal system." But Fuller went further and identified still other general purposes of a legal system. The first category of such purposes is broadly procedural and is implicit in Fuller's general theory. He claimed that, whatever the substantive purposes of a legal system, certain procedural purposes must be honored for a system to qualify as a system of law rather than as a mere regime of arbitrary and patternless exercises of state power. These purposes require that at least statutes (and other forms of made law, as appropriate):

(1) must be sufficiently general (i.e., there must be rules);

(2) must be publicly promulgated;

(3) must be sufficiently prospective;

(4) must be clear and intelligible;

(5) must be free of contradictions;

(6) must be sufficiently constant through time so people can order their relations accordingly;

(7) must not require the impossible; and

(8) must be administered in a way sufficiently congruent with their wording so people can abide by them.

Interestingly, part of the significance of the truth that a legal system must be purposive in the foregoing respects is that this constrains the kinds of specific purposes that at least officials can pursue through law. For example, once officials adopt a general rule and promulgate it, this will constrain what they themselves can thereafter do. (No positivist appears to have understood the broad implications of this.)

These procedural purposes may appear to be merely purposes of statutes. But they are more than that: they are purposes of certain other forms of "made law" such as regulations and constitutions. These purposes extend to law administration, as well as lawmaking. They may be said to be general purposes of the *legal system*.[30]

Obviously, in the daily workings of modern legal systems, these broadly procedural purposes are pursued (in varying ways and degrees) by legislators, judges, and others concerned with law. Yet these purposes do not all apply to such important forms of law as managerial directives, custom, and private contract. Is it really appropriate to say that they are general purposes of legal systems as such? Or that they are conceptually built into the very notion of a legal system? There are no wholly settled conventions for resolving these questions. Legal systems do exist partly to guide conduct and to structure interactions, functions that would be impossible if these broadly procedural purposes were not met. Further, in the clearest cases of legal systems, officials and others regularly pursue such purposes through law. Members of the society have agreed on, or at least acquiesce in, the pursuit of these purposes through statutes and certain other forms of made law, as appropriate. It is therefore at most a modest indulgence in teleological attribution to say that the *legal forms* through which this pursuit is carried out have these purposes. These legal forms must also be appropriately designed in order to serve such purposes. And it hardly seems possible that a modern legal system could get along without statutes. Thus, the social realities support this way of thinking and talking too. Further, there are precedents. For example, we regularly attribute the purposes of individuals to the groups of which they are members. In this way, we even sometimes say that a whole society has certain general purposes.

Regardless of whether it seems linguistically or conceptually appropriate to say that a system that purports to be one of law has these general procedural purposes, Fuller argued that we *ought* to say so. This device would help keep legislators, judges, and other participants in the system conscious of the justified demands of "procedural legality." Certainly standardized ways of speaking can sharpen awareness. In the case of law, there is special need for such broadly procedural consciousness-raising. There is a general tendency to focus on the substantive to the neglect of the procedural, a tendency all the more pronounced where the procedural consists of the system's own broad requirements of legality, some of which, Fuller admitted, can even be justifiably overridden from time to time. Indeed, officials in power are constantly tempted to depart from them in the interest of expediency. They may, for example, even decline to lay down rules in advance merely to preserve their own power. As Fuller noted, "By publishing a criminal statute government does not merely issue a directive to the citizen; it also imposes upon itself a charter delimiting its powers to deal with a particular area of human conduct."[31]

Being conscious of justified general purposes is one thing; knowing what to do as a consequence is quite another. Still, Fuller held that all purposes, even general ones such as the foregoing, usually have a special "direction-giving" quality. It was partly because of his belief in this quality that he laid such great stress on purposes in the law generally.[32] In various writings he offered a number of illustrations and arguments designed to show how an appreciation of the purposes of forms of law, including relevant means-end relations, could lead citizens and administrators to carry them out more faithfully and more effectively.

Further, only by regular and explicit reference to these general procedural purposes, and to the corresponding facts, can we judge the degree to which the system as a whole fulfills the requirements of the rule of law. This way of speaking and thinking keeps the relevant standards for judging legality—the various general procedural purposes—at the forefront and invites us to apply those standards to evaluate the performances of key official personnel. It might be said that in order to judge compliance with legality we need not call the relevant standards "purposes," and we need not attribute them to the system as such. But this would be to quibble. And it can hardly be denied that if we view social phenomena as having certain purposes this will invite or perhaps even solicit the question, "To what extent are those purposes being fulfilled?"

Some might ask whether there is really any threat to the rule of law that we should take such trouble over the issue in the first place. In many parts of the world, the rule of law is a sometime thing. Much of Fuller's thought about the rule of law was motivated primarily by the example of Nazi Germany. But this is only the most extreme case of a Western nation that in this century perverted law in countless ways contrary to its broad procedural purposes.

Besides, "rule of law" issues do arise for officials and citizens to resolve even in Anglo-American systems. Whether an official body should proceed ad hoc or by rule, whether a proposed law is sufficiently clear, whether a given interpretation is more congruent than another with the law already on the books, whether a proposed retroactive law will do more harm than good, whether one way of disseminating knowledge of a law is better than another—these and other such issues frequently arise in modern legal systems, and there is no reason to be complacent about official resolutions of them in the American or British system. It is an important responsibility of legal educators and the legal profession to evaluate these resolutions and to speak out critically. Fuller's purposive theory calls explicit attention to this responsibility. Of course he did not hold that the pursuit of legality can be made merely a matter of rules. The pursuit of legality—of law's general procedural purposes—is a practical art calling for repeated acts of human judgment heavily dependent on energy, insight, intelligence, and conscientiousness.[33]

Beyond these procedural purposes, Fuller held that a legal system typically has broadly substantive purposes. Thus, a "striving after justice," or the "maintenance of peace and internal order," or the "reinforcement of the family," or still other broad purposes may be pursued by a given system of law. But he did not dwell on this theme, perhaps because he thought that trying to discuss very broad substantive aims in the abstract is not very meaningful.

Fuller saw an important interrelationship between the pursuit of broadly procedural purposes in a given system and the quality of the substantive aims pursued in that system. More specifically, in his view a healthy rule of law is likely to beget sound, or at least not unsound, substantive law. As he put it, "If we do things the right way, we are likely to do the right thing"[34] (a position that we will return to in due course).

We can now readily see how Fuller might argue that law, in the sense of an existing legal system, is a vast, ongoing value-laden enterprise. We have already learned that he viewed individual legal precepts as value-laden. Insofar as a legal system is the sum of its parts, and legal precepts are undeniably part of the system, it must follow that the system itself is value-laden.

But Fuller went beyond this and took a more holistic view. He stressed the eight broadly procedural purposes of a legal system as well—the requirements of generality of rule, of clarity, prospectivity, promulgation, administrative congruity, and so forth. As applied to statutes and certain other forms of made law, each of these requirements incorporates a notion about how a legal system as a whole—the legal enterprise—*ought* to function. Now, on Fuller's view, if the system failed totally to meet any one of these requirements, or failed substantially in regard to several, that society might still be said to have a system of government, but it would not be government through or under law.[35] (For Fuller, the existence of a legal system is a matter of degree; hence a legal system might be said to only "half-exist.") Thus no matter how firmly installed a given regime might be in a particular society, this hard fact alone, this indisputable "is," could not, without more, constitute a legal system. A legal system is not just a system of ad hoc, patternless exercises of political power. A legal system does not necessarily exist just because some official person, or body, or group is "in charge" within the society. Law is not merely a "manifested fact of social power." Rather, a legal system can exist only if it functions sufficiently in accord with the foregoing eight instrumental notions of how such a system *ought* to function when making and applying statutes (and other forms of made law, as appropriate).

In short, to say that a legal system as a whole exists is to say that an "is-ought" complex of the kind discussed exists. Thus, again the question, "Is this reality a system of law?," overlaps mightily with the question, "Is this system in sufficient measure what it ought to be in terms of rule making, clarity and constancy of rule, congruence, etc.?" Again, "being" and "value" are not two different things, but two aspects of an "integral reality." A genuine legal system is thus value-laden in holistic terms. It sufficiently embodies or reflects notions of how such a system *ought* to function if it is to be truly legal.

Legal processes

Despite what has been said to this point, Fuller's primary unit of jurisprudential analysis was neither the legal precept nor the legal system as a whole. Rather, his main interest lay in the law's processes. Put in other terms, his was a "physiological" orientation to law, as opposed to the more "anatomical" concerns of most legal positivists.

Fuller devoted many years of study to various legal processes, including processes for creating and administering customary law and contract law, processes of adjudication, processes of enacting written law, and processes of managerial direction. For Fuller, these, too, are essentially "purposive human arrangements," and should be described and treated as such. Fuller did not develop a systematic account of the purposes that are essential to the definition of each basic process. Nor did he explain very fully how far a necessary purpose may fail of embodiment or implementation before we can say the process no longer exists, or has become some other kind of process. But he did offer many remarks on the purposes of different processes, and we will return to this topic in Chapters Six and Seven.

Fuller stressed the purposiveness of legal processes for pragmatic as well as theoretic reasons. He believed that by considering processes in light of their purposes, those who participate in their workings will be more likely to remain aware of the relevant purposes and see that they are appropriately carried out. Here again, he is stressing the special "direction-giving" quality of purpose. Further, he held that those responsible for channeling decisions into appropriate processes will be more likely to perform that task well. They will be more conscious of the purposes that define the nature of alternative processes and thus more likely to channel matters into the appropriate processes. What a process is suited to do inevitably depends on the purposes that inform its design and structure and thus constrain what may be done through it.

Fuller extended his thesis about the value-laden character of law to legal processes. Let us continue with the example of adjudication, a topic on which he wrote a great deal. Fuller did not explicitly specify any general substantive purposes that adjudication ought to fulfill in order for it to be genuinely adjudicative. Such a list could of course be devised—it would include, let us say, provision for the resolution of issues of fact, for the resolution of issues of law, and for the facilitation of out-of-court settlement.

Fuller did articulate certain instrumental requisites of adjudication. In order for a process to qualify as adjudicative it is not enough for it to involve just any tripartite interaction between two competing parties and an impartial decision maker. Among other things, it ought also to involve a certain kind of participation by the affected parties.[36] In Fuller's own words:

> The parties to the dispute must present their contentions to the judge in the presence of one another; each must be given the chance to know first hand what arguments and proofs his opponent is presenting and be afforded an opportunity to refute them. By this standard, the test lies, not in the formal authority of the judge, but in the participation in the decisional process accorded to those directly affected by the judge's decision.[37]

If the process does not function by such means (through such "instrumental oughts"), then it is simply not adjudicative. Rather, it is a kangaroo court, or something else.[38] It follows that a genuine adjudicative process is a further important kind of "is-ought" complex known to the law. It is necessarily value-laden and normative, and thus not reducible to mere matters of fact (e.g., functioning social roles or courtroom activity). In genuine adjudication, "being" and "value" are part of an "integral reality." And again, the question whether a process is adjudicative overlaps mightily with the question whether it is, in relevant respects, what it ought to be.

3

The morality and immorality of law

In the last chapter, we saw that for Fuller the existence of forms of law depends partly on notions of value—of what ought to be (by the lights of some appropriate person or body). A precept cannot exist as law unless it embodies an intelligible purpose and incorporates minimally sufficient means; these are notions of value. A legal system cannot exist unless it operates sufficiently through general rules that are clear, prospective, and congruently administered, etc.; these are notions of what ought to be, so they too are notions of value. And a legal process such as adjudication cannot exist unless appropriate provision is made for the affected parties to present proofs and arguments, and the decision maker is sufficiently impartial; these are notions of value. According to Fuller, then, notions of value figure in the very "existence" conditions of legal rules, a legal system, and legal processes. In Fuller's words, "being" and "value" are two aspects of an "integral reality." The phenomena of law are thus necessarily value-laden.

In the case of legal precepts, it may be noted that the full extent of their value-laden character cannot be seen if we merely concentrate on the value element in the conditions for the existence of a legal rule, for example. We must also contrast the relative potential of fiat and of reason in determining the overall substantive content of legal precepts. Value necessarily figures in reason. Fuller believed that although certain legal precepts (e.g., rules of the road or statutes of limitation) necessarily incorporate a significant element of fiat, it has far less scope for play in determining the substantive content of the law than reasoned notions of value. Indeed, in his classic essay "Reason and Fiat in Case Law,"[1] he argued that the necessary element of fiat in law is quite small.

According to Fuller, then, the law is value-laden in a double sense. It is necessarily value-laden because notions of value figure in the very existence of legal precepts, of legal systems, and of legal processes. But its precepts are, in their substantive content, *contingently* value-laden as well, and inasmuch as this content is commonly determined by reasoned notions of what ought to be rather than by any possible element of fiat, this content is, in general, heavily value-laden.[2]

It is important to pause and stress how limited Fuller's overall position is up to this point. In affirming the necessarily value-laden nature of legal precepts, the legal system, and legal processes, he is only saying that when these forms of law truly exist as law, they necessarily embody notions of what ought to be (notions of some appropriate person or body). He does not claim that these notions of what ought to be necessarily translate into notions of value in the form of moral rightness or goodness.* The same also holds for the notions of what ought to be that contingently figure in the substantive content of legal precepts.

If the "oughts" that must figure in the existence of forms of law and the "oughts" that inform the substantive content of legal precepts are not necessarily moral, then it follows that they might actually turn out in a particular society to be immoral or at least morally objectionable. Fuller was ever mindful of this, and thought that legal theorists, professors, judges, lawyers, law students, and citizens at large should thus constantly strive to see that the values informing the law are, so far as possible, good.[3] A vigilant critic of many aspects of the legal order himself, he held that a concern with "the problems of justice and right law furnishes the driving force for the whole subject of jurisprudence."[4]

Fuller was also mindful that his general thesis about the value-laden character of law naturally raises the more specific question of the relationship between law and that most important subclass of all values, moral values. In short, do the substantive and instrumental notions of what ought to be, which on Fuller's view necessarily figure in law, ever also necessarily translate into moral values? This question is another controversy-ridden staple of legal theory, and Fuller gave different answers here, depending on the variety of "law" in question: precepts, the system, processes.

Legal precepts

Although Fuller held that legal rules were complexes of "is-ought" and in this way value-laden, he did not hold that the values involved were necessarily good.[5] For him, there was no contradiction whatsoever in saying that "X is an evil law."[6]

If there is no necessary connection between law and moral worth here, might there be other kinds of connections? Fuller did argue that certain general requirements of instrumental efficacy have at least an important contingent connection with morality and thus are likely, when satisfied, to beget better law. For example, for a statute to be effective it should generally be clear, prospective, and publicly promulgated. Such requirements of instrumental efficacy are more likely to beget better law because the lawgiver in such circumstances will be loath to promulgate bad law in open and clear terms.[7]

*Fuller did not often use the word value, preferring the word ought instead. But in the context of our discussion, neither term in his usage necessarily means "right" or "good."

Moreover, Fuller was much aware that individual legal systems have their own general standards for determining what counts as law in those systems. These "local" standards must be distinguished from Fuller's universally applicable criteria of law introduced in Chapter Two (i.e., that it must embody an intelligible purpose and be instrumentally efficacious). These local standards are *additional* tests that must be met in a given system if a putative form of law is to qualify as law in that system. Furthermore, says Fuller, these may be tests of content as well as source. Thus, in a given system, the legal validity of a putative form of law may have to be tested not only against "source-based" criteria that allocate lawmaking power and specify how statutes, precedents, or contracts are to come into being, but also against standards of content. In other words, a contract clause may have to be tested for "conscionability," a trade custom for "reasonableness," a precedent for minimal "goodness" ("Is that good law?"), a statute for "substantive fairness," and so on.

Now, legal standards of content *are* frequently moral in character. In such cases, the truth of the statement, "X is the law," requires that the putative law satisfy still a further conception of what ought to be, namely, the substantive conception embodied in the legal standard of validity. The fact that a rule has an intelligible purpose and a sufficiently apt instrumental design does not alone guarantee that the rule will pass this further test. Whenever a rule, to qualify as valid law, must satisfy tests of moral worth specified in standards of legal validity, then we may say that, in the particular society involved, there is a necessary connection between the existence of valid law (law meeting these standards) and the morality of that law. Fuller did not himself make this argument explicitly, though he did hint at it in various of his writings.[8] The argument, of course, presupposes that the applicable legal standard of validity does indeed embody a moral standard. This is not an unrealistic presupposition. In our own system, for example, many operative standards of legal validity incorporate moral notions.

When Fuller argued for the value-laden nature of law, he was sometimes read to be saying that if law exists, then it must be what it ought to be, and therefore be immune to criticism. But it is wrong to read him in this way. Even had Fuller fully subscribed to the immediately preceding argument for a necessary connection between law and morals in a given society, it would not follow that the law would then be immune to criticism. The moral standard applied might be one of mere "positive morality" (i.e., commonly accepted morality) and criticizable in light of what H. L. A. Hart and others have called a more enlightened "critical morality"—an independent body of moral standards to be used to evaluate a society's positive morality.[9] Also, even if the positive or common morality was sound in all respects as judged by critical morality, it still might be only imperfectly incorporated in the law in some way, and the law would thus remain subject to criticism in that regard.

Fuller, as we know, was generally critical of the positivists and more specifically of those who constantly emphasized that "there is no necessary connection between the law as it is and the law as it ought to be."[10] Perhaps he assumed they were saying that it is simply not possible for a legal system to have criteria that make the morality of particular precepts relevant to their very existence as law. Or he may have thought they were really saying that a legal system ought not to have such criteria, for the content of the resulting law might embody objectionable morality or might render the law too uncertain, or the like. Fuller himself held that the content of the law ought to be relevant to its validity as law in many ways, some subtle and complex. He thought that positivist thinking to the contrary invited a "law-is-law formalism."[11] He worried that what the people of a society mistakenly accept as real tends to become real.[12] Thus if they come to think of law merely as something emanating from authoritative sources, they will be inviting a system in which the worth of substantive arguments is judged by whether they have been authoritatively endorsed rather than by their rational merits —a system in which the quality of law's content becomes increasingly less relevant to its validity as law. He thought it important that quality of content be generally relevant to validity.[13]

The legal system

As we saw in Chapter Two, Fuller held that eight broadly procedural requirements must be met to a sufficient degree before a legal system can be said to exist. These requirements apply to statutes and certain other forms of "made" law, and are (1) the formulation of general rules, (2) their public promulgation, (3) in prospective terms, (4) in clear and intelligible language, (5) free of contradictions, (6) in a form that citizens can abide by, (7) that are sufficiently constant through time and (8) are administered congruently with their language as announced.

Now, are these instrumental notions of value concerning how a system of law ought to function themselves necessarily notions of moral value, either individually or collectively? Fuller often called these requirements "principles of legality," and he had no doubt that taken together they were necessarily notions of moral value. Indeed, he held that these requirements of generality, clarity, prospectivity, and so on, constituted an "internal morality of law."[14] Of all Fuller's theses, this one became the most controversial and elicited the most irate reactions. One philosopher, for example, in commenting on this thesis, went so far as to remark in passing that Fuller "has tendentiously announced doctrines disputed by no one, and has denounced as misinterpretation all attempts to read his own frequently impenetrable views in a way that would join issue and make sense of his polemics."[15] This flourish of overstatement can only be explained as the exasperated reaction of a provoked adversary.

Positivists and other critics most often proclaimed that Fuller's eight requirements were merely "oughts" of efficiency, not of morality. That is, a regime ought to make rules, ought to publish them, ought to apply them congruently, and so on, merely in order to realize its ends effectively. On this view, such "oughts" have nothing to do with morals. Thus, contrary to one of Fuller's apparent claims, the principles of legality are neither individually nor collectively principles of moral value. If they were, conformity therewith must necessarily yield or be equivalent to something that is moral, good, or right. Similarly, violations must necessarily yield or be equivalent to something that is immoral, bad, or wrong. Yet neither is true. A general, prospective, publicized rule could be bad. A "rule" that is particular, retrospective, and kept secret could be good.

In answer to a letter from Wolfgang Friedmann of Columbia, who had argued along the foregoing lines, Fuller remarked: "In treating my principles of legality as mere conditions of efficacy you are in harmony with Hart, Dworkin, Cohen, Hughes and Summers. Nevertheless, in my humble opinion you are all wrong."[16] This letter, written in 1966, was followed by a formal "Reply to Critics," the title of a chapter Fuller added in revising his book *The Morality of Law* in 1969. Here he denied that his principles of legality were necessarily, far less exclusively, maxims of efficacy. He pointed out that a regime in power might actually find it effective *for its purposes* to violate the principles of legality. This had not been uncommon in the history of government, he noted, citing unpublished laws in Nazi Germany and retroactive criminal laws in the Soviet Union in the 1960's as examples.[17]

In this work Fuller sought to set forth several affirmative arguments in favor of his claim that the principles of legality somehow constitute a "morality" (i.e. necessarily translate into principles or values of moral worth).[18] But since he did not explicitly set forth the argument that seems to support this characterization most fully, let me present it here. Sufficient compliance with the principles of legality necessarily guarantees, to the extent of that compliance, the realization of a moral value, even when the content of the law involved happens to be bad. That moral value is this: the principles of generality, clarity, prospectivity, and so forth, secure that the citizen will have a *fair* opportunity to obey the law. Admittedly, the choice may be a choice to obey an evil law, but the citizen will at least have had a fair chance to decide whether to do so or not, and to act accordingly. This is in itself moral, even though, overall, what the state happens to be doing to the citizen through the substance of the law is immoral. Observe that if the principles of legality were violated, there could be a dual moral objection: the citizen could be subjected to an evil law *and* could lack any fair opportunity to know of it in advance and act accordingly. Indeed, to punish or sanction a citizen for not following an evil (or even a beneficent) law that is unfollowable is also unjust. And injustice is indisputably immoral. (Fuller did point out that when his eight requirements are not sufficiently met, the citizen can have no meaningful basis on which to discharge any general moral obligation he might otherwise have to obey the law.[19] This could be construed as an oblique way of making the fairness and injustice arguments I set forth in the text.)

Moreover, what is moral and what is immoral in this instance necessarily implicates both citizens and officials. There is not only the morality of citizens being provided a fair opportunity to comply, and the immorality of their being denied it; but also the morality of the *action* of officials in providing that opportunity and the immorality of their denying it. Fuller did point out that legal officials are governed here by a "morality of role," are trustees of state power and have a general moral obligation to use that power fairly. If they abuse their power by denying citizens a fair opportunity to obey the law, they commit a breach of trust. The officials involved include, of course, judges and administrators as well as lawmakers.[20]

Fuller sometimes referred to his eight requirements as the *ideal* of legality. Certainly this ideal is itself moral, at least in the sense that when it is realized, it follows necessarily that citizens are not denied a fair opportunity to obey the law. Because this value is merely processual, the law involved is itself not necessarily good. But even a processual moral value can be of high importance.

Fuller suggested still a further and related argument for a necessary connection between his principles of legality and moral value. Drawing on the writings of the German philosopher Georg Simmel, he contended that a legal system rests on a tacit reciprocity between lawgiver and subject. By enacting laws, a government in effect says to the citizen: "These are the rules we ask you to follow. If you will obey them, you have our promise that they are the rules we will apply to your conduct." When a lawgiver violates the principles of legality, thus breaching this understanding, the lawgiver to that extent necessarily forfeits some governmental legitimacy. Such violations could be sufficiently extensive as to deprive the government of all legitimacy. Legitimacy is itself a moral value.[21]

Though all these are arguments for *necessary* connections between Fuller's principles of legality and moral values, most of Fuller's explicit arguments supported only a contingent connection. Thus he believed that the satisfaction of his eight principles of legality generally served moral ends. To be sure, these principles were "neutral" with regard to the substantive purposes of law (its "external morality"), but observing them made it less likely that truly bad laws would be adopted. The requirement of publicity, for example, exerts a not-so-subtle pressure in favor of laws that are not on their face bad. Similarly, the requirement of generality makes it more likely that officials will act responsibly, for they must articulate the principles on which they act.[22]

Beyond this, since in Fuller's view, certain "made" law is only law if it meets these eight requirements, good law of this kind perforce requires that they be met to some minimally sufficient degree.[23] Further, the observance of principles of legality provides citizens with a stable framework for contractual and other dealings with fellow citizens and governmental personnel. Law is thus a facility that provides necessary conditions for interactional life in society and for the realization of unquestionably moral values such as freedom and fairness.[24] In sum, even in the absence of necessary connections between the principles of legality and moral values, it can hardly be said that the observance of the principles of legality is morally indifferent.

Do any of the positions Fuller sought to defend here foreclose criticism of the legal system? In arguing for necessary connections between the principles of legality and such moral values as fairness and legitimacy, one is not thereby seeking to immunize the law from criticism. To say that a legal system exists, and therefore is in some measure fair and legitimate, is to leave open the possibility that it may not be very fair or very legitimate. In addition, far from putting the law beyond criticism, some of Fuller's views appear to invite it. One reason he so stressed the principles of legality was precisely that he thought they promised to make governmental action much more fully subject to moral appraisal. A publicly promulgated rule, for example, is a pretty clear target.

Fuller sometimes called his principles of legality "principles of the rule of law." In his treatment of the rule of law in this sense of the term, he called attention to moral dimensions that have often been neglected in legal theory. This is not to say that he neglected the staples of "rule of law" writings (e.g., the law's guidance function and the value of certainty). Indeed, he carried these matters much farther than most leading thinkers have. And he demonstrated that the considerations relevant to determining the existence of a legal system are not reducible to mere matters of empirical fact such as the existence of a monopoly of force or the existence of certain configurations of official power, but require inquiry also into the degree to which values designated by the rule of law are in course of realization.

To end this section, let us look at one possible argument for a further necessary connection between law and morals that Fuller only hinted at.[25] Suppose a system satisfies all the principles of legality but utterly fails to serve human interests. One could argue that it could not then be a legal system because our very concept of law is built on the notion that law ought to serve human interests at least to some degree. In this respect, law might be likened to the practice of medicine (an analogy suggested to me by Professor Max Black). A society in which doctors regularly poisoned their patients could not be said to have a medical system. Similarly, a purported legal system that systematically and deeply diminished the well-being of its members might be said to lose not only its legitimacy, but also its title as law. Among other things, this would mean that there could be no moral obligation to obey the directives of the system.

Legal processes

Fuller devoted more sustained thought to legal processes than to any other facet of law.[26] But surprisingly enough, he did not stress the necessarily moral value of certain legal processes. Yet he arrived at this idea even earlier (1949) than he did his views on the moral value of his principles of legality, which were not published until the 1960's.[27]

Consider, for example, adjudicative processes. In Chapter Two we saw that Fuller required that certain instrumental notions ("oughts") of value be satisfied if we are to have anything that can truly qualify as adjudication (presentations by the parties in the presence of one another with opportunity to rebut each other, an impartial judge, etc.). Genuine adjudication is therefore an "is-ought" complex in which "being" and "value" are part of an integral reality.[28]

Now, do these notions of what ought to be necessarily translate into moral notions? Fuller believed that some of them do, and if he is right, then we have here a further necessary connection between law and morals. Fuller believed that if a process is genuinely adjudicative, it necessarily affords participants a fair opportunity to be heard in matters of real concern to them. Moreover, by virtue of this participation, such a process is necessarily to some degree legitimate, and this lends moral force to its particular outcomes. Fairness and legitimacy are not merely values. They are moral values.[29] The outcomes of a genuine adjudicative process are not necessarily good, to be sure. They might even be bad because (among other things) the law that was applied was bad. But this does not make the values of fairness and legitimacy involved in the workings of a genuine adjudicative process any the less moral or any the less significant in themselves.

Again, this is not to immunize adjudication from criticism. A genuine adjudicative process might be to some degree fair and legitimate yet subject to criticism precisely on the ground that it is not as fair and legitimate as it should be. That the process is what it ought to be sufficiently to qualify as a genuine adjudicative process does not foreclose all criticism even when the relevant notions of what ought to be are necessarily moral.

As we will see in Chapter Six, this same type of general analysis can be applied to various other processes. It is enough for now to cite one further example. Consider genuine legislative processes of a democratic kind. The right of parties potentially affected by a proposed law to a legislative hearing in which they may try to influence the content of the legislation, and indeed the very principle of majority rule by which legislation is enacted, are parallel to the adjudicative right to a hearing with its implications for fairness and legitimacy.

In sum, then, genuine legal processes are value-laden. Moreover, certain values must necessarily be served if certain processes are to exist or to function genuinely as such processes. Further, since certain of these values are values of moral worth, morals are necessarily a part of such legal processes.

4

The differentiation of law from non-law

One of the things Fuller most objected to in the legal positivists' approach was their excessive (to him, anyway) preoccupation with finding some all-encompassing criterion, or master test, by which law could be differentiated from non-law. (In this context, non-law is usually assumed to consist mainly of moral notions and moral argument.) He expressed these objections in some detail in his 1940 work, *The Law in Quest of Itself*, and in his exchanges in the 1950's and 1960's with H. L. A. Hart, the leading modern-day positivist.[1] The overall anti-positivist attack was carried even further in the 1960's and 1970's by Hart's own successor at Oxford, Ronald M. Dworkin.[2] Many today agree that the works of Fuller and Dworkin demonstrate that there can be no master test for law.

Fuller's anti-positivism took two forms here. First, he held that the positivist quest for a general criterion by which the law could be identified and differentiated must fail, at least in regard to such societies as the United States and Britain. Second, he held, contrary to most positivists, that whatever the manner of differentiating valid law from non-law in such societies, there can be no sharp line between law and non-law (especially morals). Although Fuller did not develop the first of these theses as fully as he might have, I will seek to elaborate it here faithfully to his evident intuitions (and also in a manner largely consistent with the anti-positivism of Dworkin). Fuller did, however, develop at some length his view that law cannot (in general terms) be sharply differentiated from non-law (especially morals), and I will provide a rather full account of that view. As we will see, he thought a great deal was at stake.

The positivist quest for a general differentiating criterion

It is hardly surprising that positivists from Hobbes to the present have not been content to identify the valid laws of particular societies merely by the fact that they are widely accepted. Among other things, any such factual "test of acceptance" could not itself very well differentiate law from non-law, for then the common morality could be classified as law too, since it consists (in part) of socially accepted precepts. Moreover, a mere test of acceptance could not account for either the bindingness of a new form of law, for it would not have had time to command acceptance, or the bindingness of certain old law that no longer (if ever) commanded acceptance. Besides, we all know that lawyers and others concerned with the law are ordinarily able to identify the law relatively accurately and efficiently without inquiring into its actual acceptance case by case. Presumably, then, there is some master test.

Many positivists envisioned a kind of two-tiered "system," in which the lower tier consists of the ordinary binding precepts of the system and the upper tier of some accepted general criterion for identifying the precepts of the lower tier. The general identifying criterion incorporates the feature or features that all and only the binding precepts of the lower tier have in common. Or as H. L. A. Hart put it, the accepted criterion (or a limited set of criteria) specifies "some feature or features possession of which by a suggested rule is taken as a conclusive affirmative indication that it is a rule of the group."[3] In this two-tiered system, the criterion itself (or a limited set of criteria) qualifies as part of the system because of its social acceptance, whereas the binding rules of the lower tier, though they also may be accepted, qualify as law by *satisfying the criterion* of valid law that is already an internal part of the system. For example, if, in Great Britain, the socially accepted general criterion is "whatever the Queen in Parliament adopts is law," then any rule so adopted is valid law in Great Britain.

The legal theorist in the positivist tradition may confront two quite distinct problems here: (1) that of devising some general test as above, and (2) that of describing the criteria at work in one or more particular systems. The first task can lead to fairly elaborate constructions, as the works of Austin, Kelsen, and Hart amply attest. Similarly, the task of providing an accurate general description of the actual law-identifying practices within a particular system can be formidable. And these practices may differ significantly from system to system. (We will later see that there is still a third task for the theorist—that of prescribing the kind of overall theory of legal validity that a legal system ought to have.)

For those concerned primarily with the first problem, a two-tiered scheme with its all-encompassing criterion has seemed an attractive solution. Not only might such a scheme explain how lawyers and citizens can efficiently identify valid law without having to determine the social acceptance of particular rules; an all-encompassing and sharp-edged criterion occupying the upper tier also promises to "nail down" the law of the lower tier and thereby mark it off from such non-law as morality. Further, the criterion seems to allow for a *system* of law that would be at once unified and coherent. At least, all the binding rules of the lower tier would somehow answer to the criterion of the upper tier. Finally, it promises also to account for the legal validity of new forms of law not yet socially accepted and of old forms no longer accepted.

With all this apparently to be said for a two-tiered scheme with its master test, it is hardly surprising that the positivist quest for such a scheme has been so persistent and intense. Fuller variously described this pursuit as the quest "for some criterion of the law that is," for "some criterion which would sharply distinguish law from morality," for "some means of drawing a sharp line between the law that is, on the one hand, [and] the law that ought to be, or is trying to be, on the other," and for "some clear and unambiguous test of law, for some clean sharp line that will divide the rules which owe their validity to their source and those which owe their validity to acceptance and intrinsic appeal."[4]

Predictably, given the long history of positivist legal thought, a variety of identifying criteria have been proposed. Thus, a lower-tier precept has variously been held to be law if and only if it

(1) is a command of the sovereign,
(2) is laid down by legislators or courts,
(3) is predictable that courts will act on it,
(4) represents an actual behavior pattern of courts,
(5) can be traced to the basic norm at the foundation of the legal order,
(6) is identifiable by reference to the accepted criteria of validity of the system in a "rule of recognition."

Nearly all the proposed tests purport to be merely factual (i.e., require that the validity of a lower-tier precept be determined solely by reference to antecedent events). Yet this factual inquiry is to be something much less than an ad hoc determination of the degree of actual social acceptance, if any, of the precept in question. Rather, as usually conceived, the inquiry is to be into whether the precept displays some feature that all and only valid precepts of the system have in common. (The criterion requiring this feature is itself assumed to be a part of the system by virtue of its social acceptance as the test for law.) Observe that each of the six tests above purports to be comprehensive. That is, each presumes to identify all the law of a given system. Observe also that source, not content, is what determines the validity of a precept in most of these tests. I will sometimes call a criterion of this kind "source-based." The source-based character of nearly all of these tests is hardly accidental, for the positivist quest stands its best chance of sharply differentiating law from non-law if a precept's membership in the lower tier can be said to be due exclusively to its authoritative origin. If the putative law can be traced to an authoritative lawgiver, then it is valid; if not, it is invalid. But if the content of a lower-tier precept is made relevant to its validity, the line between law and non-law will not be so clear. For that matter, it is not even possible to capture actual tests of content in anything that can appropriately be called a general criterion of validity, as we will see.

Failure of the positivist quest

Conceptually, there does not appear to be any inherent obstacle to the success of the positivist quest. For example, it seems possible that all legal systems might be ones in which valid law of the lower tier is identifiable solely by a general source-based criterion. But possibilities are one thing, actualities another. To begin with, the positivist conceptual framework does not satisfactorily apply to the American legal system for one simple reason: many of the applicable tests of legal validity are not exclusively source-based; they are also content-oriented. Thus, for example, a contract otherwise valid because made by legally qualified contracting parties (source) may be invalid because it is unconscionable (content); a will otherwise valid because made by a competent testator (source) may be invalid because it is in conflict with state governmental policy (content); an otherwise valid statute because duly enacted (source) may be invalid because it arbitrarily discriminates (content); an otherwise valid precedent laid down by a court (source) may prove to be invalid because it is not "good law" (content).

The tests of legal validity at work in these examples take the form of particular standards that range over relatively discrete domains. A test of this type is far from being a general differentiating criterion (or a limited set of such criteria) of the kind that figures in the usual positivist framework.[5] Moreover, since these more particular standards of validity all embody tests of content as well as of source, the American system emerges as a strikingly different arrangement from the kind of two-tiered scheme envisioned by many positivists. Yet the existence of such particular standards explains the important fact that in the American system, lawyers and others concerned with law can regularly identify the law efficiently and effectively without measuring the general acceptance of lower-tier precepts in particular cases.

A positivist might respond that in such a system, particular standards of validity of this kind can all be captured in a general differentiating criterion if one thinks of that criterion as occupying the highest of three tiers, with the precepts identified as binding law on the lowest tier and the more particular standards of validity occupying an intermediate level. We may pause to ask what might motivate such a move as this. Ordinary lawyers might well think it superfluous to erect such a third tier purporting to capture all the content of the second-tier standards in some single criterion (or a limited set of criteria). Some positivists, though, could be expected to point out that a single master test, or a limited set of very wide-ranging criteria, could be highly valuable to lawyers as providing a kind of short cut to the identification of binding law on the lowest tier. Moreover, a crowning third-tier criterion (or limited set of criteria) would conform to positivist models drawn from science. At least such a crown would qualify as a kind of parsimonious reduction of the second tier and would thus display the systematic unity and coherence of the legal order as a whole.

Whether or not the positivist's general differentiating criterion captures most source-based tests, it should be plain that particular content-oriented standards of validity cannot be captured in such a criterion (or even in a limited set of such criteria). These standards can at most be incorporated in an inventory, and an inventory is clearly not a criterion.

In the American legal system, there are hundreds of these particular standards of validity. I know of no major field of law in which they cannot be found. And even within a given field, there may be many different standards. Unconscionability, for example, is only one of several grounds on which an otherwise valid contract clause might be invalid; it might have been made in bad faith, for example, or be contrary to public policy.

I doubt whether it would even be possible (without distortion) to have one master test for each field. There is no way that all the divergent content relevant to the validity of putative forms of law could be welded together or summed up into anything that could qualify as a single, overarching criterion. Of course, one might try to "generalize" from the various individual content-oriented standards of validity to the effect that valid law must be "reasonable in content" or the like, and then state this generality in a "criterion." I am certain lawyers would find the resulting criterion highly misleading and relatively useless as compared with direct resort to more particular substantive standards of validity. It is also difficult to see how an all-encompassing content-oriented criterion could escape being vacuously general. In short, if I am right, we are up against the limits of theory here. Indeed, even if all the divergent substantive content embodied in particular standards of validity could be captured in a master test for each major field of law, this would still leave us with a vast multiplicity of criteria—far more than some systematizing positivists would be happy with. Observe that I am not suggesting that a legal system can dispense with particular standards of validity. What I am arguing is that in some legal systems we cannot capture such standards in anything that may properly be called a criterion (or even a limited set of criteria) of the kind that so many positivists have sought. Rather, the most that we can have (and all that we should ever want) is a lengthy inventory of these more particular standards.

Now, is there any evidence that Fuller himself saw the foregoing line of attack on the positivist quest for a general "criterion of the law that is"? One sentence in his book *The Morality of Law* indicates rather clearly that he was indeed thinking along these lines. Thus he said in 1964, in attacking Hart's quest for a "rule of recognition" embodying such a criterion, that he "seems to insist that . . . the rule of recognition that ascribes sovereignty to the Queen in Parliament can in some way summarize and absorb all the little rules that enable lawyers to recognize law in a hundred different special contexts."[6]

If we abandon, as we should, the reductionist quest of the positivist, we are left in some societies with a two-tiered theory in which binding precepts of the lower tier are identified as law by reference to *an inventory* of particular standards of validity on the upper tier, standards both of origin and of content. In such a scheme, positivist theory generally has it that the precepts of the lower tier are valid law because they satisfy the criteria of validity internal to the system, whereas the precepts of the upper tier—the criteria themselves—are part of the law of the system because they are generally accepted. For example, a law requiring the presence of two witnesses for a valid will would derive its validity not by virtue of its being specifically recognized as law within the society through general acceptance, but by virtue of its satisfying some criterion of validity internal to the legal system, say, "a duly enacted statute that is not unconstitutional is law" (American system) or "whatever the Queen in Parliament adopts is law" (British system). On the other hand, the general criterion of valid law at work here would itself qualify as law not by virtue of its satisfying criteria of validity internal to the system, but by virtue of its being specifically recognized as law within the society through general acceptance as such.

Fuller attacked this distinction too. He thought that it reflected an effort to impose a juristic scheme on the reality of law from without, a scheme again motivated by the "positivist quest for some clear and unambiguous test of law, for some clean sharp line that will divide the rules which owe their validity to their source and those which owe their validity [i.e. status as law] to acceptance and intrinsic appeal."[7] In Fuller's view, even some lower-tier law owes its status as law largely or wholly to acceptance and rational appeal. Yet he did not always see how to get the most theoretical mileage out of his insights here. In what follows, I offer some assistance. Consider, for example, a duly enacted statute. In the positivist scheme, this is indisputably a form of lower-tier law and therefore must owe its entire status as law to satisfying a criterion of validity internal to the system. But just what is *the law* of a statute? The law of a statute is not exhausted in its formal wording. Among other things, the content of the law of a statute derives also from the interpretations put on it by judges and others. To the extent that these influence the statute's content, the statute owes its status as law not to satisfying an internal criterion of valid law, but to notions that inform particular interpretations and are therefore *accepted* as having rational appeal. (Such notions may be very particular and ad hoc). And no sharp general line can be drawn between that part of the law of a statute that owes its status as law to having been duly enacted (satisfaction of an internal criterion of valid law) and that part owing its status as law to the influence of particular notions of what is an appropriate interpretation for the issues and the case at hand (notions legally recognized and accepted because of their rational appeal).

Suppose, for example, a new statute says that a will must be signed in the presence of two competent witnesses. Must the witnesses both be present when the testator signs? Or can he sign in the presence of one and then another? The statute does not say in so many words. A court will usually decide the issue in light of interpretational and other notions that have rational appeal to the court. Such notions inform the law of the statute and thus qualify as a form of lower-tier law, yet they do not necessarily owe any of their status as law to satisfying a general positivistic criterion of valid law internal to the system (e.g. "A duly enacted statute that is not unconstitutional is valid law"). In his book *Anatomy of the Law*, Fuller characterizes such notions as "implicit law" in contrast to the "made law" of statutes, constitutions, contract terms, and other forms of written law.[8]

Earlier, we saw that Fuller held that the validity of lower-tier made law cannot be accounted for by a general criterion of validity. Now we see that he held as well that all made law contains implicit law, and that made law therefore does not necessarily owe the validity of its entire content even to satisfying particular standards of validity, let alone a general criterion.

But equally if not more embarrassing to the positivist quest for sharp distinctions between lower-tier law owing its validity to internal criteria and upper-tier law owing its status as law to acceptance and rational appeal, Fuller identified basic categories of lower-tier law that are wholly or at least in very large measure implicit law, not merely implicit elements in made law. As such they owe their status as law wholly or at least in very large measure to acceptance and rational appeal. Although in *The Anatomy of Law* Fuller cited several examples of such implicit lower-tier law, he gave special emphasis to customary law and to common law. Neither of these forms of law is essentially or predominantly made law. (In Chapter Six, I discuss his conception of customary law in some detail.) Unlike Dworkin and others, Fuller believed that customary law is of great importance in our legal system, and not merely in commercial and business contexts. But he (and Dworkin as well) denied that the legal status of customary law, this wide-ranging form of lower-tier law, could be accounted for as the positivists would have it. According to one influential version of positivist theory, that of John Austin, custom becomes valid lower-tier law only when it satisfies a criterion of validity internal to the system: "formulation or adoption by an authorized court." But according to Fuller, customary law is law primarily because of its general acceptance by those affected. On this fundamental issue, Fuller should be allowed to speak at some length in his own words:

> Austin's treatment of custom involves something like a doctrine of second birth: custom starts as a kind of conventional morality and is then reborn as law when it is adopted as a standard of decision by the act of a court. There are a number of artificialities concealed in this apparently innocent—if tendentious—interpretation. In the first place, as we have already intimated, this is not the way the courts themselves look on the matter. It is true that not every customary practice will be accepted as a standard of judicial decision. Some customs are injurious to the public interest or are contrary to legislative enactments. The courts will, accordingly, scrutinize the implications of a custom before accepting it as law. Nevertheless, when this acceptance takes place the courts do not think of themselves as *enacting*, but rather as *recognizing*, law. There are situations in which a custom is so obviously fair and beneficial that no doubt will arise but that it would, in case of controversy, be accepted by the courts as a source of law. The outcome of litigation may be so foreseeable that litigation will not take place. In such a situation the result of Austin's analysis is to deny the name of law to custom precisely in those situations in which it is so plainly law that no legal test of its right to that designation will be likely to occur.
>
> Secondly, Austin's interpretation would lead us to suppose that when a second case arises the court deciding this case would look not to the custom itself, but to the authoritative statement of the effect of the custom contained in the first decision. But in practice this will seldom occur. Usually the second case will involve some slightly different facet of the custom, one not directly involved in the first case. The second court will, accordingly, derive its standard of decision from the custom itself, and not from the words used by the first court in attempting to describe the custom.
>
> Thirdly, customs have a habit of changing through time. Changes may come about through altered external conditions, because of technological progress, or as indirect accommodation to new forms of enacted law. However the changes occur, they are likely to be recognized and accepted in later judicial decisions. Here the doctrine of rebirth becomes, in effect, a doctrine of continuous rebirth, with all the embarrassments such a view entails for any notion that a custom is in some way wholly transmuted into a radically different thing on the date when it was first used by a court to decide a litigated issue.
>
> Fourthly and lastly, if we reject all the qualifications just made, and accept Austin's doctrine of rebirth on its own terms, there remains an element of implicit law in the doctrine itself. Austin plainly assumes that once a custom has been accepted by a court as a standard of decision, that acceptance holds good, not simply for the case at hand, but for all similar cases in the future. This is because Austin takes for granted the existence of a rule or practice—a *custom*—by which courts will follow their own prior decisions. Now this rule was never "made" by any explicit enactment; it is a part of the customary rules governing the actions of courts. Like most customary rules it has its

> fringes of uncertainty and is subject to exceptions in instances that cannot be clearly defined in advance. So that, in the end, the security of the custom reborn as enacted law against a relapse into its unbaptized state depends upon a custom implicit in the practice of courts.[9]

Fuller took a similar approach to the common law, which he characterized not as made law, but as essentially or predominantly implicit law. Common-law precepts dealing with rules of contracts, torts, property, and the like are vital forms of lower-tier law. Yet they owe their status as law in large measure to general acceptance and rational appeal, rather than to conformity with a general criterion or standard of validity entirely internal to the system (i.e., having been laid down by prior judges). The ingredients of the common law are in large part notions of reason (not necessarily sound in objective terms) growing out of the subject matter of the common-law cases that arise. And in our system, whether or not a precedent is sufficiently good to become "settled" law and therefore truly law is largely a matter of the acceptability of its ingredients to subsequent judges and to the legal profession at large. Thus common-law precepts are largely law by virtue of the acceptance of these ingredients in light of their rational appeal, not by virtue of having been formally laid down by some duly authorized state official (i.e. a judge), the positivist's usual criterion of validity here.[10]

It may appear that these forms of implicit lower-tier law cannot be known in advance—that we must wait until a judge interprets a statute, or recognizes a custom, or decides a case, before we can know the law. This would not be the result, on the positivist's theory, for criteria of validity internal to the system are known and usable in advance, a great virtue. But even if, on Fuller's view, lower-tier law owes its status as law primarily to acceptance and rational appeal, it does not follow that citizens, lawyers, and others must usually wait for a judge's ruling to know the law. Although this cannot be developed here, in my view, the grounds on which interpretational notions, custom, and common law are received *are* very largely generalizable, *are* in fact so generalized, and *are* widely understood within at least the legal profession. Thus for the law to be knowable in advance, it is simply not necessary to have the kind of system for which so many positivists seem to have yearned—a system in which law is identifiable preferably by reference to the antecedent and authentic stamp of some authoritative originator. Law can be sufficiently identified by other means.

Before we turn to Fuller's further line of argument, let us see how, if at all, his attack on the positivist quest for a master test of valid law differs from Dworkin's more recent and more celebrated attack on this same quest (though aimed mainly at the ideas of Hart). Dworkin has concentrated on a category of lower-tier law that he calls legal principles (e.g., "No person shall profit from his own wrong" and "Manufacturers of dangerous articles have a special duty to the public").[11] For the positivist, these forms of law would be law by satisfying a general criterion of validity, but Dworkin has argued impressively that they instead qualify as law by virtue of their general acceptance and intrinsic appeal, as well as by virtue of their being used as reasons *by officials* from time to time ("institutional support" not itself capturable in a criterion). This has led him to argue further that there are no gaps in the law—cases of "first impression" and the like, since legal principles (reasons) are always available to fill the gap. Thus there is always pre-existing law, and one of the parties to any case always has a legal right to the outcome in accord with the weight of relevant legal principles. Quite evidently, then, Dworkin's attack on positivism is not identical with Fuller's. Fuller does not specifically address himself to what Dworkin calls legal principles. Moreover, Dworkin sometimes suggests that principles must have some actual official institutional support *before* they can be law (though he does not consider this a source-based test). Fuller does not require such support for all the various forms of implicit law, for example. And the distinction I have sketched between a general criterion of validity and an inventory of particular standards of validity does not figure at all in Dworkin's illuminating effort.

From Fuller's private papers, there is evidence that he endorsed Dworkin's general approach (first published in 1964); but there is no indication in Fuller's own published writings that he would go as far as Dworkin in regard to principles. Although Fuller was sympathetic to the idea that some principles might become so well established as to qualify as lower-tier laws of a kind owing their status to recognition and acceptance, he did not hold that there could never be gaps in the law or claim that there is always pre-existing law. He argued that moral argument is directly relevant to deciding a case of first impression, and that such argument is not necessarily already "in the law," so to speak, in the form of legal principles *à la* Dworkin. (These interestingly different forms of anti-positivism merit a further treatment that cannot be provided here.)

Undesirable effects of the positivist quest

We have seen that for Fuller, the positivists' two-tiered conceptual framework is bound to fail on several counts. To begin with, some important systems embody many varied and particular standards of validity, some source-based and some content-oriented; the notion that a master test could account for all this variety is a fantasy. Further, the very notion of a sharp distinction between a master test owing its status as law to acceptance and lower-level precepts owing their status as law to satisfying the master test will not stand up when applied to some important systems. Thus, the elements out of which the positivist theory is constructed are inadequate. Worse yet, some of the constructions are elaborate fictions or hypostatizations. The idea of a sovereign whose commands constitute the law (Austin) and the idea of a basic norm to which all valid law is traceable (Kelsen) are examples. According to Fuller, then, all this is bad theory. Moreover, bad theory of this sort could beget bad law, bad legal method, and bad systems of law. But we are getting ahead of the story.

Fuller thought that most positivists viewed their quest as a value-neutral enterprise. After all, they took their analytical models from science, and true science is supposed to be value-neutral. The general theory of validity being constructed was addressed to social data: law-identifying practices in particular legal systems. He also thought that they were deluding themselves, that at bottom they were usually "carrying out a program," not just "constructing a theory of legal validity" or "analyzing the necessary forms of legal thought."[12] These thinkers, it seemed to him, purported to be conceptualizing reality (or a "postulated" reality with an inner logic of its own) without reference to any social purposes their efforts might serve. Fuller singled out Hobbes as an exception. Hobbes "theorized" that valid law consists entirely of the commands of the sovereign, and that morals are subordinate to and derive from positive law. Why? To Hobbes, such a source-based criterion of validity promised a closed system of law in which the lower-tier rules would be easily identified and highly determinate, thereby securing order, peace, and civil obedience. Any theory so motivated could hardly be value-neutral. But after Hobbes, rarely did theorists so openly proclaim their program. Yet such exclusively source-based criteria promise a sharper line between law and non-law than content-oriented criteria. Moreover, source-based criteria elevate the role of authority and fiat in the legal order. Law is essentially something formal that is authoritatively laid down rather than something with a certain kind of required content (moral or other). Further, such a theory has profound implications for legal argument: a good argument becomes one that has been authoritatively endorsed, not one that happens to be sound on its merits. Given the motivation of Hobbes and his successors, it should hardly be surprising that this "value-neutral" theory includes internal elements so clearly designed to serve order, peace, fidelity to law, and related values.

Fuller discerned still other motives at work in the positivists' enterprise. For one thing, many of them were moral skeptics. Kelsen, for example, sometimes suggested that justice was simply an "irrational ideal."[13] Austin seems to have thought that much of morality was not fit stuff for incorporation in law. Fuller pointed out that Austin wrote of the "uncertainty, scantiness, and imperfection of positive moral rules."[14] Small wonder that these thinkers pursued a criterion of the law that was largely source-based—that promised a sharp distinction between law and non-law. To them, non-law meant, largely, moral ideas and argument. The positivistic emphasis on the completeness and comprehensiveness of a "genuine" legal system is in the same spirit. Gaps in the law, for example, would only represent a possible entry point for imperfect moral ideas.

According to Fuller, positivists also assumed that the elegant architecture of a two-tiered or perhaps even three-tiered structure (with a single criterion of validity perched at the top) would serve still other values, namely, simplicity, unity, system, and coherence—values prominent in scientific and philosophical thought. The ragged edges of certain legal phenomena, their fragmentary character, their recalcitrance to neat systematization, were all conditions more to be pitied than to be taken account of.

Fuller noted that when positivists invoked their general theories of validity in order to describe law-identifying practices within particular legal systems, they seldom felt that they encountered any difficulty. This was apparently because they had worked out fairly elaborate constructions capable of sustaining a life of their own even when the facts failed to cooperate. Indeed, to the extent of any failure of fit with given systems, so much the worse for those systems. Although Sir Henry Maine and a few others identified various important failures of fit, it was really the work of Fuller and more recently Dworkin that enabled us to see the full extent to which positivist theories of legal validity do not apply to the facts of existing legal systems.

The failure of these theories to fit the facts was bad enough, but a more objectionable effect was this: positivists became preoccupied with them and the values they were assumed to serve, and thus failed to come to grips with the question of what kind of general theory of legal validity ought to prevail in a legal system. Fuller believed that source-based and formal theories of validity not only misrepresent legal reality, but are unhealthy as well. In his view, purportedly descriptive general conceptions of theorists, legal personnel, and citizens about what counts as valid law may ultimately shape what the law actually becomes. Thus, if a society embraces a formal and fiat-oriented theory of legal validity, it runs the risk of falling into a "law-is-law" formalism.[15] To the extent that this eventuates, it may also influence moral ideas, which thereafter reinforce the law.

In addition, Fuller denied that ideals drawn from science and logic such as simplicity, unity, system, and internal coherence can have a very strong claim on the law. More important, he denied that positivism does in fact serve the cause of peace, order, and predictability. As he put it, those interested in these values must concern themselves with

> the content of the law, and not only with the content but with the goodness of that content. The stability of a given legal system, its capacity to produce

> peace and order, will depend . . . on the layman's willingness to accept those rules as being essentially right. A law which is good for the purpose of establishing order will have to be or at least to seem "good" in other respects as well.[16]

And for Fuller, standards of validity that are largely formal cannot adequately serve the end of having law that is good in content. Nor can standards that make the origin of law the only test of its validity, thereby excluding notions of justified content—moral and other ideas. Standards of validity ought to orient legal personnel to the merits of arguments, not just to their prior official sponsorship, if any.

But let us be clear on one point: Fuller did not claim that positivists cared little about the quality of the law's content as such. He knew, of course, that Bentham, Austin, Hart, and others all cared a great deal. He claimed, rather, that a *theory of legal validity* of the traditional positivist type inherently neglects the quality of the law's content. In dwelling on such a theory, these thinkers missed an important opportunity to strike theoretical blows for the just, the right, and the good in law.

Failure of sharp differentiation

There is a further aspect of the positivist quest for a master test of valid law that we have not yet frontally considered. Most positivists wanted the kind of test that would *sharply* differentiate law from non-law, especially morals. Fuller thought this aspect of their enterprise doomed to failure, and he devoted more effort to showing this than he did to arguing that we cannot have and ought not to want a source-based master test for identifying all the law of a society.

Here Fuller launched a three-pronged assault. He offered a number of arguments and examples designed to show how and why no such sharp line is possible, at least in systems known to him. He also dug out the motives behind the positivist position, translated them into arguments, and then sought to answer them. Finally, he advanced a number of reasons of his own to show why legal theorists ought not to go around insisting on a sharp separation of law from non-law (especially from morals). Let us examine each of these lines of attack in turn. (What follows is again my own systematization of Fuller's views. He did not himself draw his thoughts together precisely in this way.)

The impossibility of a sharp differentiation. Fuller, as we have seen, simply denied that there was any general feature or set of features of the kind most positivists were seeking to capture in a master test that would enable them to differentiate law sharply from non-law (mainly morals), and so saw the positivist quest as fundamentally misguided. I will begin with his arguments, expressed or implied, concerning law in the form of specific rules and other precepts.[17]

First, in deciding whether to follow a precedent, judges, other officials, and lawyers, at least in the United States, are ready to ask whether the precedent is "good law"—whether its purposes are sufficiently good and whether it is sufficiently well designed for those purposes. Thus it is widely assumed that only precedent that is sufficiently good can become truly settled and therefore valid law. The fact that case law is authoritatively laid down or acted on does not alone qualify it as sufficiently good for it to become settled. Judge-made "law" that is not sufficiently good to be regarded as settled is likely to be overruled, or confined to its facts, or riddled with exceptions, or regularly "distinguished" away, or simply ignored. But the standard of sufficient goodness is largely determined by moral notions. It is thus not possible to draw a sharp line between a legal standard of validity purportedly incorporating moral notions of sufficient goodness and general moral ideas of sufficient goodness "outside the law" on which such standards must continuously draw.

Second, some basic standards for determining the validity of legislation find their way into admittedly legal rules (in some systems, constitutional rules). Other such standards, equally fundamental, may not be formally expressed in such rules, yet their ingredients may be tacitly accepted and thus a part of the working system. For example, in the United States it is widely accepted that a legislature must not adopt law in the course of a drinking bout, or must not pass laws and then keep them secret. Fuller claimed that such "implicit laws of lawmaking" are in significant measure matters of social morality, and that no sharp line can be drawn between them and standards explicitly embodied in the law, such as due process or equal protection. Even written constitutions cannot make the line a sharp one, for they do not embody all the essential notions. Moreover, a constitutional order as a whole must itself be imbued with a spirit of legality—moral in character—if it is to function healthily.[18]

Third, legal precepts, judge-made and statutory, must be interpreted and applied by lawyers, judges, and other officials, a task that is commonly discharged in light of applicable purposes and reasons. Yet often such purposes and reasons are not just "there" to be read off the face of a judicial opinion or a statute. In formulating applicable purposes and reasons, lawyers and officials regularly invoke moral arguments. This should not be surprising. The purported substantive ingredients of most statutes and cases are moral in character, at least in some measure. Again, it is simply not possible here to draw a sharp distinction between the argumentation that is legal and the argumentation that is merely moral.

Fourth, the law applicable to a case frequently allows leeway for different decisions. When this is so, the task of legal personnel goes well beyond merely interpreting and applying existing law. More than the usual element of creativity is involved. The judge, in the course of deciding the case, may even take the opportunity to try to improve on the substance of the law. In so doing, he will bring to bear his own notion of what the law ought to be, a moral argument. In this process he will often blend interpretation and improvement—"is" and "ought." It is impossible to draw a sharp line within this blend between these two elements. Similarly, lawyers, judges, and other officials must frequently cope with statutes, cases, and other forms of law that are, in relation to the issue at hand, only nascent, implicit, or fragmentary, and thus plainly in need of reasoned elaboration. The required elaboration that occurs is in fact regularly infused with moral notions. It is not possible to draw a sharp line between elaborations infused with moral notions that are already a part of the law and elaborations infused with moral notions that are not already a part of the law.

Fifth, some forms of law upon analysis turn out to be badly conceived or defectively drafted. They may fail in basic structure, in details of wording, in consistency with related law, in the perception of underlying facts, or in various other ways. Some judges and administrators take the view that such forms of law cannot be rescued at all. Others think rescue is possible but only to the extent that the law itself provides the necessary guidance. But there are some who will try to "make the most of" any such form of law (within limits). Now, often this cannot be done without resort to reason, including moral argument not wholly implicit in the deficient law. Here, too, there can be no sharp line between "the law that is" and the "law that ought to be."

Sixth, many legal rules incorporate concepts rooted in social morality. The ideas of responsibility and excuse that appear in our criminal law are illustrative. Yet these ideas, by their nature, cannot be subjected, even for legal purposes, to exact and standardized formulation. This is but another way of saying that they cannot be sealed off from their moral origins. In working with their legal embodiment, judges and others must often draw on these ideas as they are understood outside the law. Again, there can be no sharp line here between the legal and the merely moral.

Seventh, no one would deny that moral ideas are often relevant when making the law. Yet in the common law, for example, what constitutes a "case of first impression," in which the court must perforce make new law, is a matter of degree. There is always *some* rationally relevant legal analogy. The question is whether it is close enough to control the new point. It may not be. Something similar can be true of a statute in which the legislature has left some matter open. No sharp line can be drawn between creating new law, in which morals commonly play a part, and the identification and application of binding law, a purely legal matter (according to some positivists).

Eighth, a legal precept may at the outset only partially embody a moral principle or moral concept, which subsequently may be fully incorporated into the law by a court and applied thereafter. Such evolutionary incorporation need not occur, but frequently it does. Fuller sometimes said an evolving precept of this kind is in a "process of becoming." The precept becomes, perhaps even by imperceptible degrees, something that it was not originally. Of course, judges may also engage in more articulate and explicit collaboration in working out shared purposes over time. In any case, the reality is fluid and moving. It is not possible to distinguish sharply between notions that, as Fuller put it, "are only trying to become law and those which have succeeded—to set up a kind of finishing line, as it were."[19] At the same time, the entire moral environment surrounding the law is itself never wholly static, and as a society's values change, judges take these changes into account when they work with common law and statute. In a process of this kind, law and morals often merge, and no sharp line can be drawn between them.

Ninth, general moral principles (e.g., "No person shall profit from his own wrong") may play a role in the law without ever being adopted as law in so many words. Often it will not be possible to say whether the introduction of such a principle actually breaks new ground or merely recognizes a moral idea that has actually been "in" the law all along.

Finally, Fuller believed that an unconscious blending of "is" and "ought" frequently occurs in the law. Most judges, legislators, officials, and lawyers take their responsibilities seriously. It is only to be expected that they will, even without being fully aware of it, frequently seek to improve on the legal materials with which they work. Fuller once compared this phenomenon to the retelling of a funny story. Because we have grasped the point, when we retell the story, we often reformulate and in so doing we tend to improve on it. Frequently this process is more or less unconscious, or at least not deliberate. Fuller concluded that exactly the same kind of process could be at work in the reading of a statute or a decision.[20] In the course of transmitting a tradition, a judge may improve on it. His improvement comes about through "the is and the ought working together"—through a merging of the original legal materials with the judge's own conceptions of their true point. That the "is" and the "ought" can be sharply separated here is sheer fantasy.

Motives behind the search for a sharp differentiation. Fuller inquired into the motives behind the search for a sharp differentiation between law and non-law to see whether any of them might justify the pursuit of this goal. Again, the impetus that science gave to legal positivism must not be forgotten. Scientifically minded legal positivists were especially eager to have a "genuine subject." On this view, law, to be a real subject, must be sharply demarcated and differentiated from other things. It must be free of foreign matter and not dependent on other subjects. Kelsen and some of the American realists were proponents (often implicitly) of these subject-matter ideals.[21] Yet if Fuller's arguments are sound, the nature of law and its moral content are such that it cannot conform to these "ideals."

Many legal positivists also seem to have harbored a deep metaphysical view about the kind of substance fit for status as law. The genuine "stuff" of the law must be in the form of brute fact or reducible to brute fact. It must therefore be concerned with human conduct, not human mental states. Its existence must not be something easily debated or excessively open to controversy. As we have seen, Austin (in Fuller's view) stressed the "uncertainty, scantiness, and imperfection of positive moral rules." Holmes stressed that morals have to do with the "internal"—with motives and mental states.[22] And so on. Moral notions therefore cannot qualify as the stuff of which true law is made, and law must be sharply marked off from morals. Now, any such view must be seen for what it is, namely, an *a priori* conception of law that ignores its true character. As Fuller continually stressed, moral notions in fact pervade the law, a state of affairs in which a sharp separation simply cannot be made.

Nearly all positivists placed high value on what Fuller called "fidelity to law."[23] Thus at the minimum it should always be possible for citizens to obey the laws, and especially laws of which they might disapprove. All forms of law must be determinable and fully knowable in advance. Law cannot be confusingly entwined with moral notions not themselves law. In this light, a closed legal system, secure against further moral argument, even becomes a kind of ideal. Fuller himself conceded a genuine and "permanent element of stress" here between what Bentham called the necessary "cognoscibility" of law on the one hand and the desirability of leaving the system open to moral argument on the other. But Fuller thought that positivists greatly overstated the degree of stress. In his view, a closed system introduces stresses of its own such that the law-abiding citizen can no longer take the law at face value. And whatever the loss of cognoscibility in a system in which no sharp line can be drawn between the legal and the moral, Fuller thought this was more than compensated for by the infusion of moral ideas that improve the law's content.

A desire for law sufficiently knowable so that law-abiding citizens can be faithful to *its ends* even when those ends are not their own is one thing; a desire for law sufficiently certain, predictable, and reliable so that citizens can readily plan and interact in furtherance of *their own ends* is still another. Fuller did not reject this latter desideratum, but he assumed that some regular infusion of moral ideas was actually required to facilitate private ordering. Of course, the system could become too open-ended, too fluid, or too fast-moving. The rule of law itself requires that the law not be in such an ever-changing state that citizens have nothing to rely on.

Most positivists were also concerned to preserve the criticizability of the law. Some seem to have assumed that this requires a sharp separation of the legal from the non-legal, especially when the non-legal takes the form of those very moral standards by which the law itself is to be evaluated. But this is a misguided view. The law might be in need of criticism precisely on the ground that it is not sufficiently infused in some respect or other with morality. Moreover, a useful distinction may be drawn between a society's positive (common) morality and its critical morality. A body of law incorporating positive moral notions is not necessarily immune to criticism based on a critical morality.

Then there is the anarchist, whom some positivists seem to have feared so mightily.[24] Actually, there are two kinds of anarchists. We may call the first "legal" and the second "moral." The legal anarchist is the more radical. He argues thus: "This ought not be the law by my lights, therefore it is not, and I am free not merely to censure, but to disregard it." If the law is made very clear indeed, this may make the legal anarchist less ready to say "therefore it is not the law," and more ready to go along.

The moral anarchist, doubtless a more common type, is usually willing enough to go along with the law, but is accustomed to behaving pretty much as he pleases in mere matters of morals. According to Bentham, what is needed is a system in which both the law-abiding citizen and the moral anarchist will obey the law punctiliously, yet censure freely. However, the line between law and morals must be sharp, or else the moral anarchist is likely not only to censure freely, but to disobey as well.

Now, even if we admit that failing some sort of distinction, a moral anarchist might well mistake the law for mere morality, to the detriment of peace and order, there are replies to Bentham's position. A legal system cannot be set up and maintained merely with the moral anarchist in view. It is the law-abiding citizens we need mainly to keep our eye on. They are in the overwhelming majority. With respect to them, a sharp line between law and morals that seals the one off from the other is, according to Fuller, more likely to disserve than to serve the cause of peace and order in the long run.[25] The law-abiding citizen's willingness to obey ultimately depends on his sense that, overall, the law is essentially right or fitting. Law good for the purpose of securing order will thus have to be morally acceptable in other respects. A system of law sufficiently open to moral argument is more likely to be morally acceptable and thus capable of serving the cause of peace and order.

For some positivists, a simple fear of moral orthodoxy and moralism seems to explain the attempt to keep law and morals sharply distinct: a system of law open to morals risks the robust infusion of an illiberal common morality. Fuller denied that this was a significant risk. Moreover, he pointed out, judges and others must exercise judgment with respect to any ingredient that may enter the substance of the law, moral or non-moral. And there can be no guarantee against bad judgment. This problem is not solved by insisting on a closed system, for it would keep out good morals too.

Finally, as already noted, moral skepticism motivated certain positivists. Kelsen and some of the American realists were thus led to keep law and morals sharply distinct.

Undesirability of a sharp differentiation. Fuller discerned what he thought to be a deep ambivalence in the positivists' pursuit of distinguishing features that would separate law from non-law. In his view, many positivists seemed to waver between (1) holding that law and non-law (mainly morals) *are* in fact sharply separable in accordance with some general distinguishing feature or set of features, and (2) holding that law and non-law (mainly morals) *ought to be* sharply separated. Fuller preferred to approach the issue in the latter terms. To him, notions of what law really is (as contrasted with non-law) were not "mere images of some datum of experience, but direction posts for the application of human energies."[26]

In Fuller's view, legal theorists and others responsible for the health of a legal system ought not to be looking for a way to draw a clear line between law and morals at all. To begin with, he argued, such a separation would stifle judicial creativity. Judges, especially in the common law, have many opportunities (with the aid of lawyers) to improve on the existing law. They should stand ready to overrule, extend, narrow, revise, and fill gaps in the law. All these call for creativity, along with a lively sensitivity to relevant purposes and to the moral considerations that must figure in those purposes. Yet a judge who performs in a positivistic spirit generally wants to think of himself as merely following the law. Positivism seeks to erect a rigid barrier between that law and the morally reasonable—what Fuller called "a warning stop sign" that will keep reason from pushing "as far as it can."[27] The judge is simply to do or die and seldom to reason why; his is generally to be an uncreative role.

Fuller worried too about the broader issue of interpretation as such. He contended that positivism only increased the already serious risk that judges and others, overwhelmed by the linguistic or doctrinal technicalities of a form of law, would fail to grasp or would lose sight of the law's intent, and so would apply it mechanically. The principal safeguard against this sort of "law is law" formalism[28] and deadening literalism, he believed, lay in a view that refuses to sever the law from its moral ingredients and thus tolerates some "fusion" of law and morals.[29]

It might be argued that the solution to the fundamental problems of creativity and interpretation is not some blurring of the lines between the law that is and the law that ought to be. After all, Fuller himself admitted that the law embodies some bad "oughts." Perhaps the bad might be just as likely to infuse the law's content as the good? Now, H. L. A. Hart in fact made this very argument against Fuller, who thought it raised "much the most fundamental issue" of their whole controversy.[30] Fuller's counter to this, as I understand it, ran as follows.[31]

First, in an open-ended system of the kind he had in mind, the values that would infuse the law are not all *that* likely to be bad. On the contrary, they are far more likely to be good—to consist of "generally shared views of right conduct that have grown spontaneously through experience and discussion." Why so? To begin with, even in the most perverse regimes, there is always a certain hesitancy about writing inhumanities and intolerance into legal texts. In addition, in an open system judges and other officials are subject to demands for public justifications of what they do. These demands exert a constant pressure in favor of infusions of moral, not bad or evil, notions of what the law ought to be. Relatedly, with the "freer legal method" of this system, in which substantive rather than formal reasoning in borderline cases is the prevailing style, it would be harder for a judge or other legal official to cover up an infusion of bad or evil notions. The cover of a law-is-law formalism would simply be less ready to hand. Further, citizens need a rational and coherent system on which they can rely, even in borderline, novel, and difficult cases where some infusion of moral notions is certainly called for. The infusion of good morals will facilitate this coherence more than the infusion of bad or evil ideas, for the latter are less susceptible to patterned adoption or integration into a system that relies, in large measure, on moral acceptability; judges and others know this and will act accordingly.

Second, the immorality that would admittedly still slip through in an open system must be weighed against the immorality likely to be found in a more closed system. The restrictive and formal tests of validity needed to try to keep law and morals separate would be incapable of also keeping alive the general sense that the substantive goodness of law is and ought to be relevant to its very status as law. At the same time, in a closed system judges (and other officials) would be under far less pressure to justify their actions on substantive moral grounds. As a result, styles of legal argument would tend to become more formalistic. When called on to give reasons for decisions (especially dubious decisions), judges would find it easier to take refuge behind the maxim "the law is the law." All this might even eventually spell some loss of that "identification of law with those demands of morality that are the most urgent and the most obviously justifiable." Yet this very identification may be what largely accounts for the hesitancy of judges and other officials to write inhumanities and intolerances into the law in the first place.

5

Natural law and the role of reason

In the past hundred years, encyclopedists have often classified legal theorists into one (or more) of four categories: natural law theorists, legal positivists, historical jurists, and thinkers of the sociological or instrumentalist schools. Natural law is the oldest of these traditions, counting among its classical adherents Aristotle, the Stoics, and Cicero. Though one inevitably thinks of the great theologian Thomas Aquinas in this connection, a legal theorist may belong to this school of thought without being in the least religious.

When Fuller began writing in the 1930's, the American legal climate was not very congenial to natural law thinking. Fuller was sensitive to this. The term natural law still had about it "a rich, deep odor of the witches' cauldron," he remarked in 1942, and the mere mention of it sufficed "to unloose a torrent of emotions and fears."[1] Yet without claiming to be a "sponsor for any of the various systems of natural law," Fuller readily identified himself with that tradition. He did this perhaps most prominently in his book *The Law in Quest of Itself* (1940). Today, he is often thought of as the leading American standard-bearer of secular natural law thought.

But regardless of how Fuller was labeled, by himself or by others, was he truly a natural law theorist? The question is important for two reasons. Much of the history of legal theory in the past two hundred years has unfolded as a kind of debate between adherents of natural law and adherents of legal positivism. Now Fuller, as we know, was uncompromisingly anti-positivist. But to take a position against one side does not automatically put you on the other, so that we are still left with the question of whether he is correctly called a natural law theorist. As the very fact that there is room for doubt suggests, natural law "theory" divides into several branches, encompassing views ranging from the rather moderate to the quite extravagant. In this welter of competing claims, what is distinctly true of natural law theory can easily become obscured. I will single out the general tenets and directions of thought that have historically been associated with natural law thinking. We will see that Fuller embraced some and rejected others.

Sources of law's content and of evaluative standards

The classical natural law theorists focused on the law's content and on the substantive standards appropriate to its evaluation. This general orientation to law reveals itself directly and indirectly in a variety of related emphases that can be usefully portrayed in a kind of table, with appropriate contrasting emphases also listed:

Emphases of natural law theory	*Other emphases (especially positivist ones)*
Content and substantive standards of evaluation	Official sources
Reasoned arguments	Authoritative fiats
Moral substance	Formal pronouncement
Embodiments of values	Configurations of state power
Requirements for healthy functioning ("physiology")	Structural features ("anatomy")
Ends and means embodied in precepts	Formal properties of precepts
Religious authority	Secular authority

Looking at most of the items on this list today, we may wonder why natural law theory had such a bad name in certain legal circles in the United States at the time Fuller came on the scene in the 1930's. After all, inquiring into the content and the soundness of law is surely a legitimate concern of legal theory. Part of the explanation for the unpopularity of natural law thinking lies in the rise of the scientific ethos, which among other things tended to redirect thought about law away from "right reason" to "fact." The science-minded tended to be moral skeptics, too; and many skeptics simply could not accept the concept of *right* reason. Legal positivism, with its varied hostilities to natural law theories, would probably have been unthinkable without scientific positivism leading the way. At least in the United States, moreover, there was so violent a general revolt against "formalistic reason" that the baby (reason's just claims) tended to be thrown out with the bathwater. Then, too, natural law had been associated with religion, particularly the Catholic church. In an increasingly secular era, its religious associations were thought to diminish its claims on our attention. (This, of course, does not follow necessarily at all.)

Among the other reasons for the widespread antipathy to natural law doctrines is the simple fact that certain theorists tended to identify, quite unfairly, the whole tradition with the more extreme positions of some of the classical thinkers. To help the reader to understand the force of this reaction, I will briefly discuss the types of positions that presumably accounted for the more pungent "odors" arising from this "witches' cauldron" (as Fuller mockingly put it).[2]

First of all, natural law was assumed to entail an ideal conception of the ultimate end or good for mankind. This feature would usually take the form of some overarching value that incorporates a religious doctrine, such as the notion that the ultimate end for man is knowledge of God, an end to be secured partly through life in society under positive law. Other variations on this theme include elaborate tables of values, ranging from the knowledge of God and the preservation of life at the top of the scale to rather mundane concerns at the bottom.

Another feature of extravagant natural law theory is some doctrine about the authoritative source of natural law. Commonly, in religious versions of the theory, natural law is imputed to some extent to a supreme being. As a corollary, natural law is a "higher law," and any human law in conflict with it is invalid.

A third feature is a comprehensive ideal system of laws, fully worked out in all relevant details. This ideal system, or "code of nature," which consists largely of moral dictates deriving (partly through right reason) from God or from human nature, or both, determines society's positive laws. More than that, it serves also as the source of standards for evaluating those laws. Since it is both the exclusive source of society's laws and the exclusive source of standards for evaluating them, it is also an exhaustive source. Further, on this extreme view, the ideal system of laws would be applicable to all societies, would be immutable over time, and could not be overridden in the least respect. In short, its dictates would be absolute.

Now, to the extent that people identified natural law theory with these features, it is not difficult to explain why the theory was in bad odor when Fuller came on the American jurisprudential scene. At least to the secular-minded, *all* these claims are inarguably extravagant. Fuller himself took pains to repudiate each of them.[3] He did not subscribe to the "ultimate overarching value" thesis, or to the doctrine that natural law can be the subject of an authoritative (divine) pronouncement, or to the notion of natural law as a higher law that invalidates any conflicting human law. He rejected the view of natural law as an exhaustive and timeless system of laws, or "code of nature," susceptible of concrete application like a written code. He certainly did not hold that the laws of different societies should be the same for all time. Nor did he subscribe to a scheme of absolute values.

But we cannot on this account say Fuller was not a natural law theorist. One searches the literature of classical natural law in vain for very many thinkers who subscribed to all these doctrines.[4] Not even Aquinas and Augustine, the great Catholic church fathers, did so. The fact is, such a model of natural law theory grossly misrepresents the tradition as a whole. It is true, of course, that most of the classical theorists believed in a religious version of the ultimate overarching-value thesis and also believed that natural law was to some extent the subject of authoritative (divine) pronouncement. But it is possible to dispense with these features and still leave much of the natural law tradition intact.

If we confine ourselves to the general direction of natural law thought in which the emphasis is on the law's content and on substantive standards for evaluating that content, and if we dispense with the peculiarly religious aspects of this, can we now say that Fuller subscribed to it? Observe that what remains is not mere residue. Indeed, to many it is the heart of the tradition. It consists, essentially, of a vast body of substantive reasoning about the justified common core of content underlying all legal systems. This body of reasoning necessarily brings fundamental values into play. (Some of these values may change over time, and different laws will be needed in different societies even to serve the same general values.) The literature of natural law is replete with both summary and extended statements of this overall position. Aquinas, for example, was in part summarizing as much when he stressed that true law is "right reason."

Is there anything distinctive about this core element in the natural law tradition? There is, at least as contrasted to the thought of most legal positivists. Historically, most positivists have focused on formal sources, authoritative fiat, state power, legal structure, and the like. There is nothing against their also looking into the law's content, to be sure; but relatively few have, and that is the central point. (And even then those few, perhaps most notably Bentham and Hart, have shown an interest in content primarily in their reform proposals, not on the theoretical level.) An occasional positivist—Hobbes is a leading example—has even gone so far the other way as to argue for law's general immunity from moral criticism.

In regard to this core element, then, Fuller must be classed as in the natural law tradition. He himself wrote that the most fundamental tenet of natural law is an affirmation of the role of reason in legal ordering.[5] One of his favorite quotations was from the writings of a little known natural law theorist of the nineteenth century, William Rawle:

> Law, in all its divisions, is the strong action of Reason upon wants, necessities, and imperfections. No matter whether its ministration is by a legislative or through a judicial faculty, or by the consentaneous acts of individuals under no manifest compulsion; it is still the act of those on whom it has pleased divine Providence to bestow the attribute of reason, as distinguished from those who are guided only by instinct, and can make no rules for themselves.[6]

Fuller's stress on the force of reason and his faith in reason were perhaps the most recurrent themes in all of his writings. He most often contrasted reason not with instinct (as in the foregoing passage), but with the mere commands of officials in positions of state power. More specifically, he affirmed that law, in its general nature, is primarily an effort to apply reason rather than fiat to human relations, thus taking up an ancient natural law view held by Aquinas, among others. Of course, Fuller conceded that bad reasons might lie behind and figure in the content of a rule of law. Indeed, he thought that this might even justify disobedience.

As we saw in Chapter Four, Fuller attacked those positivists who would make the authoritative origin of a precept the one and only standard for determining its standing as valid law. In his view, this unduly divorced law's source from its content—from the ingredients of reason that in large measure must make it up. Positivism could not and did not satisfactorily cope with "the content of the law," he said, with the result that its most dangerous quality was its "denial of the force which ideas have without reference to their human sponsorship."[7]

Notwithstanding his endorsement of the natural law view that law is primarily the application of reason to human relations, Fuller sought to offer a balanced account of natural law:

> If the virtue of the natural law theory has been to keep alive faith in the capacity of human reason, its vice has often been to overstate the role rationality can play in human affairs. Reason can shape the fundamental structure of a legal system; it cannot prepare the law to deal with every twist and turn that human affairs can take. Under any legal system, embarrassing and borderline cases will arise that can, with equal rationality, or irrationality, be decided either way. To reach some disposition of these cases, we must employ a principle of *authoritative* decision and pass them over to a judge or administrator to decide, not because he will know how to decide them, but simply because somebody must. (Emphasis supplied.)[8]

Indeed, in one of his most perceptive essays, "Reason and Fiat in Case Law," Fuller even argued that every legal rule, as well as every legal institution, necessarily embodies some element of fiat.

Did Fuller go no farther in the general direction of natural law thought than to affirm the primacy of reason in legal ordering? Did he, like many predecessors in the tradition, try to identify more specific requirements of natural law? The short answer is: he did not go very much farther. He did state generally that in the case of a great many legal rules, the weight of reason is heavily on one side. Moreover, he stressed the universal importance of two broadly procedural dictates: "Keep man's purpose-forming processes healthy," and "Keep the channels of communication between men open."[9] For him these were natural laws of the most fundamental kind. The social significance of the first should be obvious, though just how positive law is to be used to achieve it is less clear. Fuller was not so sure that others would immediately see the importance of the second, though to his mind it was the "one central indisputable principle of what may be called substantive natural law."[10] Open communication was crucial, he argued, for five reasons: (1) it enables us to acquire and transmit knowledge; (2) it greatly facilitates our efforts to coordinate common enterprises; (3) it enables us to reconcile differences and reach mutual understanding; (4) it is the means by which we inherit the achievements of past human efforts; and (5) it can expand or contract the very boundaries of life itself. A life of isolation is generally inferior to one in which we are in contact with our fellows. Fuller did not, however, go on to explore how his central indisputable principle of substantive natural law might be effectively translated into positive law.

The objectivity of reason

According to many if not most classical natural law theorists, it is in part through reasoned argument or reflection that we are to identify the dictates of natural law and translate them into positive law. Again, this is not to say that reason ultimately determines all the twists and turns of particular forms of the law. As Fuller himself emphasized, mere authoritative choice or fiat must commonly play some role too.

Is this reasoned argument objectively grounded, or is it merely a matter of personal predilection? If natural law thinkers are familiar to us at all, it is likely to be for their advocacy of the existence of objective reason.[11] But the non-religious could obviously not agree with those who held this objectivity to be grounded in the word of God, and many insisted instead that it was grounded in human nature. Thus people who create or evaluate positive law are enjoined, in two words, to "follow nature."

This procedure cannot be ruled out, across the board, as unintelligible or unduly vague. It lends itself more readily to some issues of content than to others. Even one of Fuller's chief targets, H. L. A. Hart, has shown in an illuminating way how appeals to such objective facts of human nature as the general desire to survive, the natural vulnerability of humans to physical and other forms of harm, and the limited altruism of human beings can be used to justify at least the minimum content of a legal system: rules against violence, rules against theft and deception, and rules providing for the enforcement of promises.[12] Moreover, the injunction to "follow nature" need not be read as applying only to human nature. Natural law arguments can also be based more broadly on objective social facts—the inevitability (given the vagaries of human interaction) of some violent behavior in the absence of restraints, for example, or the inevitability (given a scarcity of resources) of some forms of theft in the absence of restraints. Classical theorists of natural law did not always distinguish between the broader and the narrower approach, but the broader one is implicit in the writings of many of them. In both cases, however, the objectivity of reason is grounded to some extent in appeals to "matters of fact" (as Hume would have required).[13]

Now, can it be said that this doctrine of the objectivity of reason qualifies natural law thinking as distinctive? Yes, it can—at least as contrasted to the thought of many legal positivists, including some of the most prominent ones of modern times. I do not want to suggest that positivists are logically committed to the view that reason is subjective, or that one cannot logically embrace an objectivist view without being a natural law theorist in some respect. But it is a fact that nearly all classical natural law theorists held some version of the objectivity thesis, and many positivists held some version of the subjectivity thesis. The great Austrian positivist Hans Kelsen, as we have seen, even once said that "reasoning" about justice was irrational.[14] Kelsen was probably the most influential legal theorist of this century.

In these terms, Fuller again qualifies as a natural law theorist. Although he rejected the religious view of objective reason, he embraced other versions of the objectivity thesis, often quite emphatically. He believed in "facts of the matter" on which objective appeals could be based. He believed that reasoning on some issues could be objectively grounded in human nature as such: "That is good which advances man's nature; that is bad which keeps him from realizing it."[15] Fuller did not develop in any detail what he meant by "man's nature," and his writings on this general issue are not extensive. He did, however, offer specific illustrations in support of his view that for a wide range of issues there is a "right ordering" of human relations, that this ordering can be discovered through objective reason, and that the weight of reason will often be heavily on one side. The decision maker in such cases is perhaps better thought of as a "decision finder"—one who ascertains what Fuller often called "the common need."

Let us see how convincing Fuller's illustrations are. He asks us to assume that a society is just getting started and to conclude, with him, that its inhabitants would soon have to agree that certain acts like murder would have to be subject to punishment. Here, the weight of conflicting considerations greatly favors one side. A's freedom to kill is vastly outweighed by B's interest in continuing to live. So, too, for all As in general and for all Bs in general. Society would likely disintegrate if murder and the free use of violence were not punished. The decision maker will thus "find" what Fuller called a "natural principle underlying group life" and decide accordingly.[16]

Again, let us assume that a legislator has the task of drafting a law regulating traffic. This person would search (with the aid of reason) for

> a set of rules that would keep people from running into one another, which would, at the same time, not slow traffic unduly or create impossible burdens of administration for traffic officers and traffic courts. In other words, the sources of his law would lie in the necessities inherent in the problem with which he had to deal. Given a situation, and given certain generally felt and accepted human desires about that situation, his task would be to work out a way of effectuating those desires within the compulsions of the situation to which they relate.[17]

Finally, consider still another of Fuller's illustrations dealing with a problem of quite a different nature from the other two:

> We may suppose, for example, the case of five men cast off in a motor boat in the Pacific. These men are civilians who carry into their new relationship no hierarchic ranking, and they are at the outset strangers to one another. By profession or calling they are: a navigator, a machinist, an angler, a cook, and an accordionist. Each has the equipment appropriate to his calling. All of them want to reach the nearest land in the shortest possible time, and all know what land area is nearest. They have plenty of fuel and oil and an ample supply of bread and fruit. All like accordian music; all like bread, fruit and fish; all are sane. It is possible that these men might for a considerable number of days carry on a complex group undertaking with no principle of organization other than the recognized common need. The members of the group might carry out their joint task without any captain or leader, without having occasion to take a vote, to submit a dispute to arbitration, or to strike bargains or negotiate settlements among themselves. Their actions would be dictated by the necessities of the situation and their shared understanding of what those necessities demanded of each of them.[18]

In all these illustrations, Fuller claims that the objective dictates of reason are, after careful thought, quite determinate. Yet there is nothing exceptional about these cases. Furthermore, analogous problems of legal ordering regularly crop up in almost every domain of human interaction. It is safe to say that Fuller had little patience for the kind of professional skepticism about the inherent power of reason in practical affairs so fashionable in many philosophy departments (and not a few law schools) in his day. In deciding what the law ought to be, over a wide range of issues, it would never have occurred to him to think of natural law as a "brooding omnipresence in the sky" or the like.[19] Rather, he considered himself in search of a "hard earthy reality." His approach was not that of one "doing obeisance before an altar," but rather more in the nature of "a cook trying to find the secret of a flaky pie crust, or of an engineer trying to devise a means of bridging a ravine." Such a person is "mastering a segment of reality" and "discovering and utilizing its regularities for the benefit of the group."[20]

To some of Fuller's critics, all this smacked of reasoning about means when no one had denied the possibility of objective reasoning about means, only about ends. To this, Fuller's response was that the reasoning involved extended both to ends and to means, and it is difficult to see how this is not so in the three illustrations set forth above. In addition, Fuller insisted that there is no sharp line between what counts as means and what counts as ends, and that when we are confronted with the necessity of making an actual decision, "means and ends no longer arrange themselves in tandem fashion, but move in circles of interaction."[21] Ends, then, are not to be judged entirely in isolation from means. And insofar as they are evaluated independently, reason is far from silent. At the minimum, we can readily rule out many ends as bad in themselves. We might imagine "a society in which treason, murder, and rape are officially encouraged, in which breach of contract is rewarded and its observance punished, a society where assisting one's neighbor is regarded as a heinous crime. No sane person would hesitate to call such a society bad."[22]

Fuller was highly impatient with the philosophers' doctrine that "no ought can be derived from an is." He did not interpret it as a narrow logical doctrine turning on a general theory of types or on a special technical meaning of the word derive.[23] Rather, he interpreted it as a sweeping doctrine to the effect that facts cannot tell lawyers, legislators, and judges what they ought to do. In so interpreting the doctrine, he may have created a straw man. In any case, he flatly repudiated any such notion. The existence of purposes is factual, and from given purposes we may readily argue that we ought to have one rule rather than another. Further, facts also have a bearing on the question of purposes in the first place, for the available means is factual and will quite properly be considered alongside those purposes.

Let me just add that the criticism that natural law theorists illegitimately derive "ought" propositions from mere "is" propositions appears to rest on a misunderstanding of the tradition. Many of these theorists disclaimed that they were engaging in an inferential process to begin with. They believed that basic notions of value such as life, knowledge, and sociability are self-evident.[24] (This is not to say Fuller held this view.)

Tolerance of "fusion" between "is" and "ought"

Again, the contrast to be drawn here is one between virtually all (or nearly all) natural law theorists and most legal positivists. Many positivists, as we saw in Chapter Four, sought to formulate a general test that would enable them to differentiate sharply between law and non-law. These theorists believed in the possibility of a sharp separation between the "law as it is" and whatever non-law happens to encompass, including, of course, morals—notions of what "ought to be." Their quest for a sharply differentiating criterion usually led them to try to adopt a formal test of valid law—one cast in terms of the authoritativeness of the source of any putative law. As we also saw in Chapter Four, Fuller considered this quest futile, partly because content as well as source determines the legal validity of law, in most Western systems at least. Also, on his view, it is simply not possible to draw a fine distinction between the "is" and the "ought" of law, i.e. to divorce law from morals.

Did natural law theorists subscribe to these positions? One seldom finds classical arguments articulated in the terms Fuller adopted. Yet that whole tradition stressed considerations of substantive content (as well as matters of procedural and institutional design). These theorists did not seek formal criteria that might enable them to draw the sharp distinction that so many positivists sought. Nor did they construct specific arguments designed to establish any such distinction. Their thought simply did not flow in this direction.

Further, Fuller himself claimed that "what unites the various schools of natural law, and justifies bringing them under a common rubric, is the fact that in all of them a certain coalescence of the *is* and the *ought* will be found."[25] But it is well to reiterate that Fuller did not hold that this coalescence implies that a bad law—one that combines the "is" with a bad "ought"—must necessarily be legally invalid: "Though the natural law philosopher may admit the authority of the state even to the extent of conceding the validity of enacted law which is obviously 'bad' according to his principles, it will be found in the end that he draws no hard and fast line between law and ethics."[26]

Indeed, according to one scholar who recently studied this question at length, few if any classical natural law theorists actually held the quite untenable "higher law" doctrine that an immoral law cannot be legally valid.[27] Some passages from Aquinas, for example, are often cited to the contrary, but a close inspection of his various pronouncements on this subject indicates that this view should not be attributed to him.[28]

In this connection, Fuller's position must be qualified in one respect. He did take the view that what purports to be a whole system of law can so far depart from the requirements of the rule of law—law's "internal morality"—as to make the system's particular laws legally invalid, even though individual laws might not be morally objectionable. He spelled out this position in a letter to a friend written in 1958: "The concept of the internal morality of law is essentially procedural. If my imaginary monarch by accident emitted a rule of highly moral content, the content of this rule would not make it law if it was in fact part of a system so oblivious to the internal morality of law that it was not entitled as a whole to be called law."[29]

Limits of the obligation to obey

A vital theme within the natural law tradition (though hardly confined to it) is that there are important limits to the general obligation of citizens and officials to obey the law, however valid it may be by the criteria in force in the system. Aquinas, for example, said: "Man is bound to obey secular rulers to the extent that the order of justice requires. For this reason if such rulers have no just title to power, but have usurped it, or if they command things to be done which are unjust, their subjects are not obliged to obey them; except, perhaps, in certain special cases."[30]

Thus he, like many others in the natural law tradition, severed the issues of legal validity and obedience. A subject might have no obligation to obey a valid law. Very few legal positivists have differed with this view. But they have been far less willing to discuss the limits of the obligation to obey than natural law theorists. This is not at all difficult to explain in the case of moral skeptics like Kelsen and his followers. The limits of the obligation to obey are defined in terms of moral notions. One who does not believe that moral argument can qualify as rational argument is unlikely to devote many pages to the issue. It is true that some legal positivists, such as Bentham, have not been moral skeptics. Yet not only did these thinkers say relatively little about the issue compared with natural law theorists; what they did say frequently took the form of underscoring the obligation rather than identifying the reasons for ignoring it. Bentham himself popularized the maxim, "Obey punctually, censure freely."[31]

Of course it is possible to define the limits too narrowly and thus encourage anarchy. Fidelity to law is an important value, and the positivists, or at least many of them, have done well to stress it. But certain theorists of natural law have contributed here, too, for they have helped to make room for the many cases in which a valid law may be unsound or perhaps even bad, with a duty to obey nonetheless remaining intact. Those who hold that an immoral law cannot be legally valid obviously leave no room at all for such cases.

Overall, Fuller's scattered remarks on the general obligation to obey the law align him more with the spirit of classical natural law. Although he never treated the subject in any systematic way, he was primarily interested in the question of the limits to that obligation. As already indicated, he went beyond the many classical theorists of natural law who distinguished between the issue of legal validity and the issue of a moral obligation to obey. He denied, for example, that certain laws enacted by the Nazis, "considered as laws and in abstraction from their evil aims, were just as much laws as those of England and Switzerland." In his view, the moral obligation of German citizens to obey many of these laws was not merely diminished, but obliterated, for they contravened basic principles of the rule of law: some were not even published; many were extraordinarily vague; they were often not interpreted in ways at all congruent with any plausible meaning they might have. In short, they were not law, and so could not possibly lay claim to a moral obligation of obedience.[32] Again, Fuller's position here must be distinguished from that of the few natural law theorists who have totally collapsed the distinction between the issue of validity and the issue of obligation. Fuller was not saying that a bad law is not a law. He was saying that a *regime* may so depart from the law's "internal morality" that at least certain of its enactments cannot be considered law and thus cannot give rise to obligations of obedience.

"Technological" natural law

We have seen that Fuller believed in (1) what might be called a form of "right reason," (2) general principles dealing with "purpose-forming processes" and with communication, and (3) the objective determinability of "right orderings" of human relations (within limits). He sometimes referred to the sum of these views as "substantive" natural law. This sum translates into laws against murder, violence, and theft, and in a society like ours, into laws regulating traffic flow, for example. As noted above, in Fuller's view, those concerned with the law, no less than engineers, carpenters, and cooks, must master "segments of reality" to discern and use their regularities for the benefit of the group.

But Fuller extended this analysis and these analogies beyond substantive law to encompass "processual" arrangements as well—what he called "basic forms of social order," such as customary practice, contract, legislation, adjudication, and electoral methods. He did not agree with those who saw these basic forms or processes as more or less unlimited in number and infinitely pliable, without any inner integrity of their own. Instead, he believed that they were governed by objectively determinable "laws," and that these laws were "natural" in the sense that "they represent compulsions necessarily contained in certain ways of *organizing* men's relations with each other" (emphasis supplied).[33] By this, Fuller meant, for example, that the enactment of statutes requires that they be clear and prospective, and that they be administered congruently with the spirit of their texts; these requirements may be thought of as "laws of lawmaking." Adjudication requires that the fact finder be impartial; this is a kind of "law" determining the constitution of an adjudicative process. Similarly, an electoral process of the one-person-one-vote type requires that provision be made against counting a person's vote more than once; this is simply an "internal" compulsion of the arrangement, a requirement easy enough to recognize, but not always so easy to implement.

Now, in Fuller's view, these examples illustrate a kind of technological or organizational "natural law" that determines the constitution and utility of forms of social ordering. The next three chapters of this book are devoted to Fuller's contributions to the study of this subject, which he thought of as a branch of natural law theory. By the time he arrived on the scene in the 1920's, this technological branch of natural law had all but fallen from view. In the Middle Ages, Aquinas had interested himself in it; and in the seventeenth and eighteenth centuries, it even became a prominent subject of study and debate. Yet viewed against the long history of natural law thought, it had never occupied more than a modest place at best. Fuller changed this.

6

Law's means and ends: A "processual" theory

Means-end relationships were a central focus of Fuller's thought. Although we saw in Chapter Three that he stressed the purposive nature of law, he wrote very little on that staple of political and legal theory, "general social ends." One does not even find an essay on justice. Fuller was skeptical of the value of discussing social ends in the abstract. Characteristically, in the only systematic work he did on any general social end—two essays on freedom—he emphasized the "means" aspect. Thus:

> The choices men can make [exercises of freedom] without requiring collaborative social effort for their realization are trivial. Our more important choices are meaningless if there is no way of carrying them over into the larger social order on which we are dependent for almost all our satisfactions. But, to give social effect to individual choice, some formal arrangement, some form of social order [some means], is necessary.[1]

Fuller believed that the study of socio-legal means had been unduly neglected in the history of political and legal theory. He defined this study as the "theory of good order and workable arrangements" and christened it "eunomics."[2] Eunomics, as he conceived it, is a concrete and highly practical enterprise addressed to the legal realization of social ends, but it

> involves no commitment to "ultimate ends." To be sure, it may reject particular ends as presenting what Michael Polanyi calls "unmanageable social tasks." It may, in other words, reveal that there are ends which seem in the abstract desirable, but for the attainment of which no social form can be devised that will not involve an obviously disproportionate cost. But the primary concern of eunomics is with the means aspect of the means-end relation, and its contribution to the clarification of ends will lie in its analysis of the available means for achieving particular ends.[3]

Insofar as previous legal theorists had addressed eunomics, they tended to concentrate mainly on the nature and varieties of substantive and procedural law, on the structural elements that make up a legal system, and on adjudication, if they in fact took up processes at all. Fuller, on the other hand, concentrated on the basic processes of socio-legal ordering as essential legal means, and believed that adjudication was only one of a handful of basic processes. The ones on which he concentrated, with their corresponding forms of law and other outcomes, are as follows:

Process	*Forms of law and other outcomes*
Customary interacting	Customs
Contractual ordering	Contracts
Democratic legislating	Statutes, etc.
Electoral decision making	Designation of officials, approval of referenda, etc.
Administrative or managerial direction	Orders, decrees, regulations, etc.
Adjudication (including arbitration)	Case law, authoritative interpretation, decisions, etc.
Mediating	Contracts, etc.

Fuller's study of these processes was one of his most original contributions to legal theory. Unlike modern jurists of the so-called analytical school, he went far beyond the mere analysis of the constitutive and regulative rules that define and govern these processes. In his study of each basic process, he addressed several difficult and, in my view, more important questions: How do we decide that something counts as a distinct process? What are its dominant purposes? What gives it and its outcomes legitimacy? Is it in part constituted by rules or other precepts that necessarily serve moral values? How do affected parties participate in it? What is the role of any decision maker or "manager," and what constraints shape that role? What is the nature of the substantive ingredients that go into the forms of law (or other outcomes) that the process yields? What is the nature of these forms of law, and how do they differ from those of other processes? What are the conditions for the most effective use of the process? When does it operate with maximum moral force? What problems are beyond its proper scope? What are its significant interrelations with other processes?

These are not the only questions that could be raised, to be sure, but they are in themselves a very large undertaking. A body of answers to such questions must surely qualify as a general theory. Fuller did not address these questions comprehensively and systematically, or even in ways that were always consistent, but he did delve into many of them, especially in regard to legislative, customary, contractual, adjudicative, and managerial processes.

Six main considerations appear to have motivated Fuller's emphasis on the processes of socio-legal ordering. First, and contrary to the usual legal positivist, he held the processes from which rules and other outcomes derive to be the primary units of jurisprudential analysis within a legal order, rather than the rules and outcomes themselves. Second, he was especially interested in the differing sources of legitimacy and moral force that legal processes might have. He rejected a narrowly instrumentalist view that legal processes are to be judged solely by the quality of their outcomes; the workings of the processes themselves involve important values. Third, and of closely related interest, he believed that some processes, such as adjudication, were constituted in part of rules and other precepts that necessarily serve important general moral ends, and that if they fail to serve these ends, they simply could not be what they purport to be—could not qualify as adjudicative (or whatever). Fourth, he was concerned that societies recognize the appropriate uses and the limitations of the various processes: their special "institutional competence." Fifth, he thought there might be a kind of natural (and exhaustive) division of labor between processes, and he was concerned to discover whether this was so. Finally, he believed that his emphasis on processes as social means would provide a valuable corrective to the traditional overemphasis of theorists on social ends and also a corrective to their tendency to divorce ends from means. This last point calls for some elaboration.

Fuller singled out John Stuart Mill in the nineteenth century and Sir Isaiah Berlin in our own time as social theorists whose views illustrate many of the emphases and tendencies to which he objected. Mill contended, for example, that "all action is for the sake of some end, and rules of action, it seems natural to suppose, must take their whole character and colour from the end to which they are subservient," a view that is echoed by Berlin: "Where ends are agreed, the only questions left are those of means, and these are not political but technical, that is to say, capable of being settled by experts or machines like arguments between engineers or doctors."[4]

Fuller refused to separate means and ends in this fashion, insisting that they form a continuum. Further, unlike Mill and Berlin, he insisted on the parity of means. To him, it was just as important, if not more important, to study the nature, provinces, and limits of the processes that order society (and their corresponding forms of law and other outcomes) as to study ultimate ends such as freedom, justice, security, and equality. Social ends can only be realized to the extent that available processes allow. And we must know what is possible before we can seriously move on to what is desirable. Some effort to identify and circumscribe available means at the outset is essential to liberate the creative spirit. One can often sharpen the judgment only by narrowing the range.[5]

Further, many ends cannot be understood or appropriately defined if abstracted from all means of their realization. This is plainly so in the case of the most prominent end of our own era—equality. How can we even talk about equality without introducing the social processes and forms of order through which it is to be realized? Indeed, some ends and means may even be so intimately associated with each other that it becomes artificial if not impossible to distinguish or at least to draw a sharp line between them. This is true of many forms of freedom (as well as of equality). Quoting an example from the English theorist Michael Oakeshott, Fuller stressed that "the freedom of an Englishman is not something exemplified in the procedure of habeas corpus; it is, at that point, the availability of that procedure."[6]

Fuller believed that the processes and forms of socio-legal ordering are not merely inert conduits directing human energies toward certain desirable end states, but part of the very patterns of our lives with highly important side effects. Democratic electoral processes and forms of legislation, for example, communicate and symbolize democratic values that shape our lives in many nonpolitical contexts. Moreover, the very workings of these institutional arrangements can generate valuable social assets. Participating in adjudicative processes, for example, may give lawyers the capacity to judge matters of fact relatively objectively in many non-legal settings, thereby increasing their usefulness as a group to society generally.

Social thinkers make a fundamental mistake in neglecting the parity of means for another reason, Fuller argued. In legal ordering, we encounter many conflicts of ends, and typically these are concrete in character. We can of course imagine conflicts between abstract ends, say freedom versus equality, and we can try to establish general priorities between such basic ends. But we would rarely be content with a trade-off that saw one unit of a high priority goal realized at the expense of many units of a lower priority goal in conflict with it. To see what the choices really are we must concretely sort out the alternative means. We must consider what we lose on each (the "means-deficit") and what we gain (the "means-surplus") and decide accordingly. We cannot approach the problem responsibly simply by drawing up a set of general priorities for abstract ends.[7]

Fuller had still another concern in arguing that means were as important as ends. He thought that the processes and forms of socio-legal ordering have a certain inner integrity that needs to be studied and understood. If this integrity is not grasped—if social architects merely assume that the institutional means at hand is infinitely pliable and can be bent to just any purpose—then that means is sure to be misused. For example, when adjudication is bent to serve the ends of negotiation and mediation, misuse often results. To Fuller, eunomics was the study of *good* order and *workable* arrangements. The misuse of institutional forms would only bring bad order and unworkable arrangements.

Because Fuller stressed the means aspect of means-end relations, one is tempted to think that he viewed basic ordering processes *merely* as means. As we will see, however, he considered several of these ordering processes to be complexes of means and "internal ends." For example, adjudication is a complex of institutional forms (means) in which a certain kind of fair participation by affected parties (internal end) is realized.

Let us turn now to Fuller's treatment of specific processes. Electoral decision making and mediation will not be considered. Fuller wrote relatively little on the first, and though mediation is of major significance as an ordering process, it has few of the complexities of the other processes.

Customary interacting

Francisco Suárez, John Austin, Henry Maine, James C. Carter, and other legal theorists wrote illuminatingly on custom, but few accorded it the importance that Fuller did. Although in his own substantial writings on this subject, he drew in part on the work of another legal theorist, Eugen Ehrlich, and on such "interactional sociologists" as Georg Simmel,[8] Fuller's views on the subject are not any the less original or significant. It can even be said that he expanded our very concept of law.

For a start, Fuller believed that customary law can arise from the ways people interact in almost any context.[9] To cite one of his many examples:

> If . . . A and B occupy separate apartments in the same building and share a common entryway, then a practice might grow up whereby A was expected to lock the entry door at night, while it was anticipated that B would unlock it in the morning to let the milkman in. Conceivably such a practice might arise without any words being spoken and yet it might come to represent for both sides a settled division of labour on which each was entitled to rely in guiding his own actions. It would then become for those affected by it something like a miniature system of customary law.[10]

Fuller thought we could say, then, that A and B incurred obligations to each other, and saw such obligations as deriving from a "stabilization of interactional expectancies" by which the parties come to "guide their conduct toward one another."[11] Such interactional practices are often open-ended and oblique at the outset, and become refined and fixed only by a gradual process of adjustment and accommodation. They commonly "glide into being imperceptibly." In their incipient stage, they may be too ephemeral to deserve the name law. The stabilized practices that ultimately emerge are typically tacit, yet recurrent. And they reveal deep continuities between the "social" and the "legal."

It seems appropriate enough to call such interactional practices "customary." If we agree with Fuller that obligations do arise in this way, might we not still say they are not legal, but merely social or moral? For one thing, they are not laid down by an official. Customary law, if it is law, is created through social interaction. As such, it fails any test of legal validity that requires all law to be created and laid down from above by an official. But by such a test, contract law (the terms of agreements) could not be law either; yet in our system contract terms count as law, at least in the sense that courts will provide remedies for their violation. Can we say, then, that unlike contract law, customary law is not enforced by courts, and so it cannot be law? We cannot, for it is simply not true. The custom involved in our example would probably not be enforced, but many other customary practices are. Those in commercial dealings come immediately to mind. Customary practices often determine what courts treat as reasonable in various branches of tort law, too. In any event, Fuller rejected the assumption that to qualify as law, a rule must be enforceable by a threat or by the use of state power (as through a court). To take this view would be to "define law by an imperfection." It would force us to deny the name of law to an arrangement that "works so smoothly that there is never any occasion to resort to force or the threat of force to effectuate its norms."[12]

In his great essay "Human Interaction and the Law," Fuller presented the following model of how he thought the processes of customary interaction work, though, as he acknowledged, in a theoretical construction of this sort one might be describing something that never "fully" exists:

> Where by his actions toward B, A has (whatever his actual intentions may have been) given B reasonably to understand that he (A) will in the future in similar situations act in a similar manner, and B has, in some substantial way, prudently adjusted his affairs to the expectation that A will in the future act in accordance with this expectation, then A is bound to follow the pattern set by his past actions toward B. This creates an obligation by A to B. If the pattern of interaction followed by A and B then spreads through the relevant community, a rule of general customary law will have been created. This rule will normally become part of a larger system, which will involve a complex network of reciprocal expectations. Absorption of the new rule into the larger system will, of course, be facilitated by the fact that the interactions that gave rise to it took place within limits set by that system and derived a part of their meaning for the parties from the wider interactional context within which they occurred.[13]

The rules of law arising in the processes of customary interaction achieve their legitimacy partly from the simple fact that they serve the general purpose of meeting "some need felt by those who first shaped their conduct by them."[14] But Fuller thought that the legitimacy of customary law lay also in part in the principle of consensual reciprocity of expectations, in the principle of autonomous self-governance, and in collective preference.

What are the attributes of the kind of law that emerges from customary interaction? Because this law arises out of diverse situations, its substantive ingredients may vary across the whole subject matter of life and may even be amoral in nature. Often, however, the form of law involved will capture and particularize some conception or norm of rightness in human interaction. Yet seldom does this conception or norm take the form of anything like a "miniature statute." Usually, it will remain implicit and unverbalized unless a violation occurs that triggers a court to attempt to give the practice formal expression. But even in its formulated state, customary law may become the object of dispute and interpretation. Indeed courts have long had experience in this.

The general conditions under which customary law can emerge and persist can be sketched. Of course, the occasions for interaction must be sufficiently recurrent. These occasions must have the potential for giving rise to mutual interdependence. The actions of the parties must also be in the nature of responses and counterresponses, and it must be possible for the parties to predicate expectations on such actions.

When does a process of customary interaction and the law that emerges from it have maximum moral force? At least the following would be true. As the practice "grows up," both parties come to have a full understanding of it. Reciprocal expectations emerge and persist. The parties benefit as contemplated. Neither takes advantage of the other in the course of the practice. Neither carries an unfair burden.

Customary law in the foregoing sense can emerge in virtually any setting, Fuller believed. It is "at home completely across the spectrum of social contexts, from the most intimate to those of open hostility."[15] Indeed, in this last connection, he speculated that the most important function of customary law may be setting limits to conflicts between enemies. If it has not eliminated these, it has often helped to lift warfare above mere blind reciprocal destruction.[16] According to Fuller, it is in the middle of the spectrum between hostile contexts on the one hand and intimate contexts on the other, namely in the varied and frequently complex fields of commercial dealing, that we witness the most "active and conspicuous development of customary law."[17] Customary law occupies niches that explicit contracts fail to fill, and it can even supersede the literal words of a contract. But customary law also very often arises in contexts where, in Fuller's view, contract law would be inappropriate, for example, the family. It is in fact pervasive in this and other intimate contexts, where it not only governs specific acts, but sets roles and divisions of labor as well.

On the other hand, Fuller drew a distinction between the general aptness of an ordering process and its availability in particular circumstances, so that customary law, though it is generally apt, is not always an available option. Some forms of customary interaction, Fuller thought, may simply not lie "within the experience of the parties so as to enter into their repertory of possible responses."[18]

Contractual ordering

H. L. A. Hart has held that contract is a relatively minor legal institution.[19] Fuller, a teacher and scholar of contract, did not agree. In most of his later theoretical writings on the subject, he put to one side the ordinary contract of exchange (including "form" contracts) and concentrated instead on longer term arrangements providing for the continuous collaboration of the contracting parties: partnership agreements, franchises, labor contracts, contracts for the supply of goods over the long term, and the like. Thus when he wrote of the processes involved in "contract law," he generally meant the terms of such agreements as these. He also meant what we often call property: bank accounts, bonds, insurance policies, and other essentially long-term contractual claims. Fuller defined such contract law as law in more or less explicit form made through a process of more or less explicit bargaining.[20] The parties who negotiate such law are a kind of miniature legislature, and their law a miniature statute.

Although no sharp line can be drawn between contract law and customary law, Fuller thought one could describe important differences between many forms of contract law on the one hand and many forms of customary law on the other. As he suggested, customary law is the inarticulate older brother of contract.[21] Often the terms of a merely customary relationship are not spelled out unless it is violated in some respect, whereas in contract law the terms are generally relatively explicit, and so the parties are more apt to know far more precisely where they stand. Contract law is also normally more precise in respect to duration and scope than customary law. To a large extent, these differences reflect the different processes that produce these two forms of law. Contract law (of the kind Fuller had in mind) is usually the result of explicit and progressively refined bargaining, and is tailored to specific dimensions at the outset, whereas customary law evolves gradually out of social, often nonverbal, interactions and adjustments.

On the other hand, contract and customary law are alike in that neither is imposed by a third party, or from above, as it were. Both develop, rather, when a situation arises in which the parties involved have or come to have needs that can be met through mutual reciprocation.

Again, as with customary law, Fuller did not require that contract law be enforceable in a court to qualify as law. In fact, some important forms of contract law cannot be so enforced. The parties may stipulate against judicial enforceability, or their arrangement may be too indefinite to qualify. Yet such contracts may be lawful contracts or, in any event, serve as ordering devices. What is even more important, the overwhelming majority of contractual arrangements go forward without any resort to courts. This is mainly because they are mutually advantageous, not because of any threats of force.

Again, it is possible to identify elements of a model contracting process. (Of course, many variations that remain contractual will not conform to the model in some respect.) Each participant brings some degree of bargaining power to the interaction—"the capacity to give or withhold something desired by the other." Negotiations do not get under way until matters become sufficiently explicit that each party knows of some desire of the other and knows what would be likely to satisfy that desire. In theory, no third-party mediator is necessary. The parties themselves negotiate directly, explicitly, and often through highly specific rather than vague and open-ended proposals and counterproposals. A variety of extraneous or chance factors may still affect the outcome. One party may be a better "wheedler" than the other, or more of a brinksman, or better prepared. But the process requires a certain "attitude of mind and spirit" on the part of the participants. Each must try to understand why the other makes the demands he does even as he strives to resist or qualify those demands. (Oddly, in his writings Fuller did not systematically treat the nature of contract drafting that figures so prominently in contractual ordering. This is itself an art, and one integral to the process by which contract law is made in many cases, even when lawyers are not involved.)

The general purposes of processes of contractual ordering are multiple. From the point of view of society, they include the efficient production and distribution of goods and services, the overall increase in social satisfactions that occurs when parties trade with each other and thereby give up what they value less in return for things they value more, and social solidarity. From the point of view of the parties, the purposes of contracting include the meeting of felt needs, mutual enrichment, and the exercise of free will.

Contractual ordering processes and the law emerging from them achieve their general legitimacy in part precisely because they do serve these kinds of purposes, but also because contract law accords with the moral norm that promissory obligations should be kept. In the spirit of Adam Smith, Fuller thought that contracting processes derive some legitimacy as well by tending to "keep vivid in men's minds the reciprocity that must underlie all life in society. A society of men accustomed to do business with one another is a society that perceives the interrelations of men's activities, and sees the reasons why some give and take is essential to living in common."[22]

What are the conditions for the most effective use of contract as a principle of order? Several are already implicit in what has been said. Of course, the parties must be legally free to engage in the type of contracting at hand. Also the parties must know what is in their own interests, and there must be some common or agreed-on general measure for valuing what each proposes to provide the other. There must also be sufficient political, economic, and legal stability, yet enough fluidity to permit the harmonizing of differing interests. The parties must be at a proper "social distance" from each other—neither truly hostile nor too intimate (on which, more later).

Although Fuller did not systematically address himself to this question, it may be said that a contracting process and the resulting contract have maximum moral force under the following circumstances: both parties have other options and are free of all coercion; both parties are well informed, and equally so; neither party overreaches the other in any way; each participates directly in arriving at the agreement; each fully understands and agrees to all terms; the agreement is not one-sided; and the subject matter of the agreement is free of all taint.

Although some contractual ordering may take place in almost any context, this process has its limits. Contract does not work well where, for example, the desired patterns of give and take cannot be imagined or foreseen well enough to be settled on in advance. Nor, according to Fuller, can contract work very well where the relationship between the parties is one of intimacy, as in the family. Here, the resort to contract would be likely to imply distrust or would unhappily pose the parties as bargaining adversaries. Either would quite likely damage the relationship. At the same time, contract is simply not an option where the parties are too hostile to bargain with each other. Further, Fuller argued that contract can be inappropriate where the parties consist of a superior and an inferior, because of the risk of compromising the required authority of the one over the other.

Fuller believed that in all these situations in which explicit bargaining and contract probably would not work, some form of customary law or other tacit interaction might work quite effectively. Even when parties cannot bargain with words, they can still frequently "half bargain with deeds." In such circumstances, understandings will emerge in place of verbal commitments. They may even occur between hostile parties. For example, they may adopt tacit restraints on ways of expressing their hostility.

The interaction of contractual ordering with other forms of order was of great interest to Fuller. We have already seen some of the relations between contract and customary law. The very legitimacy of adjudicative processes may rest partly on contract. This is true of collective bargaining and commercial agreements providing for arbitration. Contract may also define the limits of processes of managerial direction in respect to employment. For example, contractual job descriptions and statements of skill level may perform this function. Explicit contract may even be used between legislators as a way to organize their positions preparatory to compromising in the legislative process. At the same time, legislative and adjudicative processes can yield forms of law that either facilitate or frustrate the healthy functioning of contracting processes between private parties.

Democratic legislating

Fuller often termed the law made by elected legislatures (and the agencies to which they delegate legislative power) "enacted" law. In his famous essay "Human Interaction and the Law," he tended to use the term narrowly to refer only to those laws that facilitate, direct, or forbid behavior—that provide "baselines for self-directed" actions and interactions of citizens or rule out certain untoward activity such as crime.[23] Thus he excluded, for example, all law dealing with the ownership and operation of public utilities, the running of public schools, and the redistribution of income through transfer payments.[24] Moreover, he did not, by "enacted" law intend even to include all forms of written law dealing specifically with behavior as such. Thus, for example, a statute setting price controls would not, in Fuller's framework, be a form of enacted law. Now this is of course an idiosyncratic usage, but it need not cause the reader difficulty. Fuller was merely focusing on the process of democratic legislating as it relates to one important type of law.

Although Fuller did not specify what entered into the processes of democratic law-making, his scattered remarks indicate it would at least involve the following: participants would be duly elected, public participation would be provided for, provision would be made for rational deliberation on proposed bills, and majority vote would be decisive.

Enacted law (in Fuller's usage) differs from both contractual and customary law in the sense that it is made by and imposed by officials—most often on citizens. Accordingly, it is widely perceived as a mere one-way projection of authority. But Fuller had a different perception of his special brand of enacted law. For such law to fulfill its purposes, legislators must act subject to important constraints. They must make "followable" laws; this means they must not set standards that are too high. They must make clear and prospective laws, and they must publish them. They must do what they can to see that the law actually applied in and out of court accords with the law declared. They must not change the law too often. As we have seen Fuller called these requirements "principles of legality."[25]

Further, the very idea of enacted law implies, not a unilateral relationship between legislator and citizen, but a kind of reciprocal, "contractual" relationship. The legislators say to the citizen: "These are the rules we expect you to follow. If you follow them, you have our assurance that they are the rules that will be applied to your conduct."[26] On this analysis, the legislators—the decision makers in the process—occupy not a position of unlimited official power, but a role subject to significant constraints.

The dominant general purposes of enacted law, then, are to create (1) rules that facilitate customary, contractual, and other forms of human interaction, and (2) facilitative rules of social control such as the criminal law. Enacted law, in Fuller's special sense, always has one or the other of these two general purposes.[27]

Fuller was always much interested in the question of the general sources of a process's legitimacy, and in his earliest writings on the processes and forms of enacted law he stressed that in Western societies, anyhow, the source of their authority lay in their being the work of a democratically elected body.[28] Maximum legitimacy requires that citizens not only elect legislators, but participate in the law-making process as well, through hearings and in other ways. Later, however, Fuller came to the view that the principles of legality such as clarity, prospectivity, and publicity were necessary too—that, as in Nazi Germany, a legislative body could depart so far from these principles that its enacted law would not qualify as law at all or as only "half law."

On Fuller's view, there is a distinction to be made between the mere legitimacy of a process and the moral force it exerts in a particular case. For example, enacted law would have maximum moral force if the legislative process not only involved a democratically elected body that adhered to the principles of legality, but also satisfied certain procedural maxims of rationality, and the outcome itself was substantially sound. Although he did not identify the relevant procedural maxims, they would presumably include appropriate advance notice of pending legislation, due opportunity for deliberation on it, and the act of deliberation itself.[29]

Enacted law, for Fuller, is a special form of legislation. It ordinarily includes no justificatory or argumentative matter,[30] but simply provides that some course of action is forbidden, required, or authorized. It commonly establishes or contributes to reasonably well-defined rights and duties. And it is something that has to be interpreted before it can be applied (a special and often complex process).

In what context is Fuller's enacted law most effective? Fuller considered the true home ground of enacted law to be far narrower than that of customary law. Its proper domain, he wrote, "coincides largely with what we have already found most congenial to the organizing principle of contract, that is, with the middle area of the spectrum of social contexts—the region populated by friendly strangers, whose relations with one another generally stand open in the sense of not being prestructured by bonds of kinship or the repulsions of a shared hostility."[31] He considered enacted law most effective in facilitating interactions—in providing frameworks for social (including legal) life. Here he had in mind rules facilitating contract, agency, and property; rules on the validity of divorce; and rules of court procedure. This is not to say that the criminal law and other such forms aimed at social control are not sufficient to that purpose; it is only that these tend on the whole merely to give formal expression to conceptions of right and wrong already widely held in the community.

Enacted law is not without its limits, even though it has the force of the state behind it. Even more than contract, it is quite unsuited to regulating family life, the affairs of many private associations (at least in non-procedural matters), and the like. Enacted law fails in such cases because it is "too blunt" an instrument, or it is irrelevant because it is "external," or it is inappropriate because the parties' relations are interdependent in ways that cannot be "organized by set rules of duty and entitlement."

Fuller sometimes wrote as if he believed there was a kind of "natural" division of labor between customary law, contract law, and enacted law. Customary law generally organizes and orders realms that contract and enacted law cannot organize and order. In a mixed economy, contract is often a more effective way to resolve problems of allocation and distribution than enacted law. On the other hand, enacted law may either facilitate the private ordering of relationships that contract organizes and orders, or, as in the case of the criminal law, order activities that contract generally cannot reach.

Again, one kind of ordering process may be in some way dependent on the workings of others. If enacted law and its processes, for example, fail to control wrongdoers sufficiently, contract and customary law will not thrive. Also, one kind of ordering process (and its corresponding form of law) may act as a drain on the moral force of another ordering process. For example, the moral force of contract would be undermined were a general statute passed relieving parties of certain of their obligations because of market imperfections.[32]

Finally, resort to one of the processes of ordering so far considered—customary law, contract, and enacted law—does not necessarily mean that the others are then ruled out. Often more than one can be fruitfully brought into play from various angles to accomplish the task at hand. Custom, contract, and enacted law all three may even be brought to bear on problems of international relations.

Fuller's treatment of enacted law and its processes calls for this further observation. As we have seen, he tended (at least in his later writings) to address only a subclass of statute law as enacted law. He appears to have ignored the remainder because he felt it was not concerned with facilitating behavior or was inappropriately managerial. I do not think that this was purely for the sake of analysis, but rather that he tended toward a minimalist view of the function of legislation. His preference seems to have been for law made primarily through customary and contractual modes of interaction. In this respect, then, we could call him a traditional rather than a latter-day liberal.[33]

Managerial processes

According to Fuller, a rough definition of a managerial directive might be formulated as follows: an authoritative order of a superior to a subordinate to accomplish ends set by the superior.[34] This definition encompasses official administrative directives, certain forms of bureaucratic regulation, and the orders of corporate, military, business, and other hierarchically organized functionaries. Managerial directives, then, are far different from enacted law (in Fuller's special sense), in terms of both the relationships involved and the goals to be accomplished.

As one would expect, the processes involved also differ substantially. Like the legislators, the superior in a managerial process must communicate his wishes. And what he says must be relatively clear, free of contradiction, and possible to carry out. But not all of Fuller's "principles of legality" apply. The manager's directives need not be general. This is solely a matter of expediency. Further, they need not conform to earlier directives he has issued. And the manager need not judge the subordinate's actions as if legal rights and duties were at stake, for they are not (except with regard to the outer boundaries). Managers need wide discretion if they are to cope with shifting conditions. Also, the broad prohibition against retroactivity is simply inapplicable.[35]

Managerial direction is far more of a "one-way projection of authority" than is most enacted law. But the manager is subject to at least one constraint: if he acts too one-sidedly, he may lose the acquiescence and cooperation of his subordinates.

In discussing the process of managerial direction, Fuller was especially interested in governmental management. He did not, however, treat systematically the sources of legitimacy for the directives of governmental managers. Two classes of people are affected by such directives: (1) government employees, and (2) citizens affected by the acts of governmental managers and employees. In the first case, the legitimacy of the directives can be traced to the consensual nature of the employment relation. In the second, to the extent that directives affect citizens, their legitimacy, for those citizens, can be traced to the legitimacy of the very law that allows the managers to issue directives in the first place. Presumably, a governmental directive would have its maximum moral force when, in addition to meeting the requirements of clarity, consistency, and the like, the manager who issues it has consulted with the subordinate who must carry it out.

Managerial direction appears to be most appropriate as an ordering process when the subject matter requires that individuals or a group be called on to apply directives in order to further managerial objectives. This will be the case at least when the manager must consider several interdependent and interacting factors in deciding on and carrying out a plan of action. Michael Polanyi, whose work Fuller thoroughly admired, used the term polycentric to refer to a managerial problem of this type, and Fuller adopted it.[36] An example of a polycentric problem that Fuller himself cited is the allocation of local television licenses to competing private applicants. This process calls for the decision maker to consider a wide variety of related factors, including the applicants' proposed network affiliations and program commitments, their financial resources, and their record and promises in regard to balanced programming. Moreover, a sound decision requires that the decision maker take into account the interdependence of such factors. Thus, for example, an applicant's capacity for providing balanced programming will depend to some extent on his resources.[37]

But the process of managerial direction is hardly confined to polycentric tasks. Many forms of governance merely require that a superior organize and direct inferiors to carry out a legislative program. For example, one could hardly conceive of a public welfare program being carried out without heavy dependence on the issuing and implementation of countless bureaucratic directives.

Managerial direction sometimes comes into play as an ordering device more or less by default. For example, the circumstances and the relationships of the parties to be affected may be so unstable, or the results of alternative processes so unpredictable, that no other form of ordering could be rationally resorted to. In these circumstances, the resilience and flexibility of managerial direction may qualify it in a special way. The conduct of foreign policy toward certain nations is an apt example. But domestic examples may be readily cited as well. The task of adjusting interest rates in times of inflation is one of the most obvious.

Of course, managerial direction must be confined within proper boundaries. Fuller concluded that it tends to burst its bounds and usurp domains better left to other ordering processes. It is generally inappropriate in most of those settings in which customary law and contract law are truly at home. A sign, but not the only sign, that we may be in such a setting is simply that we there value individual autonomy highly—so highly that neither managerial direction nor enacted law seems at all appropriate. Managerial direction is also out of place where the task is to create and maintain relatively stable right-duty relationships.

Managerial direction and the other forms of socio-legal ordering so far considered have numerous and diverse interrelations. Various forms of enacted law plainly require that some subordinates be recruited and directed in various ways to carry out this law. The control and coordination of air space to prevent collisions and facilitate traffic flow is an elementary yet important example. Countless others could be cited. Thus enacted law may be partly dependent on managerial direction for its implementation, even though the primary purpose of enacted law (in Fuller's special sense) is to set standards for personal interaction.

Contract may define the scope of managerial direction. Thus an employment contract specifies in what ways an employee is subject to a manager's orders. At the same time, managerial direction may itself lead to or require contracting. For example, the conditions under which private parties can lend and borrow money in consumer transactions rest in part on what is a "directive process," namely, a system for controlling the money supply.

Customary law may enter importantly into the process of managerial direction. Many superior-subordinate relationships are based purely on an informal understanding. To cite a banal but telling example, a superior may tolerate laxness at certain times in exchange for a subordinate's full performance when the need arises.

Fuller sometimes seemed to be saying that governmental managerial direction should not even be classed as a legal ordering process, and that as a result, the orders of a governmental superior to his subordinate were not really a form of law. He pointed out that certain of his "principles of legality" do not apply to managerial directives, and that managerial direction, unlike law, is more of a "one-way projection of authority." But in the end, he acknowledged that a legal system may be heavily dependent on forms of managerial direction. If Fuller sometimes wrote of managerial direction as if it were non-legal, it was largely for a very special (and somewhat polemical) reason, I think, namely, that of explaining away legal positivist philosophies as preoccupied with managerial direction rather than with the rule of law as such.[38]

7

Law's means and ends: Civil adjudication

Fuller devoted more thought to the adjudicative process and its outcomes than to any other type of process.[1] Adjudication, as he saw it, is essentially a process in which opposing parties whose interests are to be affected present proofs and arguments to an impartial third party, who then decides in favor of one side on the basis of this presentation. The main purposes of adjudication are twofold: the resolution of a particular dispute arising out of the past, and the declaration of law for the future. Even when the decision maker does not explicitly declare law, his decision is likely to enter into the future relations of the parties, especially if they may again appear before him or a similar decision maker. (This is not to say that adjudication is the only process with purposes such as the foregoing.)

In his studies, Fuller did not confine himself to court adjudication. He broadened his inquiry to include decisions by certain hearing officers, commissioners, administrative boards, arbitrators in commercial and labor cases, informal adjudication within families and social groups, and the like. This chapter will be confined to his work on civil adjudication in ordinary courts.

Fuller often called the law declared in civil adjudicative processes "adjudicative law." Although such law includes authoritative interpretations of statutes, regulations, contracts, and other forms of written law, he was most interested in adjudication in common law cases and therefore in common law. This kind of law appears in judicial opinions and is made by judges solely out of the raw materials of adjudication itself, including proofs and arguments presented by the litigants. Common law has been a prominent form of law in Anglo-American systems for many centuries and until quite recently made up the bulk of our law.

Features of a civil adjudicative process

Fuller thought that, as with all the other basic ordering processes, it is well to develop a model in order to distinguish adjudication from other processes and to think effectively about its uses and abuses. To him, the most important element of a civil adjudicative process is the adversarial presentation of proofs and arguments by the parties to be affected (or by their lawyers).[2] The decision maker (including the jury) bases his decision on his understanding of the positions of the parties as shown in their own proofs and arguments. A vigorous and sympathetic presentation from each side is therefore essential. It would be psychologically impossible for a decision maker, by successively adopting the point of view of each party, to argue each side as persuasively as possible to himself and make a determination in a way that could adequately replace adversarial presentation. Adversarial presentation also institutionalizes the suspension of judgment until the decision maker has heard both sides. If he were to undertake to make these presentations himself, he would, perhaps even in many cases, tend to make up his mind before the "presentations" were over. Further, the out-of-court preparation by the opposing parties for adversarial presentations helps ensure that the public trial is the real time and place of decision, as in principle it should be for issues going to public trial. If the decision maker were himself to prepare the presentations of each side prior to the trial, he would very likely already have his mind made up on arriving at the courthouse. In that event, the proceeding could not be a genuine *public process of decision*. Finally, one function of adjudicative procedure is to narrow and refine the issues that truly separate the parties. The parties, through their representatives, are supposed to be the ultimate judges of what truly separates them. The decision maker should therefore leave this matter largely to them, via adversarial interaction. All in all, the decision maker's role is a relatively passive one until the time comes for decision.[3]

A related feature of Fuller's adjudicative model is that it demands a special kind of rationality. Decisions that emerge must be explicitly principled ones—or at least ones that can be stated in terms of applicable principles or standards. Otherwise the parties who appear before the decision maker will have no criteria of relevance, and thus will not be able to present their proofs and arguments meaningfully. This is not to say that the principles the decision maker invokes must always be ones that have already been authoritatively recognized prior to the dispute. But the affected parties must at least put forward positions or claims that may be converted into issues of principle—issues resolvable through some justifiable generality transcending the case at hand. Fuller summed up this requirement by saying that the claim a party puts forward must be a "claim of right," and that the controversy must be organizable in terms of definable "rights" and "wrongs." It follows from this that if the relationship between the parties or the field of human endeavor involved is not one that can "endure" a delimiting of rights and wrongs, then it is not susceptible of adjudicative determination.[4]

Further, the decision maker must not, according to Fuller, initiate the process of adjudication himself. Among other things, this might influence him to prejudge—to form premature conclusions about what happened or about who was in the right. He will be less able to bring to the public hearing an uncommitted mind. This, in turn, will reduce the effectiveness of adversary participation through proofs and arguments.

In addition, Fuller thought that the process must provide at some appropriate point for a decision maker to give reasons for the result reached. For one thing, this helps ensure that he has understood and taken into account the parties' proofs and arguments. The nature of the reasons given necessarily reveals a good deal in these terms. If the reasons fall entirely outside the proofs and arguments presented, this indicates that the adjudicative process "has become a sham," for the element of party-participation has lost most of its significance. It may also put future litigants in doubt about how they are to prepare, and what they are to present in the way of proofs and arguments.

Another feature of Fuller's model process is that the decision maker must be impartial. For example, he must have no strong emotional attachment to one of the interests involved, and he must not have a "blind spot" that may prevent him from getting the point of testimony or argument. Without this impartiality, again, the participation of the parties cannot be meaningful.

Finally, the decision must generally be both retrospective and prospective. It must be retrospective at least in its impact on the parties before the court, if it is to resolve their dispute. It must be prospective if it is to lay down law for the future. Yet it must not be unduly prospective. It must not purport to bear on future cases other than those relevantly similar. Otherwise it will go beyond what an adversarial presentation can justify. After all, the litigants represent only themselves and their own interests, and they participate in the decision only through proofs and arguments addressed to a discrete historical episode. Courts are not legislatures.

Of all the features of his adjudicative model, Fuller stressed the appropriate participation of affected parties the most. As he saw it, "the essence" of this matter is to give each side a chance to know what the other is saying and to afford each an opportunity to refute the other. Without this feature, we simply do not have adjudication. It is hardly surprising that in our system this feature is "institutionally defined and assured" in various ways. The rules and other devices that secure this feature are in large measure constitutive of adjudication. A genuine adjudicative process is thus an "is-ought" complex incorporating a notion of how the parties ought, in fairness, to participate.

Of the other features in Fuller's model, perhaps the most important is a corollary of the participatory feature: the requirement that the decision maker respond to adversarial participation by basing his decision entirely or almost entirely on the proofs and arguments presented by the parties. Indeed, adversarial participation and its corollary appear to mark what is most distinctive of genuine adjudication in comparison with other ordering processes. These features together strongly ensure that what the parties say before the tribunal will be taken seriously and thus that the ultimate decision will resolve *their* dispute, one of the two basic functions of adjudication. They also serve the other basic function, too: the declaration of law for the future. As Eisenberg (a student of Fuller's) has pointed out, however, the declaration of sound law will sometimes require that the decision maker not base his decision solely or even very largely on the proofs and arguments of the parties, as when the parties present their case on the basis of an existing rule that the decision maker thinks should no longer be followed.[5]

Civil adjudicative processes can take other forms than the Fullerian model, including those of a more "inquisitorial" nature familiar in Western Europe. In certain European systems, adversaries participate less actively in the proceedings than in the Anglo-American system, but the processes involved remain adjudicative. There is little evidence that in his work on adjudication Fuller gave much thought to these alternatives. His own description of the Anglo-American process reflects considerable penetration and is largely faithful to the realities of at least traditional "common law" adjudication. He was, of course, aware that, as a model, it of necessity described something that "never fully exists."

Sources of legitimacy and maximum moral force

The legitimacy of an adjudicator's decision can derive from various sources. It can derive indirectly from the democratic principle when judges are appointed by elected officials (though Fuller did not himself say so). It can also derive from the perceived social utility of adjudication as a process of resolving disputes and as a mode of lawmaking. Of course, the legitimacy of adjudication in the form of private arbitration derives in good measure from contract, rather than majority rule.

In his early writing on adjudication, Fuller was much interested in determining not only when the process is generally legitimate, but also when it operates in particular cases with maximum moral force—with maximum capacity to command respect. He thought the maximum moral force of adjudication was "different in kind" from that of contract and enacted law. It is hardly possible to improve on his own summary:

> Adjudication involves a complex of factors that may appear in various combinations and that may be present in varying degrees. We may, however, say that the moral force of a judgment of decision will be at a maximum when the following conditions are satisfied: 1) The judge does not act on his own initiative, but on the application of one or both of the disputants. 2) The judge has

no direct or indirect interest (even emotional) in the outcome of the case. 3) The judge confines his decision to the controversy before him and attempts no regulation of the parties' relations going beyond that controversy. 4) The case presented to the judge involves an existing controversy, and not merely the prospect of some future disagreement. 5) The judge decides the case solely on the basis of the evidence and arguments presented to him by the parties. 6) Each disputant is given ample opportunity to present his case.

It is seldom that all of these conditions can be realized in practice, and it is not here asserted that it is always wise to observe all of them. What is asserted is merely that adjudication as a principle of order achieves its maximum force when all of these conditions are satisfied. Some of this moral or persuasive force may be sacrificed when other considerations dictate a departure from the conditions enumerated above, and where the tribunal, as an agent of legitimated power, has the capacity to compel respect for its decision.

The connection between the conditions enumerated above and the moral force of the judgment rendered is not something irrational and fortuitous. The key to it is found in the fact that men instinctively seek to surround the process of adjudication with those conditions that will tend to insure that the decision rendered is the closest possible approximation of the common need. This obviously explains the conditions of disinterestedness on the part of the judge, and the opportunity for a full hearing of both sides, that is, conditions 2 and 6 in the enumeration above. Underlying the other four conditions is a single insight, namely, that men's interests and desires form a complex network, and that to discover the most effective and least disruptive pattern of order within this network requires an intimate acquaintance with the network itself and the interests and desires of which it is composed. In other words, these conditions are designed to obviate an evil that may be broadly called "absentee management." The judge must stick to the case before him (condition 3), because if he ventures beyond it he may attempt to regulate affairs on which he is inadequately informed. The judge must work within the framework of the parties' arguments and proof (condition 5), because if he goes beyond these he will lack the guidance given him by the parties and may not understand the interests that are affected by a decision rendered outside that framework. The case must involve a present controversy (condition 4), because neither the parties nor the judge can be sure that they fully understand the implications of a possible, future controversy or the precise interests that may be affected by it when it arises. The first condition (that the judge should act on the application of the parties) is perhaps the most difficult to justify. It arises from the fact that the judge who calls the parties in and himself sets the framework of the hearing lays himself open to the suspicion of planning a general regulation in which the controversy on which he hears evidence and arguments appears as a mere detail. Thus a violation of condition 1 tends to carry with it a strong suspicion that condition 3 is being violated.[6]

Why did Fuller think it so important to try to define the conditions in which an adjudicative process would operate with maximum legitimacy and moral force? He held that a society has only a finite set of basic ordering processes, each with its own special province. That province is definable in terms of the conditions in which the legitimacy and moral force of the process are likely to be considerable (if not maximal). Resort to a given process in the absence of such conditions does not merely risk ineffectiveness; it also erodes respect for law, a social essential. Respect for process is itself a form of respect for law.

The nature of adjudicative law

Fuller wrote most about that form of law declared in the course of adjudication called "common law."[7] He saw that when new cases arise and old ones come in for renovation, the raw materials of sound common law must consist not merely of reasons appealing to authority, but of substantive reasons appealing directly to some moral, economic, social, or other consideration. He even had a general theory, it seems, about the basic sources of substantive reasons. These sources are twofold: the "perceived common need" and the "norm of reciprocity." For example, in deciding contract cases, courts must fashion rules that preserve a wholesome "regime of reciprocity."[8] And courts must on a case-by-case basis advert to notions of common need in creating a viable system of federalism like ours, for example. Fuller did not work out his distinction with regard to the sources of these reasons or consider to what extent they might be exhaustive. But in this he was not alone. We do not yet have a general theory of justification for common law cases, and it may be said that the subject is still in its infancy.

Fuller thought that the ingredients of reason in the common law differ somewhat from those in customary and contract law. For example, there can be no general test of the rationality of contract terms "considered in abstraction from the interests of the parties." It is not similarly so in the common law. Indeed, the judge is supposed to test the viability of more general and reasoned principles that would cover not only the case at hand but future cases. Beyond this matter of generality, the judge is also to evaluate the substantive merits of the principles argued for.

The ingredients of reason in common law are likewise of a different order from those in statutory law. For one thing, the text of a statute rarely includes justifications or argument, whereas common law opinions are full of this matter. Indeed, in a common law opinion, the rule applied to the case and the reasons for it are often intertwined and difficult to distinguish. Further, much statutory law rests on compromises and is thus likely to be less principled in character. Relatedly, it commonly incorporates elements of fiat.

Fuller stressed still other differences between common law and statutory law. Unlike common law, statutes take explicit authoritative form, which makes for differing approaches to their interpretation and application. This also helps to explain why judges usually have more freedom, and consequently more responsibility, in fashioning a decision in common law cases than they do when interpreting and applying statutes. They also have the benefit of being able to draw more heavily on statements of facts in precedents and dissents and on multiple opinions, all of which allows more scope for the construal and reworking of relevant precedents.

Much in a common law opinion is retrospective and thus oriented specifically to facts that have already taken place. Statutory law, on the other hand, often looks mainly to the future. And it makes far more demands on human foresight. (Some of these issues will be discussed in more detail in Chapter Nine.)

The province and limits of adjudication

According to Fuller, whose main focus was on adjudication in common law cases, the true home ground of this ordering process is in those controversies in which (1) the subject matter is not beyond the technical competence of judges, lawyers, and the affected parties; (2) the dispute involves more or less two-sided issues to which the litigants can readily address their proofs and arguments in adversarial fashion; (3) insofar as the dispute is factual, it relates mainly to an episode now over; (4) principled grounds of decision are available and can be appropriately related to the circumstances; (5) the dispute calls for and will endure a definitive delimitation of the rights and wrongs of the matter; and (6) the dispute is of a kind that permits full and informed adversarial presentations. Cases involving negligently caused injuries and simple breaches of contract are the kinds in which adjudication is most at home.

Again, it will be seen that the true province of an adjudicative process in Fuller's scheme of thought corresponds very largely to those circumstances in which the legitimacy and moral force of the process is likely to be considerable. This is hardly an accident. Fuller's adjudicative model is largely one whose features secure legitimacy and moral force.

Fuller's writings on the limits of adjudication are the most suggestive and thought-provoking of any in the history of Anglo-American legal scholarship. This is no small tribute, especially in view of the vast amount of American legal writing on court-centered subjects. Fuller was much troubled by the powerful tendencies of American officials and citizens to induce courts to take on non-adjudicative tasks, to create new processes based on inappropriate adjudicative models, and to judicialize existing processes that do not lend themselves to adjudicative methods. The failure to adjust means to ends not only gives rise to ineffectiveness, he contended, but also involves an illicit trading on the moral force of true adjudication; it distorts analysis and brings irrelevant standards of criticism into play; and it breeds hypocrisy. With all this at stake, Fuller was moved to think hard about the limits of adjudication. One of his best-known essays, published shortly after his death, is "The Forms and Limits of Adjudication," but by then he had already written much on the subject.[9] In these works he identified a number of contexts, relationships, and subjects that are not well suited to adjudication. Let me discuss six of these briefly, and then take up in more detail a seventh—the problem of "polycentricity."

First, and especially in a pluralistic and democratic society, adjudication alone is not well suited to introducing new basic aims or to launching society in new directions. Fuller did not elaborate on this point, but the most important reason for the limitation is probably this. It is generally illegitimate to assign such functions to an adjudicative process (at least in the absence of some clear statutory or constitutional mandate). The litigants represent only themselves and are in no position to represent the interests of society generally. Moreover, judges are not, in general, supposed to act as political representatives and accordingly are not politically accountable for their decisions.

Second, when issues to be litigated are ones on which the society is deeply divided, adjudication is less likely to be effective. This is largely because in such circumstances the litigants will be either entirely or to some degree unable to come to a meaningful "joinder of issues" (as lawyers put it). They will tend to talk past one another, so that what each says to the court seems quite irrelevant to the other's conception of the true issues. Fuller did not hold that there must be a broad social consensus on an issue before any aspect of that issue can ever be appropriately before a court, only that the differences be clear enough to be discussed in court in terms that each side can understand. Without this, legal intervention is still possible, but the legislature would be the appropriate forum.

Third, adjudication's effectiveness is considerably reduced within areas of rapid social change or drastic reordering. Fuller did not give his reasons for thinking this. He appears to have believed that the "leisurely" nature of adjudication was a factor. He also believed that adjudication "declares rights, and rights to be meaningful must in some measure stand firm through changing circumstances."[10]

Fourth, adjudicative processes are less appropriate where a relationship cannot withstand or endure a delimitation of rights and wrongs, but depends instead for its wholesomeness and effectiveness on spontaneous and informal collaboration. Fuller cited the husband-wife relationship as an example. Courts have generally refused to adjudicate disputes over the internal organization of the family. Such matters are better left to customary law and to private managerial direction (including co-direction).

Fifth, adjudicative processes are relatively less appropriate where, after a decision, the opposing parties must continue to work with each other. The hostility that adjudication's vigorous partisan advocacy can provoke may persist long after a case is decided. An example that illustrates Fuller's point is the adjudication of tenure disputes in universities and the public schools. After the decision, the administrators and teachers who may have been "defendants" in the tenure case on the one hand, and the teachers who have succeeded in securing tenure through a court decision or arbitration on the other hand, must thereafter work together as members of the same group. Their prior adjudicative confrontation is almost certain to make this more difficult. Again, it is probably better to resort to managerial direction or some other method for resolving such disputes.

Sixth, Fuller once suggested that a court is not well suited to drawing up institutional designs for basic structures of governance, public or private. It could not, for example, "write a constitution." Again, he did not elaborate. Presumably he thought that adjudication simply does not lend itself to the kind of accommodation and compromise that institution-building requires.

Finally, we come to the relative incapacity of adjudication to cope satisfactorily with what Fuller called polycentric problems. I have already introduced this concept in the preceding chapter, so let us begin not with a re-definition, but with one of Fuller's illustrations of the type of polycentric problem least amenable to adjudication.[11]

Suppose a wealthy art collector dies and leaves a vast collection of valuable paintings to seven galleries in the city of New York "in equal shares," her will indicating no method of apportionment, and the beneficiaries then fall into dispute over who gets what. Fuller saw this as a polycentric problem mainly because any given disposition to one beneficiary has different repercussions for some or all of the others. For example, if A gets the Renoir, C may be less interested in the Cezanne and E more interested in the Matisse. Preferences here will be influenced by numerous complex factors, including the beneficiary's holdings and the available combinations within the set of bequeathed paintings. An arbitrator or judge called in to decide who gets what could not simply list the preferences of each beneficiary for given paintings in rank order and then distribute paintings in a fashion that would give equal weight to each beneficiary's overall rank orderings. The preferences of each beneficiary are interdependent and thus alter as each painting is distributed.

To Fuller it seemed that such full-fledged polycentric problems were not fit for adjudication for essentially three reasons, all having to do with the likely ineffectiveness of the participation of the litigants. As we have seen, he believed that the very essence of adjudication lies in the adversarial presentation of proofs and arguments. Whatever impairs the meaning and force of that type of participation impairs the integrity of adjudication itself. Yet in our case, there is no single clear-cut issue, or even a discrete number of clear-cut issues, to which the parties can address their proofs and arguments. Any projected disposition of a painting would almost certainly have differing implications with respect to the distribution of any of the remaining paintings for some of the galleries. It would be exceedingly difficult (if not impossible) to organize a hearing so that each side could fully argue out these implications. Further, there would be too many affected parties to square off for argument on a whole series of alternative divisions.

Not all of the features of this case are required for a problem to be significantly polycentric. For example, if there were only two competing beneficiaries rather than seven, the problem would still be polycentric. Moreover, a multiplicity of parties does not alone spell polycentricity. If a reward were offered for information leading to the capture of a criminal, the appearance of ten claimants would make for a cumbersome hearing, but it would not make the problem polycentric.

Fuller also saw clearly that polycentricity is generally a matter of degree, and that most litigated cases have some element of polycentricity:

> Suppose a court in a suit between one litigant and a railway holds that it is an act of negligence for the railway not to construct an underpass at a particular crossing. There may be nothing to distinguish this crossing from other crossings on the line. As a matter of statistical probability it may be clear that constructing underpasses along the whole line would cost more lives (through accidents in blasting, for example) than would be lost if the only safety measure were the familiar Stop, Look & Listen sign. If so, then what seems to be a decision simply declaring the rights and duties of two parties is in fact an inept solution for a polycentric problem, some elements of which cannot be brought before the court in a simple suit by one injured party against a defendant railway. In lesser measure, concealed polycentric elements are probably present in almost all problems resolved by adjudication. It is not, then, a question of distinguishing black from white. It is a question of knowing when the polycentric elements have become so significant and predominant that the proper limits of adjudication have been reached.[12]

But Fuller held that society is shot through with significantly polycentric problems. They even abound in the sports world. One of his favorite examples was the case of baseball coaches and managers who must decide what players to play at which positions. The decision maker cannot simply select the starting line-up solely in terms of a relative ranking of each player in terms of overall ability. He must take into account how the choice of Jones at second base (a strong fielder but a weak hitter) will affect the choice between two outfielders, one of whom is a stronger hitter than the other. Fuller's list of polycentric problems included, besides the selection of athletes for positions, setting prices and wages in a managed economy to produce a proper flow of goods; redrawing the boundaries of an election district to make them correspond to shifts in population (and perhaps other factors); designing a system of throughways into a metropolitan area; allocating scarce funds for projects of scientific research; allocating air routes among various cities; drawing an international boundary across territory marked by complexities of geography, natural resources, and ethnology; and allocating radio and television channels to make balanced programming as accessible to the population as possible.[13] Fuller, of course, did not hold that because polycentric problems are unsuited to adjudication, they are unsuited to every other mode of resolution. In his view, most if not all could be dealt with appropriately through contract or managerial direction. And if there is a statute in the background, this too could make a difference.

Today, a number of legal scholars have taken up Fuller's writings on polycentricity and have sought to develop them further. They include Melvin Eisenberg, Paul Weiler, James Henderson, Rod MacDonald, and Marc Galantner. In his writings on adjudication, Fuller did not touch on other types of factors that can limit its suitability. He did not discuss the problems arising from the narrow range of remedies that courts may provide, for example, or consider the necessity for a "live case or controversy," a limitation that much interested his Harvard colleague, the late Henry M. Hart. We still do not have a comprehensive study of the uses and limits of adjudication. In any that is published, we may expect Fuller's writings to play a prominent role.

Interrelations

As with the other processes discussed, adjudication can be interrelated to one or more of the other ordering processes. For example, adjudication may rest on contract, as in labor and commercial arbitration. Then, too, much adjudication is concerned with the very wholesomeness of other processes. For example, courts in contract cases are concerned to build a healthy "regime of reciprocity." And much enacted law would be meaningless without adjudicative processes to interpret and apply it. Also, adjudication regularly draws on customary law and translates it into common law.

Certain ordering processes, such as negotiation and mediation, often take place in the shadow of adjudication. It is natural that adjudicators should take an interest in these other processes, for if they fail or break down, the disputes will often then have to be adjudicated. Indeed, some judges frequently try first to mediate certain disputes that come before them. This tendency worried Fuller. He suspected that a judge who first tries to mediate (and thereby learns the facts of the case) and then seeks to determine the facts as an adjudicator may not only fail as fact finder, but also forfeit some degree of impartiality, thereby tainting the process.

8

Law's means and ends: General assessment

The virtues and potential of Fuller's general theory of the main processes of socio-legal ordering are, in my view, numerous and beyond doubt. He never drew these together and summarized them, and that must now be done. Thereafter I will briefly explore several lines of criticism.

Virtues and potential

Fuller was the first legal theorist to set forth a general theory in which the primary units of analysis consist of processes rather than precepts (or of law's systemic features). Although American pragmatic instrumentalists like Holmes, Pound, and Llewellyn were much interested in adjudicative processes, none of them sought to develop a general theory of processes in the way Fuller did. Most theorists of the legal positivist school have addressed law as if it were primarily a system of rules. And no natural law theorist has focused in a comprehensive way on legal processes.

Yet the realization of social ends almost always requires resort to some ordering process. The basic ordering processes known to society are relatively few in number and, as we have seen, include customary practice, contract, legislation, mediation, adjudication, and managerial direction. Such processes function to create law, to administer it, and to change it. They also function to settle disputes. In the largest sense, these are means through which the ends of law are realized. (Yet most of these processes are not merely means; they are complexes of means and internal ends, as we have seen.)

Of course, processes have not been totally neglected in the history of jurisprudence. But particular thinkers have tended to concentrate on a single process when they have concerned themselves with processes at all. As already suggested, many American theorists followed John Chipman Gray and sought to "pour everything through the funnel of adjudication." Theorists in the tradition of John Austin have stressed legislative processes as sources of "sovereign commands." Hans Kelsen, according to Fuller, sought to "pour everything through the funnel of legitimated power."[1]

Fuller addressed all the main socio-legal processes and sought to construct a general theory of their nature, uses, limits, and interrelations. True enough, he did not finish his theory or draw all his efforts together in a single book, as he planned to do. Nevertheless, as is evident even from the summary account I have offered in Chapters Six and Seven, and despite the very great complexity of the subject matter, he carried much of his theory quite far. Among other things, he appears to have identified and differentiated a very large proportion of the totality of leading socio-legal processes. He also studied the anatomy and physiology of each and offered many perceptive observations in these terms. He reflected on the uses and limits of most of these processes and tried to identify the conditions under which they are best used, and the conditions under which they should not be used. He addressed the sources of their legitimacy and moral force. He took up their interrelations. In purpose, scope, coherence, structure, and degree of development, Fuller's thinking about socio-legal processes qualifies as a general theory at least as readily as most bodies of thought that pass for theories in jurisprudence. On the most fundamental level, it is fair to say that his theory enlarges our very concept of law. After Fuller, no theorist can afford to neglect basic processes and their roles. Of the many things that law is, it is importantly a set of relatively discrete and distinctive ways of doing things.

The legal realization of social ends, then, calls into play one or more socio-legal processes. Indeed, on Fuller's view, such processes and their outcomes, including precepts, largely exhaust society's legal means. It is through our understanding of them that we can learn whether we can or cannot achieve a given end through law.[2] The ends realized are also shaped and stamped by their means of realization. And in thinking about what ends to pursue, there is constant interaction between ends and possible means. It is a serious mistake to treat ends in abstraction from all means of realization. It is similarly mistaken to treat the aptness of means as if this were merely a matter of technical implementation sharply separable from the choice of ends. The problem of ends must be kept in a "sufficiently intimate contact" with the problem of means. Indeed, in the ordering of human relations through law, means have parity with ends.

At the same time, Fuller was very much aware that it is misleading to characterize socio-legal processes merely as instrumental means to external ends such as the deterrence of crime, the reinforcement of the family, or the facilitation of contract. There are ends of still another kind, ends internal to those processes, which are realizable in the course of their workings. In truth, some degree of realization of these internal ends is essential to the very existence of certain processes. Processes are not and cannot be neutral or indifferent to the realization of such ends (in contradistinction to external ends). For example, an internal end of adjudication is fair participation by affected parties. Many procedural rules purport to serve this end. An internal end of democratic lawmaking is the realization of democratic self-rule through elected representatives. Many rules purport to seek this end. An internal end of contracting is the vindication of personal free choice and fair reciprocation, also the objects of many rules. Now, such rules as these, that purport to secure ends that are internal to a given process, may be said to be in part constitutive of that process.[3]

As indicated, the internal ends of a process are to be distinguished from the external ends that the process is used to serve. Adjudication may be invoked to apply rules that themselves purport to further a vast diversity of external social ends. The same is true of democratic lawmaking. And contracting processes similarly serve the radically diverse range of ends that the contracting parties may have. The realization of one external end may even in some circumstances conflict with some other external end. Fuller thought it a "great mistake" to treat legal ordering merely as posing problems of weighing different external ends against each other.[4] Internal ends have their own just claims too, and must not be sacrificed lightly. In a highly result-oriented age, these strictures take on special meaning.

All three of the examples of ends internal to and constitutive of processes cited above are moral ends: adjudicative fairness, democratic self-rule, and contractual liberty. Note that the moral values implicated here are widely accepted and almost entirely uncontroversial. Also, their status as moral values is not dependent on some debatable general moral theory. In the case of those legal processes constituted in part by precepts embodying moral values such as fairness, democracy, and free choice, Fuller thought it entirely appropriate to say that we have not just an intersection of law and morals, but a necessary connection between them. As Stanley Paulson has pointed out,[5] his insistence on this was probably his most important single contribution to the ancient and continuing debate on the relationship between law and morals.

At the same time, Fuller's study of legal processes led him to an original general theory of the legitimacy of governmental action (a theory he hinted at as early as the 1940's but never articulated at all fully). In much political and social theory, one encounters generalized analyses of the sources of the legitimacy of "government," or of the "legal order," or the like. Most of this theory has centered on the notion of democratic approval. Fuller thought this approach far too monolithic and undifferentiated. In his view, society is not held together (insofar as it is held together at all) by some "single strand." Rather, it is held together by many diverse strands, and the nature of these varies with the sociolegal processes that yield the various forms of law. Thus, the processes for creating statute law derive much of their general legitimacy from the "democratic principle." But this is not true, as we saw in Chapter Six, of such processes as contractual ordering and customary ordering, which derive their legitimacy from the exercise of free choice and reciprocity. As for adjudication, its legitimacy derives from a complex of factors, with fair participation by affected parties at the forefront.

Implicit in Fuller's overall analysis is an important distinction between the general sources of legitimacy of a socio-legal process and the moral force with which it operates in a particular case.[6] He stressed that the overall capacity of a process both "to help hold society together" and to command respect for, and acceptance of, its outcomes depends on both its general sources of legitimacy and its moral force in a specific case. Compulsory adjudication, for example, is indirectly sanctioned and authorized by the populace. It may also be well designed to operate, and may in fact generally operate, through the fair participation of affected parties. These factors lend the process legitimacy in general. But it is also important that the process operate with moral force in a particular case. The better the quality of participation by affected parties, the more legitimate the process and its outcome in that case.

Several factors motivated Fuller's interest in the general sources of legitimacy and in the moral force of processes in their operation. Perhaps the most important was this. He thought it was possible for those who designed and used legal processes to put what he called a "moral overload" on a given process at a given time. He worried, in particular, about the tendency of Americans, officials and citizens alike, to place a moral overload on adjudication. He also thought that a society could similarly go too far with legislative action and thus place a moral overload on a democratic legislature. (He cited as an example, highly redistributive tax statutes.) In Fuller's view, those who use the law's resources should take care to observe the limits on what a social system will bear.[7]

According to Fuller, each of the basic types of legal process—adjudication, contracting, managerial direction, legislation, and so on—is to some degree distinctive not only in whatever moral content it may embody, but also in structural integrity. Each has a kind of inner order of its own. Adjudication is necessarily tripartite, for example. Contracting necessarily involves exchange. Majority rule requires voting and a system of counting. But not all such compulsions are matters of logical necessity. Some, such as the prohibition against personal out-of-court contacts with the adjudicator, the requirement of at least the rudiments of reciprocation in contracting, and the proviso against double counting in a one-man-one-vote system, are "internal" compulsions that do not rise to the level of logical necessities. Fuller characterized such compulsions as "natural laws" of social order "contained in certain ways of organizing men's relations with one another."[8] The rational construction of a socio-legal process must conform to any of these natural laws that apply peculiarly to that process.

Fuller believed the identification of these natural laws to be more a matter of discovery than invention. Though the respective roles the two play in identifying any of these laws can be endlessly debated, it seems to me almost certainly true that some of them are to some extent matters of discovery. It also seems almost certainly true that we have not yet discovered all there is to be discovered about the "compulsions" that are "contained in certain ways of organizing men's relations with one another." Once a "compulsion" of a process is recognized and understood, Fuller contended, those who participate in it or have responsibility for its working may well find that affirmative effort is required to secure the healthy functioning of the process in that respect. One of Fuller's favorite examples had to do with the familiar problem of the courtroom clash between the seasoned veteran and the neophyte. Here the judge not infrequently must take affirmative steps to offset the advantage and thus help secure fair representation for both sides.[9]

If Fuller is right in all this, an important doctrine popular among certain American theorists of a pragmatic and instrumentalist orientation is simply false. That is the doctrine of "the infinite pliability" of social processes. According to this view, given sufficient agreement on ends, processes can always be arranged so as to accomplish any conceivable combination of ends. Society is just what we "choose to make it." "Natural laws" of social order do not limit us. All limitations are merely self-imposed. Anything is possible through law.

Of course, on Fuller's view it is possible to misuse a legal process—to bend it in ways that offend its "constitution." An adjudicative process might be assigned a managerial task, for example, and this process will then function in particular cases with less than its usual moral force—less than its true capacity to command respect and acceptance. And its legitimacy will suffer, too. But more than this. The process is very likely to be less effective, and might even be positively destructive in some ways. It may yield less than satisfactory outcomes, including "bad law." And this misuse may at the same time breed hypocrisy.

Fuller thought there were strong connections between the general quality of a process and the general quality of an outcome. These connections are of two kinds and can be easily illustrated from processes for creating enacted law. The first connection is broadly procedural in the sense that a procedurally bad process may produce a procedurally bad result. Thus a legislature may depart from one of the general requirements of legality, prospectivity, to produce a retrospective statute that wreaks havoc. The other kind of connection is of a more substantive kind. Suppose a legislature in working on a certain law chooses to ignore the principle of publicity. Some lawmakers might then be led to work less conscientiously at improving the law than they would have done under the public eye, so that the quality of the final product is not what it could and should have been.[10]

Fuller might have developed a short list of "maxims of process" for officials and citizens to use. Had he done so, that list (each item of which would require much elaboration) would have included the following:

(1) Do not divorce thought about ends from thought about means.

(2) Be alert to possible interactions between ends and their means of realization.

(3) Be careful to identify any internal ends a process may have, and be mindful of what is required to implement those ends.

(4) Do not needlessly sacrifice the realization of internal ends on the altar of external ends.

(5) Seek to maximize both the general legitimacy of a process and whatever moral force it may have in particular cases.

(6) Do not impose a moral overload on a process.

(7) Do not put a process to uses beyond its limits.

(8) Assume any necessary affirmative responsibility for keeping a process in good working order.

(9) Design processes in light of any "natural laws" of social order that are applicable.

Fuller's work had considerable implications for the general educational system and for legal education in particular, and Fuller himself saw many of those implications. Indeed, immediately after the Second World War, when he began his studies of legal processes, he saw his work on legal processes as part of a program to help Americans understand the superiority of their own system of government. For him, that system translated into a number of basic processes of governance with their corresponding outcomes and forms of law. Fuller held that Anglo-American systems were superior, not just because of the ultimate ends to which they were directed, but also because of the superiority of their institutional processes.

Yet Fuller warned in the late 1940's that our own fragmented educational system was not serving us well in matters of process. The law schools concentrated on adjudication, the departments of political science on legislation and electoral processes, the economics departments on the market economy and contractual ordering (except in their fringe legal aspects), the business schools and schools of public administration on managerial direction, and so on. Fuller concluded that "this specialization has resulted in there being no department in the university that has the task of making a comparative study" of socio-legal processes of ordering. In his view, this specialization had actually "destroyed the institutional background [required] for a study of the basic problems."[11] Fuller believed, moreover, that it was not enough merely to educate lawyers in these matters, that non-lawyers also needed to develop some understanding of the nature, functions, and limits of socio-legal processes.[12]

The educational system today, as we know, is as fragmented as ever and perhaps even more specialized that it was when Fuller took aim at it. Yet it can fortunately be said that many thinkers have worked on or are continuing to work on questions of process that Fuller identified. They include, besides the theorists interested in polycentricity mentioned in Chapter Seven, John Coons, whose concern is court-imposed compromise; Philip Selznick, who has written on institutional methods of reducing arbitrariness in management-labor relations; Frank Sander, whose interest lies in alternative means of resolving disputes; and Albert Sacks, who has focused on the legal process as such. Several of the scholars working along these lines were inspired in some part by Fuller's work.

Limitations

Fuller's rich and innovative work on the law's essential means was not without limitations. Most exasperating, perhaps, to those who choose to work with his writings on this subject, is the simple fact that he did not draw them all together into a single book. Consequently, one must sometimes fish out scattered passages and piece them together into a whole, and even, on occasion, read between the lines.

There are other, more serious deficiencies. Let me try to identify at least some of them. Here I can be little more than suggestive. Although Fuller is the premier proceduralist among legal theorists, he did not develop a comprehensive general theory of legal process—one that extends to all the various stages in the overall sequence through which law is created and then translated into effective precepts. Yet one could formulate a comprehensive general theory in just these terms. Such a theory would incorporate not only the types of processes Fuller identified, but certain others as well. For example, there are processes of setting goals for basic guiding law, of getting organized to implement such law, of recruiting needed personnel, of communicating the law's content, of monitoring its observance, and so on. Fuller did not treat these basic processes. Indeed, he did not even treat the law's processes for providing remedies or imposing sanctions. And he failed to consider in a systematic way the whole question of how these processes relate to what has typically "gone before" and what typically will "follow after."[13]

Fuller seems to suggest, in the processes he did analyze closely, that there is one "master" sequence involved in the making and implementing of law. But customary and contractual ordering, for example, may be represented instead as *one* among several basic legal techniques by which important kinds of law are made and implemented. I have elsewhere called this the law's "private arranging" technique, because it essentially involves the creation, administration, and implementation of law by private parties. Adjudication figures in this technique, but only secondarily—mainly by way of assuring coercive "backup" when private agreements break down, by way of providing ground rules for healthily functioning "regimes of reciprocity" (as Fuller put it), and by way of clarifying private arrangements when disputes arise over their meaning. Actually, the private-arranging technique is only one of five basic techniques known to the law (if I am right).[14] The others are the grievance-remedial, the distributive, the regulatory, and the penal.

Several of the "processes" Fuller studied are, in reality, merely integral parts of one or more of law's five basic techniques. Managerial direction, for example, plays a major role in the distributive and regulatory techniques. Adjudication is the very core of what one may call the grievance-remedial technique, though it plays some role in each technique (as does legislation). Had Fuller thought of his processes as parts of larger wholes, it might have sharpened his treatment of various questions that greatly interested him such as the peculiar uses and limitations of different institutional forms. For example, the limits of adjudication take on different aspects depending on whether adjudication functions as part of an overall technique for the remedying of private grievances (defined as such either by common law or by statute) or functions as part of an overall technique for the regulation of some business or governmental activity.

It is of special interest that official personnel play a role in each of these basic techniques (though a limited one in the private-arranging and grievance-remedial techniques), and thus there is a need for some process for recruiting and retaining them. Here there are basically two opposite approaches: individual contracting between the governmental body involved and its employees, or collective bargaining between the governmental body and union representatives of the employees. The second alternative was generally not recognized in public employment in the United States until well after the Second World War, and full-fledged collective bargaining is still not the practice in public employment at the federal level. However, as a result of state legislative action, public-sector collective bargaining became widespread at local and state levels in over half of the states between 1960 and 1975. This profoundly important new process is ostensibly concerned merely with labor relations, but in reality involves a colossal redistribution of political power from elected representatives to private unions, power to be exercised in accord with collective bargaining rather than parliamentary procedures. By this new process, public school policy is made, police and fire protection policy is made, and much else. If Aristotle were to chance upon the American scene today, he would no doubt wish to classify American public-employee collective bargaining as a new basic form of local government. Yet Fuller, who had a keen interest in labor relations generally, wrote almost nothing about this development.[15]

In his writings on legal process, Fuller did not develop a general theory of "process values." These may be defined as values that attach to the workings of a process and are desirable in themselves. Fairness and participation are examples. Various features of our legal processes are designed to protect process values. Thus a right to a hearing, for example, secures the process value of participation, something worth having even if this participation does not affect the outcome. A general theory of process values would address these questions, among others: Which values can qualify as process values? Why are process values desirable? What is their importance compared with other values? How may they be secured? These are large and difficult questions. Fuller's interests plainly extended to process values such as legitimacy and participation. He was also much interested in the maximum moral force of a process's operation and the integrity of processes generally. With a fully developed theory of process values, he might have articulated his views on the moral facets of legal process even more persuasively.[16]

In his study of socio-legal processes was Fuller enough of an empiricist? To cite an example of potentially major import, in his work on adjudication, Fuller reveals little sign of having specifically addressed what Abram Chayes has called cases involving "public law litigation"—ones in which courts adjudicate disputes over public school desegregation, over systems of air and water pollution control, over the management of public prisons and hospitals, and so on.[17] Chayes has identified many apparent differences between public law adjudication and Fuller's essentially "private law" process. Perhaps, then, we ought to talk about different types of adjudication. But a case can be made that much of what Chayes calls public law litigation is not really adjudication, given that the decision maker is not really required to base his decision more or less entirely on the proofs and arguments of the parties. And even if this is adjudication, the fact that Chayes has discerned the differences he has does not alone show that adjudication is being properly used in public law litigation generally. Still, the form of litigation Chayes has singled out might represent a type of ordering process with its own distinctive sources of legitimacy and moral force.

Others have addressed some of Fuller's specific ideas about the limits of various processes and the conditions required for their effective functioning. For example, did Fuller overemphasize the role of the affected parties participating in adjudication?[18] Even without their full participation, might not adjudication still be reasonably well suited to a given task? And what is to count as participation, anyway? Over the past twenty-five years, many new kinds of cases, including the class action, have appeared. Of course, Fuller's theory might be revised in some way to take account of these developments. This and many other related tasks await neo-Fullerians.

9

Legal method

Fuller was much interested in general questions about how existing law is to be applied, and about when new law may be made. It is not only the judges who must face these issues. So must lawyers representing clients, legal educators, law students, and treatise writers. Most of what follows will be a summary account of Fuller's central views on common law method. In the final section we will look at some of his general thoughts on statutory interpretation.

Interpreting and applying precedent

The common law judge is generally expected to follow precedents. But how he is to interpret and apply them is a basic problem of legal theory.[1] At the time Fuller began teaching law a great battle was raging over this problem. As he later put it:

> During the period from about 1870 to 1920, it was quite common to encounter in legal discussions statements like these: An offer is by its very nature revocable. It would be a violation of logic to permit a person who is not a party to a contract to sue on it. The legal nature of a claim to damages does not permit an assignment of it. Holmes once described this method by saying that the schools "take their premises on inspiration and then use logic as the only tool to develop the results."[2]

Many educators, including Christopher Columbus Langdell and Samuel Williston of Harvard, took a formalistic approach to legal method. Langdell, for example, claimed that the precedents on the revocability of offers to enter contracts must be read to mean that an offer is always revocable at the will of the offerer, regardless of the extent to which the offeree may have justifiably relied on the offer. In support of this, he argued that the very "logic" of the term offer as it appeared in the precedents signified that an irrevocable offer is a "legal impossibility."[3]

Similarly, Williston, like Langdell, a contracts scholar, held that the inherent "logic" of common law principles on contract compel judicial decisions, and that it is the judge's job to read the precedents to divine this logic. In his great treatise on contracts, Williston argued, for example, that any contractual obligation is a "right-duty relation," that the breach of a contractual "duty" simply entails a lost expectancy,[4] and that the damages suffered must therefore be measured, not in terms of out-of-pocket costs, but in terms of this lost expectancy. The kind of reasoning on which Langdell and Williston relied was not by any means confined to legal educators. It appeared with some frequency in judicial decisions as well.

Formalism, as this general approach to legal method is conventionally called, was hardly confined to the common law of contract. It may even have had its greatest impact within constitutional law. Formalism came in many varieties and seems to have been motivated by a number of factors. Hence it cannot be defined in simple terms.

Formalism provoked a vigorous and vocal reaction.[5] During the early decades of this century, a new general theory of law and its use was coming into being whose adherents were resolutely anti-formalistic. Leaders of this new school of thought, which I prefer to call pragmatic instrumentalism, though it is also sometimes referred to as sociological jurisprudence or legal realism, included Judge Oliver Wendell Holmes Jr.; Roscoe Pound, who in 1916 became dean of the Harvard Law School; John Chipman Gray, also a Harvard faculty member; the philosopher John Dewey, and in the field of contract law specifically, Arthur L. Corbin of Yale and Karl N. Llewellyn (a pupil of Corbin's). These men wrote hundreds of pages in an attempt to demonstrate the errant ways of Langdell and his followers.[6]

Fuller eventually joined the fray. His 1939 review article on Williston's contracts treatise became famous. In it he gently chided the great master of contract law for his over-reliance on the "syllogistic marshalling of traditional concepts" and neglect of "underlying social and ethical desiderata."[7] He himself saw nothing logically inevitable about a court's using Williston's measure of lost expectancy. The mere out-of-pocket expenses a plaintiff incurs in anticipation of a defendant's performance might be quite appropriate in certain cases. Such recovery might in fact be especially appropriate where the plaintiff had not accepted the defendant's offer, yet had reasonably relied on it.[8]

In Williston's contract treatise, said Fuller, he had ignored a great many decisions in which courts had reimbursed plaintiffs for out-of-pocket expenses incurred in reliance on promises, cases that failed to fit Williston's concept of contract based almost entirely on obligations arising from deals fully formed through "offer" and "acceptance." Fuller pointed out that judges and lawyers do not enjoy the treatise writer's luxury of being able to ignore "freak" cases that do not fit some preconceived view of common law contract liability. Moreover, such cases may turn out not to be freaks. The reliance cases are not. They rest on basic notions of rightness, as Fuller himself had already demonstrated in "The Reliance Interest in Contract Damages," a classic article he had published (with William Perdue) a few years earlier.[9]

In the same general vein, Fuller was skeptical of the American Law

Institute's various Restatements of the Law, then beginning to influence the courts. Williston was Chief Reporter of the Restatement of Contracts, which included many capsule formulations in boldface type. Fuller characterized these restatements as law "intentionally abstracted from its purposes in the process of exposition, on the theory that this divorce is conducive to certainty in application." And he expressed a fear that judges were not "thinking through the implications of the cases before them, and [were] acquiring a taste for the abstract and ready-made formulas of the Restatements." [10]

How, then, is a precedent to be interpreted and applied? Strictly speaking, a precedent has no "face value," Fuller thought.[11] Certainly a judge is not to seize on words and phrases in an opinion, abstract them from their context, and apply them more or less in accord with some assumed literal meaning that they might be thought to have. Rather he is to "look behind the words of a precedent" to what influenced the court, or would have influenced the court if it had perceived the importance of certain factors or could have foreseen the sequence of the cases that were to arise.[12]

In the common law, a judge is not required, as he is in the interpretation of statutes, to try to adhere even in a general way to the language of a precedent, Fuller maintained. A precedent—a decided case—is something that has purportedly been *justified* either by reference to previous cases or by direct appeal to substantive reasons, or both. The rule applied and the reasons purporting to justify it are ordinarily "two aspects of a single reasoning process." [13] The rule is frequently stated by the deciding court more than once and not always in the same terms. In addition, a judge may misstate what he is actually deciding, and may even fail to articulate his reasons clearly. This is a far cry, indeed, from the "statutory mode," in which there is a set and singular form of words with which the court must work. Common law is unwritten law. And it follows that nothing approaching the so-called plain-meaning rule, one basic method of statutory interpretation, could even be remotely credible as an approach to the application and interpretation of precedent. The application of a precedent is inherently something that must be argued for.[14]

What, then, is to guide the later court in this process? There is no simple answer or pat formula. One general approach draws on Fuller's important insight that all case law rules can be viewed as a mix of "reason and fiat." [15] In his famous essay "Reason and Fiat in Case Law," Fuller observed that some case law doctrines partake more of reason than fiat, and others more of fiat than reason. For example, the choice of a time period of five rather than six years for the recognition of title by adverse possession (squatter's rights) is inherently more a matter of fiat, the choice of reliance damages rather than expectancy damages for breach of contract more a matter of reason. When interpreting precedents, a court will do well to observe this distinction.

To the extent that a problem requires reasoned resolution, the court can always seek to put itself in the place of its predecessors and try to reason things out by the prior court's thinking. But precedents do set certain limits. A court is not wholly free to substitute its own reasoning for that of the prior court, with all that this might imply in the way of an altogether different solution for a similar problem.

To the extent that a problem falls within the realm of fiat, the later court must adhere rather more closely to the lines laid down by the prior court, if what the later court is doing is to count as interpreting and applying prior law. In Fuller's terms, "established fiat is itself a reality that reason bids us take into account in our reckonings."[16] The philosopher David Hume had similarly noted that "the slightest analogies are laid hold of [by judges and lawyers] in order to prevent that indifference and ambiguity, which would be the source of perpetual dissention."[17] Of course, the line between the two realms may be hard to draw. And the court may have to work its way through converging precedents to some kind of sensible synthesis. Or a prior opinion may partake of fiat when the issue should have been ruled by reason, or vice versa.

In his teaching, and to a lesser extent in his writings, Fuller stressed the vital importance of hypothetical cases in legal reasoning. Let us consider the problem of determining the scope of a precedent in a field in which reason (rather than merely fiat) may be decisive. Such a precedent must stand for something more than just a decision "on the facts." In these circumstances, a judge can hypothesize cases to which the precedent must apply, if it has any genuine scope at all, just as he can imagine cases to which it would be absurdly applied. By a process of comparative analysis (often complex) he may then be able to plot the case at hand on a kind of legal continuum, and to arrive at a principle that includes neither too much nor too little. In all this, the facts of the prior case must loom large, for they (along with values) generate reasons, and also serve as bases for the construction of hypothetical cases.

A similar general approach is perhaps possible even when the case confronting the earlier court fell primarily within the realm of fiat. Certainly the scope of such a precedent is not unlimited, and hypothetical cases may be similarly useful in plotting its limits.

Most of these ideas, it must be said, are found (or implied) in the articles and books Fuller wrote in his middle period, particularly his profound essay on reason and fiat. Some of his earliest writings are not wholly consistent with them. Thus he once stressed that if a court is to determine what a prior court decided, it must, within limits, determine "why it decided as it did." Yet if this inquiry is "pressed too far," he suggested, it tends to end in an "imbroglio of conflicting and overlapping motives in which all orientation is lost and from which the case seems to decide everything at the same time." Here, Fuller thought that "it may be necessary for logic to carry the burden."[18]

The ingredients of reason and fiat and the imaginative resort to hypotheticals do not exhaust all matters of relevance to a judge who must decide what a precedent means. Fuller would have said that no precedent is an island. It is virtually always a part of a larger field of thought and action, including other precedents. The terms and concepts that pervade or cut across this field also lend meaning and significance to the precedent at hand. Furthermore, one view of a precedent will often be more consistent or cohere more faithfully with the law of the whole field than others. Fuller put this as follows: "The rules applied to the decision of individual controversies cannot simply be isolated exercises of judicial wisdom. They must be brought into, and maintained in, some systematic interrelationships; they must display some coherent internal structure." And he was at pains to emphasize that all this is not merely a dictate of logic, of symmetry, or of *elegantia juris*. In part, it is a requirement of "justice itself," namely, that like cases be decided alike.[19]

Fuller's writings on common law method might be faulted in several respects. Ironically, for all his emphasis on reason (as opposed to fiat, force, or intuition), he never sought to develop a general theory of the nature, kinds, and limits of substantive reasons at work in common law. Yet this is now seen as a fertile and highly promising field of legal theory.[20] Nor did he work out a systematic account of the kinds of substantive reasons behind the general doctrine of precedent itself, of their comparative general force, and of how they may themselves be used to justify adhering to a precedent even if it is wanting in some way. Further, although in his classroom teaching on contracts, Fuller dwelled on the idea of synthesizing related cases into something more (or less) than they would be if each stood alone, his published writings are largely devoid of insights into this complex art.

Fuller of course recognized that the subsequent court has "considerable" freedom in dealing with precedent. He identified various sources of this freedom, including the later court's prerogative to accept the decision of its predecessor but not its justification, or to accept the justification but assert that it was misapplied, or to reinterpret the justification (especially in the face of multiple opinions). Fuller perceived that a key element in all this freedom is the full statement of facts in the prior opinion. As justifications are interpreted or altered by the later court, certain facts become more important, others less so. "A truncated factual statement, cut to fit a particular theory of the case, would ill serve the process of growth and rearticulation that is an essential characteristic of the common law."[21]

Fuller was fully aware that judges very often faced a difficult task in drawing a line between applying precedent and making law. As he saw it, the common law is a "body of living material,"[22] and essentially unfinished. Judges usually view the work of earlier judges as something "to be reformulated and improved in the light of experience and sober second thought."[23] According to Fuller, judges participate in a collaborative process in which they articulate purposes shared with their predecessors. This whole process is frequently obscured from view because the evolutionary reform of the common law has "a way of creeping up on us, and at any point it is difficult to say whether the court is announcing a new rule or only making explicit assumptions which lay implicit in the old rule."[24] To Fuller, the common law includes much that is implicit, inchoate, nascent, and evolving. It is thus pregnant with implications for future cases.

As late as the early 1900's, there were prominent legal educators and judges in the United States who saw little scope for judicial lawmaking, some because they believed that existing law is more or less complete, others because they were against making law in any circumstance. For both, only legislatures have the authority to make law. The instrumentalists considered this general outlook formalistic, also, and subjected it to heavy attack. By the end of the 1930's it was widely agreed, at least among legal theorists and legal educators, that judges have vast scope for creativity. Cases of first impression are not uncommon. Gaps in the law regularly appear. Precedents accumulate and conflict. Original error and misjudgment occur. Society changes. Interpretation is unavoidable. All these call for various forms of creativity.[25]

In judicial lawmaking, Fuller stressed the relevance of "social and ethical desiderata." He held that the weight of reason was frequently heavily on one side, though judges might have to do some careful thinking before they could discern this. Moreover, the reasons that should be decisive are often moral reasons. Fuller was emphatic that judges should not view these as "extra legal," for to him they were the very raw materials of lawmaking. One simply could not maintain a sharp distinction in this way between the common law and the ingredients that make it up. Fuller held that "if we look to those rules of morality which have enough teeth in them to act as serious deterrents to men's pursuit of their selfish interests, we will find that far from being 'extra legal' they are intimately and organically connected with the functionings of the legal order."[26] He cited as examples the moral notion that we should keep our promises and the moral notion that in such daily activities as driving our cars we should keep a proper lookout for others. At the same time, he stressed that the law's daily functioning reinforces these moral notions, so that they become partly creatures of law and thus are not extra legal in another sense.

Nor are the materials that figure in the making of the common law merely the subjective concoctions of individuals who happen to be judges. According to Fuller, the relevant considerations are commonly quite objective. The perceptive judge sees that "there are external criteria, found in the conditions required for successful group living, that furnish some standard against which the rightness of his decisions should be measured."[27] In a society with a division of labor, for example, some provision for redress of broken promises is required, as it is for wrongs to property, too.

How far is the judge's task in making the common law one of discovery rather than invention? For Fuller, "criteria of rightness" are in substantial measure external and thus might be said to be discoverable. The need to provide redress for broken promises, for example, is something judges can discover. They do not merely invent it or make it up. As we have seen, Fuller held this to be true in regard to the processes of social ordering, too. Thus, in making law, judges must discover and respect the inner order and integrity of such basic forms of social ordering as contract, legislation, and even adjudication itself. Judges who fail to do this will make unsound decisions and bad law.

In various of his writings, Fuller went out of his way to attack the "bad man" theory of law set forth by one of the country's most influential judges, Oliver Wendell Holmes Jr.[28] According to Fuller, this theory implies that the judge's creative role is essentially that of designing minimum restraints to keep the bad man in check. Fuller rejected this view. In deciding cases, the judge is not merely laying down a system of "minimum restraints designed to keep the bad man in check, but is in fact helping to create a body of common morality which will define the good man. When he sees his office in this light, the judge will realize, I think, how significantly creative his work is."[29]

Legal fictions

No summary account of Fuller's views on judicial method in common law cases would be complete without some treatment of his views on legal fictions. His book by this title, published in 1967, consisted of three articles (essentially unchanged) that he wrote in 1930–31, when he was only twenty-eight years old. They display a remarkable sophistication and insight, as well as an intellect precociously versed in philosophy, linguistics, and European legal scholarship.

Fuller defined the usual legal fiction as a statement of fact or of a legal relation that judges know to be false but think has utility. The history of the law of tort provides many examples. Assume that a rule says there is no duty of care to trespassers. A man has an abandoned railroad turntable on his land. Unknowing youngsters are attracted to it and while playing on it, one boy crushes his foot, and the landowner is sued. The judge characterizes the injured boy as an "invitee" rather than a trespasser because, he says, the turntable is an "attractive nuisance," the very existence of which invites the plaintiff onto the defendant's land. Here the judge utters what appears to be a statement of fact, namely, that the plaintiff has been invited by the defendant to enter the premises. Yet in truth the defendant issued no such invitation, and the judge is fully aware of this. The fiction has utility, however, for it enables the judge to escape a seemingly hard and fast rule and do justice in the case.

Fuller identified three functions of the legal fiction. First, it may usefully "bridge a gap between concept and reality" in circumstances in which the judge would not otherwise be able to articulate, or would be fearful of articulating, the rationale behind it. In our turntable example, it does appear there is a special circumstance for which the defendant should be responsible, namely, the increased risk to youngsters of keeping a turntable on one's property. The judge's resort to fiction takes account of this and allows him to reach the result he thinks just, when he might otherwise have found himself without the requisite legal resources or without the necessary courage.

Second, a judge may resort to a fiction because he thinks this may make his decision more acceptable. And in some cases he will no doubt be right. The reference to a rule, even a fictionalized one, is an appeal to authority. Also, it may placate those who have a narrow conception of the judicial role. In cases like our turntable example, those who oppose judicial lawmaking might be led by the fiction to accept a decision for the plaintiff. Of course, here the function is to some extent that of concealment.

Finally, judges may rely on a fiction as a way of satisfying themselves that harmony and stability are being preserved, especially in a time of change, when they may feel uncertain of their bearings.

Of course, judges who resort to fiction must be wary of misleading themselves or later judges. Suppose, for example, that a second turntable case arises, one in which the evidence shows that the injured youngster was fully warned in advance of all risks and had even been evicted from the premises on occasion. Should the fiction be employed to grant recovery? Probably not. Fuller quotes the great English jurist Lord Mansfield: "But fictions of law hold only in respect to the ends and purposes for which they were invented; when they are urged to an intent and purpose not within the reason and policy of the fiction, the other party may show the truth."[30]

Fuller thought that judges should generally avoid fictions. But he recognized that, given the limitations of judicial intellect, the inadequacies of language, and the conservative tendencies of the law-trained, fictions can provide an avenue for needed growth in the law. Better that the law grow through fiction than that it not grow at all. And in time, most judges will come to see a fiction for what it is and drop it. Of course, in the meantime, they must remain conscious of the hazards. These include the risk of overextension and the possibility of confusion in analysis.

The interpretation of statutes

In some legal systems, notably those of Anglo-American countries, legislatures have given courts a relatively free hand in interpreting statutes.[31] In others, strict attention to the letter of the law is often required. Where courts are not under such strictures, judges may differ substantially in their approaches. But a uniform approach within a system is clearly desirable: if lawyers have some firm idea of how judges are going to interpret statutes, they can advise their clients more effectively than they can when the interpretation could go any which way, and trial judges can follow appellate judges more consistently. The task of legislative draftsmen is also made easier, for they can anticipate how the language they choose will be approached. In Fuller's words: "If the legislative draftsman is to discharge his responsibilities, he, in turn, must be able to anticipate rational and relatively stable modes of interpretation."[32]

Legal theorists seldom undertake merely to describe interpretational practices; usually they also sort out the different approaches and prescribe one over the others. Three basic approaches have been particularly prominent. The first, and the least popular among legal theorists, might be called the "delegation" theory, and holds that when the legislature enacts a statute, it delegates a broad grant of power to the judiciary, giving it a more or less free hand limited only vaguely by the statutory words. But even then, partisans of this theory view these words not as obligatory, but only as guidelines. At various times in the United States, this approach has found considerable favor. Indeed, in our own day even some of the U.S. Supreme Court justices have practiced it. Of all competing approaches, this one accords least deference to statutory language. Yet it is not utterly without defense. Judges are closer than legislatures to the circumstances of actual cases that arise, and thus may have a more intimate understanding of the problems posed. And, in any case, general language is almost always to some extent an imperfect means of conveying solutions in advance.

A second basic approach is often called the "plain-meaning" technique. Here, the task of the judiciary is considered to be that of determining the meaning of the words in a statute largely in light of conventional usage, on the assumption that most words have single plain meanings of relevance. One of the most lively debates in modern times took place in 1958 in the pages of the *Harvard Law Review* partly over the desirability of a version of the "plain-meaning rule," as advocated by H. L. A. Hart. In that debate, Hart stated: "A legal rule forbids you to take a vehicle into the public park. *Plainly* this forbids an automobile [for] the general words we use—like 'vehicle' in the case I consider—must have some standard instance in which no doubts are felt about its application." (Emphasis supplied.)[33]

Fuller attacked Hart's plain-meaning approach and advocated a third theory of interpretation, one that is often called "purposive." On this approach, interpreters are to determine what the purposes of the statute may fairly be said to be, to read the statute in light of those purposes, and then to decide accordingly. Thus whether the word vehicle excludes an automobile would depend on the automobile and on the statute's purposes. Assume, for example, that the purposes of the statute are to reduce noise in the park, and to increase safety and cleanliness (as ascertained from legislative minutes). In that event, Fuller claimed, if "some local patriots wanted to mount on a pedestal in the park a truck used in World War II . . . in perfect working order," this would not offend such statutory purposes and thus would not, on a purposive approach to interpretation, be contrary to the statute.[34] But, it seemed to Fuller, on Hart's plain-meaning approach, the truck would "plainly" qualify as a vehicle and thus be excluded from the park. Even a Park Authority truck brought in to haul off litter might be excluded.

From the foregoing, it can be seen that purposive interpretation requires that even the features of the *standard* case to which the statute applies be determined by reference to statutory purposes. Contrary to Hart's view, those purposes are relevant in standard as well as borderline cases.

Fuller was particularly scornful of Hart's focus on a single word, "vehicle," and its alleged plain meaning. Few words have single plain meanings unaffected by context. "Vehicle" takes its meaning from being in a sentence that is in turn inside a statute with identifiable (or rationally attributable) purposes. The meaning of a statute is not the sum of the meanings of its particular words. Rather, the statute as a whole is a device to achieve purposes, and these purposes infuse the parts of the statute with meaning. To determine the purposes of the statute it is at least necessary to consider the statutory scheme as a whole, for only as an integral whole can we see the statute as an instrumentality with some overall purposive design. To use one of Fuller's examples, assume that a statute reads: "All improvements must be promptly reported to . . ." Now, the meaning of the word improvements would differ depending on whether you fill in "the head nurse" or "the Town Planning Authority."[35] We cannot determine the meaning by conventional usage in ordinary discourse. Interestingly enough, it is quite possible for the language of a statute to be such that no single word suggests its principal purpose. True, the word park (not "vehicle") in the earlier example does suggest the intent, for a park is usually intended to be a quiet, safe, and clean place. But the word park does not have to appear in the statute. It could merely state "all that area bounded on the north by Adams Boulevard, on the east by Third Street," etc.[36]

According to Fuller, the purposes of a statute may change. Consider further our park example. A "wholly extra-legal change in the uses made of parks may gradually bring about an alteration in the meaning of 'park.'" A statute cannot be "cut loose from the developing life into which it is projected." But this problem of the statute with an evolving purpose should be distinguished from the problem of the "absolute" statute. Fuller did not think that the best interpretation would necessarily keep the statute "up to date." On the contrary, it is the "inevitable fate" of many statutes to become out of date. For him, the practical issue was "whether amendment should be accomplished by the judiciary or the legislature." And he held that if the preference is for judicial amendment, "the reason for this preference should be made explicit."[37]

Fuller did not pretend that American judges always used a purposive approach in interpreting statutes. He merely argued that they *ought* to adopt that approach, insisting that it was more congruent with the substantive purposes ("oughts") of the text and more likely to yield sound results in particular cases. He associated the plain-meaning approach with positivism, and once remarked:

> When rules are treated in terms of their purposes, "is" and "ought" inevitably get mixed; conversely the attempt to preserve an appearance of rigid separation of "is" and "ought" inevitably results in our treating rules as something distinct from their purposes. From the standpoint of diagnosis, when men treat rules of law as disembodied entities without regard to the ends they serve, what is the reason for this perversity? I think that the explanation is to be found in the influence of the positivistic philosophy, which teaches men that they must keep distinct the law that is from the law that ought to be.[38]

Again, Fuller did not work out a comprehensive theory of interpretation. Nevertheless, one finds many useful insights in his scattered writings on the subject, and we may profitably look at several of these.

Theorists of interpretation have frequently assumed that if a statute and other relevant subject matter (including legislative history) reveal no specific intent about how the statute is to be applied in a given situation, then whatever the judges say is in truth no interpretation, but only legislation "to fill up *casus omissi*." Fuller roundly condemned this view. Taken seriously, such a "pointer theory of meaning" would require, for example, that "the intention of the draftsman of a statute directed at 'dangerous weapons' [be construed] as directed toward an endless series of individual objects: revolvers, automatic pistols, daggers, Bowie knives, etc." Yet this would misconceive the nature of statutory purpose. Statutory purpose is ordinarily more general and systematic, and the statute designed accordingly. In resorting to that design to punish the use of a weapon not normally viewed as dangerous but clearly so in the context, a judge carries out the draftsman's intent, even if the draftsman never had the particular weapon in mind as a prohibited one.[39]

How are general purpose and design to be determined? Here again, Fuller stressed "the putting of hypothetical cases." He believed that "by pulling our minds in one direction, then in another, these cases help us to understand the fabric of thought before us."[40] They enable us to make a statute a "coherent, workable whole." He also believed that the wisest interpreter is one who understands the processes by which statutes are made. Such a person will not be misled by manufactured evidence of legislative objectives, will not take obvious political compromise too seriously, and will pay particular attention to what seem to have been shared assumptions about the problem the statute was passed to deal with.[41]

As we have seen, Fuller was insistent on the creative role of judges. A statute is not a mere thing whose sense is all "in the statute book." And no sharp line can be drawn between merely discovering the statute's purposes from textual and other evidence on the one hand and justifiably *attributing* purposes to it on the other. The sound determination of statutory meaning will frequently require imaginative analysis (often through resort to hypothetical cases falling within and outside the statute). Choices between conflicting purposes will call for thought that did not occur to the legislator. The language of the statute will need to be infused with purpose and creatively construed. It may even have to be adjusted to some extent to unforeseen changes. Much will be implicit. Fuller believed that no form of "enacted law ever comes from its legislator wholly and fully made."[42]

It is often said that even purposive interpretation must cease where the language of the text ceases. Or in other words, the text of the statute must be able to "bear" the proposed interpretation.[43] This is rather metaphorical. But it might be possible to assemble a wide range of cases, actual and hypothetical, in which we could justifiably say the texts do and do not appropriately bear the contemplated interpretations, and then construct some useful principles for drawing a general line of this kind. Fuller did not, however, attempt to carry out such an enterprise.

Fuller stressed on several occasions the importance of not interpreting a statute in ways that would unfairly surprise those private parties who might have relied on it. This, and the requirement that the text "bear" a proposed interpretation, qualify his basic approach.

It would be foolish to deny that statutes are sometimes vague. Here Fuller advocated a blending of "interpretation and improvement," or, as he also put it, a "blending of is and ought." He considered this effort to "serve the ought" entirely justified, and pointed out that much positivistic legal theory has nothing salutary to say on this important question, unless it be to take refuge in some form of literalism.[44]

Fuller was of course aware of numerous vagaries and complexities in purposive interpretation. Purposes could be hard to determine. They might be left quite implicit. Or the available evidence of purposes might be fugitive. Also, the ascertaining of purpose not infrequently requires an imaginative marshalling and weighing of argument. And even when purposes are articulated in the law in some form, they may be unduly vague. One of Fuller's favorite examples of an "unlawlike purpose" is Congress's charge to the Federal Communications Commission to act "in the public interest." Or if not unduly vague, several conflicting purposes might emerge, making it necessary to articulate and weigh arguments to determine the priority of one purpose over another. Often the true light of determinative purposes in a given branch of the law might not even emerge until the end of an extended period of groping by a number of different judges or other officials for the relevant means-end relations. And, of course, purposes change over time.

Fuller did not fail to appreciate the risk that some judges or other officials might take the purposive approach as a kind of blanket invitation to impose their own idiosyncratic conceptions of purpose, and hence law, on litigants and citizens generally. For example, in the guise of interpretation, judges of a religious persuasion might construe a statute forbidding public sporting events on Sundays to require people to go to church (his example). But Fuller believed that any such risk is not high, for statutes and other forms of law have discernible boundaries ("structural integrity") on which nearly all can agree. Moreover, the appellate process provides checks and opportunities for sober second thought.[45]

Critics have occasionally even suggested that Fuller believed officials should generally have discretion to impose their own personal purposes in place of those of the lawgivers. He brushed this aside with a curt response: "This criticism would be justified only if the view I am advocating permitted the interpreter of a statute or precedent to read into it any purpose he saw fit. No such abandonment of ordinary principles of interpretation is here proposed or implied."[46]

Of course, any general approach to interpretation has its limits. We should expect only so much from a general method and no more. A theory of interpretation cannot *decide* concrete cases. It can only specify steps to be taken and structure the exercise of judgment. The presuppositions of a general approach may fail in particular cases and thus limit its efficacy. For example, the means-end hypothesis in a statute may be so faulty that a purposive approach can provide but little guidance. Fuller pointed to the statute of frauds as an apt illustration of this phenomenon.[47]

10

Contract jurisprudence

Although the formalist-minded Samuel Williston of Harvard was the generally acknowledged *doyen* of contract law in the early 1930's, two of the other prominent American contract specialists of the day, Arthur Corbin of Yale and his former pupil Karl Llewellyn of Columbia, were among the leaders of a revolution in contract thinking, a revolution that was part of a much larger instrumentalist movement in American legal thought. So significant was the shift in thinking, in fact, that Fuller was prompted to remark, as early as 1934:

> One seldom encounters a law review article today of the type so common ten years ago, in which the writer starts with an inquiry into the "nature" of some legal concept and ends by deducing all sorts of important consequences from the supposed inner nature of the concept—without more than a passing reference to the practical effects of his conclusions, and then with an air of condescension, as if to compliment the facts for showing good judgment in conforming to his theories.[1]

Fuller himself practiced a sophisticated instrumentalism in several respects. We saw in Chapter Six how he viewed contract as one of the basic processes of socio-legal ordering; and in Chapter Nine, how he repudiated a formalistic legal method. In his work on contract law, though he aligned himself with the instrumentalist spirit of Corbin and Llewellyn,[2] he displayed considerable independence of mind and originality. His writings on contract law are few in number. They consist mainly of his justly famous article "The Reliance Interest in Contract Damages"; his review of Williston's treatise; his article on the doctrine of consideration and the requirements of form in contract; and his own casebook. Corbin and Fuller agreed in the late 1930's to co-author a new edition of Corbin's casebook and even signed a publishing contract; but the project never materialized, apparently in part because Fuller wanted to open the book with some cases on remedies, and Corbin was not enthusiastic. Fuller followed through on the idea when he published his own casebook, *Basic Contract Law*, and many considered this a major advance. Among other things, the book focused on the basic alternative rationales for judicial intervention where a promise is broken (relief for unjust enrichment, reimbursement for justified reliance, and compensation for lost expectancy where this is just), and it cut through the verbiage of doctrine to expose the different measures of damages actually available "in contract." It also exploded the "contract–no contract" dichotomy, demonstrating that liability "in contract" fell rather along a continuum, and that the appropriate remedy was determined by the circumstances of the case.

In this chapter we will see that Fuller made new or fresh contributions to our understanding of the substantive and formal grounds of liability "in contract"; of the field of contract remedies, especially the interplay between right and remedy; of the independent significance of the reliance interest in contract law; and of the role of intentions and tacit assumptions in contract analysis. Scant as Fuller's writings on contract law and contract teaching are, they have had an enormous impact. His ideas have influenced the courts, and also the second Restatement of Contract, promulgated in 1981. His casebook is still widely used (and copied), though in the current edition, Fuller's co-author has chosen not to open with remedies; and "The Reliance Interest" is the most frequently cited article in American contract literature. He has influenced many scholars, including the most important scholar in the field today, Patrick Atiyah of Oxford University. No doubt part of this influence is due to Fuller's having also been a leading legal theorist. But that is really beside the point. In any event, this is hardly the first case in which a marriage of contract and legal theory has proved extraordinarily fertile.

The substantive and formal bases of liability in contract

Liability in contract is an ancient problem to which several of Fuller's contemporaries also contributed, including Roscoe Pound, Karl Llewellyn, and the philosopher Morris Cohen. The problem is essentially one of formulating broad rationales that justify providing a remedy for some broken promises but not others. Most of the ingredients of Fuller's own contribution are not novel, but he did restructure, interrelate, and synthesize them in new ways. The actual (and potential) rationales for enforcing promises in Anglo-American law show themselves, often imperfectly, in the working clothes of such contract doctrines as the requirement that an enforceable promise must be supported by "consideration" (e.g., be part of a bargained-for exchange), that reliance on a promise not supported by consideration must be justified if there is to be recovery, and (in former times) that certain promises be "under seal." Of course these rationales are authoritatively reflected in specific judicial decisions reached in the names of such doctrines. Fuller remarked that we hear of proposals to "abolish consideration" or to abolish the seal, or the like. He certainly sympathized with those who held that the doctrine of consideration was really many different doctrines. But he insisted that the *problems* these doctrines attempt to solve "cannot be abolished." Indeed, if anything needs abolishing, he remarked wryly, it is a conception of legal method that assumes that a legal doctrine such as consideration "can be understood and applied without reference to the ends it serves."[3] Thus he held that the very scope of the rules of law falling under the rubric of consideration depends on the reasons behind this rubric. Judges are to apply these rules up to the limits of such reasons, no more and no less, and the quality of results that they reach in the name of these rules is to be judged partly in light of this basic principle of scope.

Fuller had his own way of breaking down and analyzing the various rationales behind the doctrine of consideration and its corollaries. He distinguished between what he called "substantive" and "formal" reasons for enforcing promises. Formal reasons pertain merely to the circumstances surrounding the entering of an agreement, such as whether the parties acted with due caution. Substantive reasons have to do with the nature and significance of the specific promise made. According to Fuller, there are three kinds of substantive reasons.

One kind draws its authority from the "principle of autonomy"—the notion that some species of regulation of men's relations is always a necessity. A contract is a form of self-regulation and thus should be honored. After all, the parties "considered that [their transaction] set their rights and were prepared to act accordingly."[4] Fuller did not fully explore just why the so-called principle of autonomy is a justification for enforcing contracts. Did he mean that the justification lies in the mere fact that the parties assented to their own private form of self-governance? He did not go into this. At one point Fuller also stressed a notion of reciprocity, which would seem to be a reason as much in the name of fairness as of assent. At other points, when an exercise of autonomy involved an exchange of values, he seemed to be thinking of the production of wealth and the facilitation of a division of labor as possible justifications: "Men *ought* to exchange goods and services."[5] And he also suggested the possibility that a promise might be binding because it "excites an expectation," a quite different rationale from the other two. Here Fuller may, in the name of "the" principle of autonomy, have been unconsciously imposing a spurious unity. The foregoing rationales are diverse, and each seems to qualify as a source of justification (within limits). Of these sources, Fuller seems to have stressed the normative principle of autonomy the most, thereby joining in a great tradition that includes, among many others, Kant and Hegel.

A second substantive reason for imposing liability "in contract" is detrimental reliance—a justified change of position by one party based on the prospect that the other would go forward. Though reliance can serve as a measure of recovery, too, that is not our concern here. Again, Fuller did not explore at any length the nature of the justification involved, speaking mainly of "healing losses caused by broken faith." But the central point appears to be this: one party ought not to be allowed, without more, to cause another with whom he is dealing to incur a loss, for this is simply a form of injustice in dealings among men. To make a promise and thereby induce another to rely on it to his detriment and then go back on the promise is one important way of dealing unjustly with another.

Fuller usefully identified the relationships between the reliance principle and what he called "the" principle of private autonomy.[6] Reliance may be the sole basis of liability in a given case. Or the two principles may conflict, as where a promisee has "seriously, and, according to ordinary standards of conduct, justifiably relied on a promise which the promisor expressly stipulated should impose no liability on him." Or reliance may reinforce autonomy. And, occasionally, the two principles may serve as alternative and independently sufficient bases for imposing liability, as when a court suggests that the likelihood of reliance or the fact of agreement would each alone suffice.

Fuller saw as a third substantive reason for granting contract relief the need to prevent unjust enrichment of the promisor. For Fuller, this was an "aggravated form of reliance." But he acknowledged that in contract law this is sometimes a distinct ground of liability, as in a suit for the restitution of the value of the benefit conferred where the promise is unenforceable under the statute of frauds. As he noted:

> The restitution interest, involving a combination of unjust impoverishment with unjust gain, presents the strongest case for relief. If, following Aristotle, we regard the purpose of justice as the maintenance of an equilibrium of goods among members of society, the restitution interest presents twice as strong a claim to judicial intervention as the reliance interest, since if A not only causes B to lose one unit but appropriates that unit to himself, the resulting discrepancy between A and B is not one unit but two.[7]

Although any of these three substantive reasons for imposing liability may be enough to justify a remedy, Fuller recognized that certain "formal grounds" of enforceability also commonly figure in the courts' decisions. Judges worry about the circumstances in which a deal was made, in particular (1) whether there was sufficient evidence that the defendant made the promise sued on, (2) whether the defendant in making his promise was acting with sufficient caution, and (3) whether the promise fell within appropriate "channels" or "frameworks" of enforceability.[8] The English jurist John Austin observed that the first two grounds are present in the typical contract of exchange: "In bilateral contracts [inconsiderateness] is supposed to be prevented by the mutuality: each party contracting for his own pecuniary advantage; contemplating a quid pro quo; and therefore, being in that circumspective frame of mind which a man who is only thinking of such advantage naturally assumes."[9]

A promise might qualify as enforceable on one or more substantive grounds but not qualify on any formal ground, and vice versa. In the ideal case, at least one of the substantive rationales is met, and all the formal ones. An obvious example is a written contract for the sale of land: the principle of private autonomy is met; there is no evidentiary problem; the parties can be expected to act with caution; and the deal is a stereotypical transaction. But courts must grapple with many borderline cases that are less clear. Fuller believed that they would be aided in this if they analyzed such cases in terms of the substantive and formal grounds involved. But even this analysis might not be enough. Judges, particularly in borderline cases, should also take into account a third category of considerations, what Fuller calls "substantive deterrents to legal intervention": (1) the costs to be expended in bringing lawyers and courts into action, and (2) the need to keep some domains of intercourse free of legal intervention.[10]

Thus judges should not merely throw the word consideration and similar terms around when deciding on the enforceability of promises. They are to reach results and justify them in light of the rationales behind such language. Fuller's account of these rationales and their interrelations is salutary. His overall framework has explanatory power as well. It readily explains the general unwillingness of courts to enforce the casual gratuitous and unrelied-on oral promise. Here no substantive rationale is satisfied, and all formal grounds are absent. Further, many contract cases involve the so-called half-completed exchange, in which the plaintiff has performed but the defendant has repudiated. Here all bases of liability are commonly present, even the formal ones. Fuller put it that the delivery and acceptance of the performance is a kind of "natural formality" that satisfies the evidentiary, cautionary, and channeling purposes of formal requirements. What about the case of a wholly unexecuted exchange of promises that has been repudiated by one party? Here there is no unjust enrichment and (let us assume) no reliance. Yet the principle of autonomy applies. Although evidentiary safeguards may be largely lacking, still the deal is an exchange and not a gift, and this serves both the cautionary and channeling functions. It took courts a long time to come around to enforcing such promises. Although this is the right outcome, at least in business contracts, we can readily explain centuries of judicial reluctance in Fullerian terms.

Where the element of exchange is absent, the case for enforcement diminishes all the more. Still, in the types of cases falling in Section 90 of the first Restatement of Contracts, courts have often reimbursed unbargained-for reliance with only a general concern for whether the promisee had substantially relied on the agreement and for whether the promisor could have reasonably foreseen this. Section 90 provided: "A promise which the promisor should reasonably expect to induce action or forbearance of a definite and substantial character on the part of the promisee and which does induce such action or forbearance is binding if injustice can be avoided only by enforcement of the promise." Fuller's analysis would appear to require more for recovery than section 90—for example, "Were the desiderata underlying the use of formalities satisfied?"[11]

Note that the "nominal consideration" cases in which courts uphold what are in substance promises of a gift, "supported" only by the promisee giving a dollar or one cent, can also be readily explained on Fuller's analysis. At least two of the desiderata underlying the use of formalities are ordinarily satisfied in these cases. That is, the giving of the nominal consideration is evidence of the promise itself, and this also usually signifies that the promisor was not acting impulsively in making the promise. Further, there are so-called moral obligation cases in which, say, one party at considerable cost to himself comes to the aid of another, who thereafter reneges on a promise of reimbursement. Here, courts frequently uphold the plaintiff. Again the circumstances "naturally" motivate the promise, and these circumstances are objectively provable. And here, too, the promisor is seldom acting impulsively. Fuller put it that "we in effect assert the existence of a substantive ground."[12]

Remedies

This highly practical subject may appear to have nothing whatsoever to do with legal theory. But Fuller himself viewed his work on it as an "excursus into legal philosophy."[13] He considered this effort to be continuous with the ancient philosophical problem of the justification of promissory obligation. He also considered it to be a fertile field for inquiry into the relationship between substantive rights and judicial remedies in the law generally, itself an ancient jurisprudential issue.

In the absence of any readily administerable remedy for a contract failure, Fuller contended, a court may justifiably decide that there was no contract at all, even though some of the so-called substantive and formal grounds of promissory obligation may be satisfied. Indeed, he thought some decisions were to be explained precisely on this basis. And it is interesting to note that the Uniform Commercial Code in section 2-204 explicitly recognizes as much even in regard to that all-important type of transaction, the contract of sale. Of equal significance, if a court determines that damages are warranted, it is not bound to choose one remedy rather than another. The basic remedial approaches are several, as Fuller pointed out in "The Reliance Interest in Contract Damages." (This essay first appeared in 1936 but, curiously, was not widely read until the 1950's.) The key passages on this subject are worth setting out in full:

> It is convenient to distinguish three principal purposes which may be pursued in awarding contract damages. These purposes, and the situations in which they become appropriate, may be stated briefly as follows:
>
> *First*, the plaintiff has in reliance on the promise of the defendant conferred some value on the defendant. The defendant fails to perform his promise. The court may force the defendant to disgorge the value he received from the plaintiff. The object here may be termed the prevention of gain by the defaulting promisor at the expense of the promisee; more briefly, the prevention of unjust enrichment. The interest protected may be called the *restitution interest.* For our present purposes it is quite immaterial how the suit in such a case be classified, whether as contractual or quasi-contractual, whether as a suit to enforce the contract or as a suit based upon a rescission of the contract. These questions relate to the superstructure of the law, not to the basic policies with which we are concerned.
>
> *Secondly*, the plaintiff has in reliance on the promise of the defendant changed his position. For example, the buyer under a contract for the sale of land has incurred expense in the investigation of the seller's title, or has neglected the opportunity to enter other contracts. We may award damages to the plaintiff for the purpose of undoing the harm which his reliance on the defendant's promise has caused him. Our object is to put him in as good a position as he was in before the promise was made. The interest protected in this case may be called the *reliance interest.*
>
> *Thirdly*, without insisting on reliance by the promisee or enrichment of the promisor, we may seek to give the promisee the value of the expectancy which the promise created. We may in a suit for specific performance actually compel the defendant to render the promised performance to the plaintiff, or, in a suit for damages, we may make the defendant pay the money value of this performance. Here our object is to put the plaintiff in as good a position as he would have occupied had the defendant performed his promise. The interest protected in this case we may call the *expectation interest.*
>
> It will be observed that what we have called the *restitution interest* unites two elements: (1) reliance by the promisee, (2) a resultant gain to the promisor. It may for some purposes be necessary to separate these elements. In some cases a defaulting promisor may after his breach be left with an unjust gain which was not taken from the promisee (a third party furnished the consideration), or which was not the result of reliance by the promisee (the promisor violated a promise not to appropriate the promisee's goods). Even in those cases where the promisor's gain results from the promisee's reliance it may happen that damages will be assessed somewhat differently, depending on whether we take the promisor's gain or the promisee's loss as the standard of measurement. . . . If, as we shall assume, the gain involved in the restitution interest results from and is identical with the plaintiff's loss through reliance, then the restitution interest is merely a special case of the reliance interest; all of the cases coming under the restitution interest will be covered by the reliance interest, and the reliance interest will be broader

> than the restitution interest only to the extent that it includes cases where the plaintiff has relied on the defendant's promise without enriching the defendant.
>
> It should not be supposed that the distinction here taken between the reliance and expectation interests coincides with that sometimes taken between "losses caused" (damnum emergens) and "gains prevented" (lucrum cessans). In the first place, though reliance ordinarily results in "losses" of an affirmative nature (expenditures of labor and money) it is also true that opportunities for gain may be forgone in reliance on a promise. Hence the reliance interest must be interpreted as at least potentially covering "gains prevented" as well as "losses caused." (Whether "gains prevented" through reliance on a promise are properly compensable in damages is a question not here determined. Obviously, certain scruples concerning "causality" and "foreseeability" are suggested. It is enough for our present purpose to note that there is nothing in the definition of the reliance interest itself which would exclude items of this sort from consideration.) On the other hand, it is not possible to make the expectation interest entirely synonymous with "gains prevented." The disappointment of an expectancy often entails losses of a positive character.[14]

The main differences between the three basic measures of damages can be illustrated through a simple example. Assume that Edgar contracts with Betsy to build a house on uncleared land for $50,000 at a cost to him of $40,000. If Betsy repudiates before Edgar begins, Edgar should (without more) get damages measured by his lost net expectancy—$10,000. Assume that Edgar's expected costs were $50,000, so that he had no net expectancy, but that prior to Betsy's repudiation he had bought $10,000 worth of materials salvageable for only $7,500. Here he would have $2,500 of recoverable damages measured by net out-of-pocket expenditures incurred in reliance. Now assume, finally, that when Betsy repudiated, Edgar had merely cleared her land, and that the value of this benefit to her was $1,500. Betsy would be unjustly enriched in this amount, and Edgar could recover this sum.

Fuller thought that generally the remedy for breach of contract should be measured by lost expectancy rather than by mere reliance expenditures or losses, or by the extent of unjust enrichment. He justified this mainly on the footing that people need to know in advance that they can rely on promises. Damages measured by lost expectancy are most likely to reimburse the plaintiff fairly for acts and forbearances that make up his total reliance, and are generally easier to prove than reliance expenditures or losses (particularly those requiring proof of forgone opportunities). Moreover, damages measured by lost expectancy are more likely to deter breach, and whatever deters breach also prevents reliance losses.[15]

Fuller believed that damages measured by lost expectancy were most clearly justified in cases involving exchanges of economic values in a market, but that this measure was often not at all appropriate for certain other kinds of cases, a truth he thought had not been sufficiently recognized. For instance, Williston in his great treatise on contract and in his work on the first Restatement of Contracts generally assumed that any measure other than lost expectancy was somehow aberrant. Fuller insisted that reliance expenditures were neither inappropriate nor aberrant as the sole measure of recovery in some cases. Similarly, in still other cases, a defendant's unjust enrichment at the plaintiff's expense would be a better measure of recovery than either reliance or lost expectancy. Not all substantive rights are of the same character, even "in contract," and legal remedies should vary accordingly. We will see how this is so in the next section.

It is not infrequently suggested today that Fuller's interest in the subject of remedies in the 1930's demonstrates that he was then really a legal realist at heart, alongside Llewellyn, Cook, Bingham, and the others. After all, the "real law" is ultimately that which translates into the hard facts of a specific remedy backed up by judicial coercion. In my view, this suggestion is without firm support. Fuller's interest in remedies appears to have originated quite differently. His concern was with the main types of justifications for judicial intervention in cases of broken promises: to remedy *unjust* enrichment, to provide relief for *justified* reliance, and to compensate lost expectancy when it is *just* to do so. It was this same concern that led Fuller to open his casebook with the subject of remedies. This interest in justificatory rationales as such is hardly in the spirit of legal realism.

The independent significance of reliance as a measure of damages

Fuller vigorously attacked Williston's Restatement of Contracts (and various treatises and texts) for failing to give full due to reliance expenditures and losses as a basis for assessing damages. Many courts had already allowed rather full reliance recovery, and at the very least something that called itself a restatement ought to recognize as much. Basically, the first Restatement of Contracts fully recognized as remedies only the lost expectancy and unjust enrichment interests. Section 333 did allow "the amount of the plaintiff's expenditure, reasonably made in performance of the contract or in necessary preparation therefor, [to be] included in compensatory damages" in the face of difficulties of proof for the recovery of lost expectancy. But a plaintiff was not allowed to recover reliance expenditures if damages for lost expectancy were not in principle recoverable in contract as, for example, when the "contract" was not in writing under the statute of frauds. Fuller disagreed: merely because lost expectancy could not in principle be recovered, it did not follow that no remedy should be available. A good number of courts were in accord. Even when lost expectancy damages were in principle recoverable, and even in the absence of difficulties of proof of lost expectancy, some courts had, for varying reasons, confined the plaintiff to reliance recovery. Fuller held this to be appropriate, too.

Further, Section 333 did not allow a plaintiff to recover "incidental reliance" expenditures and losses, those not incurred in "performance of the contract or necessary preparation therefor." Again, Fuller disagreed. He called expenditures "reasonably made in performance of the contract or in necessary preparation therefor" "essential reliance," and he demonstrated that judicial decisions were "legion" in which courts went beyond granting recovery for what he called "essential reliance" and allowed reimbursement for "incidental reliance"—expenditures and losses not incurred in "performance of the contract or necessary preparation therefor." He cited numerous seed warranty cases granting plaintiffs the costs of planting and cultivation, cases allowing aggrieved business lessees to recover losses for moving costs and for laying in stocks of goods, cases reimbursing buyers for expenditures made in anticipation of the arrival of goods, and many others.[16] In such cases, lost expectancy might be too difficult to measure. But regardless, the aggrieved party should, in a proper case, be allowed to recover not only any "essential reliance," but also "incidental reliance" expenditures and losses. That Williston and his co-workers on the Restatement did not see the justice of this was due in part, Fuller thought, to their inability to relate such incidental reliance expenditures and losses to the "conceptual cover of contract." These expenditures and losses seemed simply too remote from "true" contract damages in the form of lost expectancy and too far removed from direct performance obligations under the contract. The restaters here, it seemed to him, had become mired in the deadly bogs of conceptualism and formalism, and were simply unable to accommodate incidental reliance, case law notwithstanding.

It is true, Fuller noted, that the Restatement did, in Section 90 (quoted earlier), recognize reliance as an independent substantive ground of promissory obligation. But Williston himself held (at least for a time) that the relying party recovering under Section 90 should necessarily receive damages measured by lost expectancy.[17] Here, the restaters in pursuit of doctrinal unity were seeking to assimilate Section 90 theory to that of ordinary recovery for lost expectancy. Yet parties who merely acted to their detriment in reliance on promises falling under the principle of Section 90 not uncommonly sustained expenditures and losses well below what lost expectancy recovery would yield. Perhaps Williston thought that we simply could not live with a legal system that failed to provide a simple and neat division between contract recovery, in which damages "must" be in terms of lost expectancy, and tort recovery, in which damages "must" be for some worsening of one's position owing to the actions of another. Of course, there was still more at stake: justice. Fuller expressed the fear that a court applying Williston's view of Section 90 might grant a plaintiff lost expectancy when much less by way of reliance damages would make him whole, or might balk at granting lost expectancy merely for acts in reliance and therefore choose to grant nothing even in the face of serious losses.[18]

In 1982 a contract theorist, Robert Hudec, wrote: "No scholarly work during the period between the first and second Restatement of Contracts had more impact on the law of contracts than Fuller and Perdue's 1936 article 'The Reliance Interest in Contract Damages.'"[19] It should not be surprising to find this influence in the new Restatement itself. A number of its sections (mainly 344, 349, 15, 86, 87, 89, 90, 139, 158, 272) authorize less-than-expectancy remedies—usually some form of reliance damages—either as relief where lost expectancy would not be available or as an alternative to full expectancy recovery.

The contract–no contract dichotomy

In 1938 Fuller said, in a letter to Karl Llewellyn: "I consider the contribution made in my article on the reliance interest to lie, not in calling attention to the reliance interest itself, but in an analysis which breaks down the Contract-No-Contract dichotomy and substitutes an ascending scale of enforceability."[20] The importance of this contribution to contract theory cannot be overemphasized. Treatise writers, commentators, judges, lawyers, and others had previously tended to pose issues of liability in this field in an all-or-nothing fashion: either there is a contract, and hence liability—usually measured in terms of lost expectancy—or there is no contract, and hence no liability.

Fuller's analysis enabled us to see the crudity of this dichotomous approach. Some cases pose strong claims for the most complete relief—a half-completed exchange, for example, in which there was mutual assent, free bargaining, full compliance with formalities, essential reliance benefitting the other party, and easily measurable and serious expectancy loss. Here, at the very top of the ascending scale of enforceability, the most appropriate remedy is of course a recovery measured by lost expectancy. But very near the lowest end of the scale we may still have some form of liability and recovery. We might have no exchange, no mutual assent, no bargaining, and no formalities, yet still grant relief in the form of reimbursement for certain out-of-pocket expenses reasonably incurred in reliance on some kind of undertaking by the other party. Here we might not even want to say that we have a contract, though we have reasonable reliance on an undertaking that was not fulfilled. Whether the recovery is called contractual is really quite secondary.

Fuller continued his crusade against the contract–no contract dichotomy by opening his casebook with the subject of remedies rather than, as traditional, with the question, "Did the parties make a contract?" The very posing of this question in this way had led some of Fuller's predecessors to think about the matter in dichotomous terms. Students learning the subject from Fuller's book eventually saw that the question is misleading. A court might not impose full-fledged contract liability in the form of lost expectancy damages. Indeed, it might only impose liability for expenditures or losses incidentally incurred in reliance. Yet the full remedial range ought to be studied in the "contracts" course. Moreover, the remedies available to a court may well influence its answer to the question whether any form of liability "in contract" should be imposed. Thus section 2-204(3) of the highly influential Uniform Commercial Code adopted in virtually all states before Fuller's death was truly Fullerian in spirit: "Even though one or more terms are left open a contract for sale does not fail for indefiniteness if the parties have intended to make a contract and there is a reasonably certain basis for giving an appropriate remedy." Fuller's approach, then, also had the further merit of alerting the student to the general interplay between remedy and right in contract law.

Fuller's rejection of the contract–no contract dichotomy was characteristic. As we have already seen in this book, he bore an animus toward black-and-white thinking generally. His resolution of the matter did not always take the same form, however. In place of the contract–no contract dichotomy, he substituted an ascending scale or continuum; in place of the "is-ought" dichotomy, he substituted the notion that "being and value," in determining the existence of a legal rule, are but "two aspects of an integral reality"; in place of a sharp line between law and non-law, he demonstrated various respects or ways in which the line fades away.

Intentions, expectations, and tacit assumptions in contract analysis

Our law of contract has long been in need of the kind of sophistication deriving from what philosophers and a few legal theorists call the philosophy of mind. In many branches of contract, psychological terms appear in the language of legal rules and in judicial opinions: "mutual assent" in contract formation, "what the parties intended" in the interpretation of written agreements, "expectations" or "assumptions" in the law of frustration and impossibility, "undue influence" in the law of capacity to contract, and so on.

Judges, lawyers, and others are sometimes misled by psychological language of this kind into thinking that proof of (or "judicial notice" with respect to) actual mental states is necessarily required, or into thinking that these states must be of a given form, for example, states of consciousness. In his contracts casebook and in his contracts teaching,

Fuller offered words of caution.[21] Quoting from the Austrian scholar Wurzel, he stressed that laymen, as everyone knows quite well, enter their transactions without any thought for the psychological implications of the language used in the applicable rules. To cite Wurzel's European example (included in Fuller's casebook), the usual layman has not the slightest inkling of the legal differences between a fiancée's loan and the advancement of a dowry. Similarly, the usual layman has no care at all for the distinction between covenants and conditions precedent as set forth in contract doctrines. Realism, then, dictates that the psychological language in some rules not be taken literally. Fairness comes in, too. For example, "mutual assent" is even today sometimes said to be a requirement of contract formation, but it is a familiar demand of fairness in this branch of the law that courts will, in a proper case, find a contract even though one party did not in fact intend to enter a contract.

Further, even in those cases in which the law should be construed to require proof of psychological fact, it does not follow that this must be a positive state of consciousness. For example, in that branch of contract law in which a non-performing party claims an excuse because his performance has become "impossible," judges often will not grant the excuse unless they find that what both parties "contemplated" was destroyed without fault of either. Do they mean the parties must have consciously contemplated as much? Fuller stressed that the answer is "no." Their tacit assumptions will be enough. In a textual note in his casebook, Fuller explored the tacit dimension in contract law with much insight. The late Robert Braucher, Fuller's co-editor of a subsequent edition of the casebook, served for several years as Reporter for the second Restatement of Contracts. It is hardly a coincidence that this new version frequently substitutes non-psychological language for the wording of the old Restatement, or that it introduces Fuller's concept of tacit assumption in various places when this is what the law really intends.[22] (This is not to say that the new Restatement forgoes all psychological terminology.)

Some afterthoughts

Important as Fuller's work on contract jurisprudence is, it remains rather curious in several respects. Although in much of his legal theory, he emphasized the role of moral reasoning in law, and although in contract opinions moral reasons of "rightness" abound, Fuller did not in his contract writing emphasize such considerations to the degree he might have. In the bulk of his work on the grounds of promissory obligation, he stressed reliance, admittedly a rightness idea. But the result was that he did not develop an even more fundamental ground of promissory obligation—*pacta sunt servanda* (bargains are to be kept), also a rightness idea. Indeed, some of Fuller's work on remedies is, at least in orientation if not in spirit, Holmesian and thus even somewhat hostile to the norm of *pacta sunt servanda*. (Holmes had sought to analyze rights and duties away, and thereby dissolve them in remedies.)[23]

Of course, Fuller did write (briefly) of the values of private choice and autonomous self-ordering, and did identify these values as one source of contract duty. But this was not where his emphasis lay. He stressed reliance theory. It may be, as Atiyah has suggested,[24] that Fuller did not appreciate the extent to which reliance theory introduces community values apart from and even inconsistent with (in particular cases) the values associated with autonomous choice and "contract as promise."[25] Not all reliance is, even loosely speaking, contract reliance. Moreover, even contract reliance introduces social values into the decision on the reasonableness of the reliance. These values may have little directly to do with the private choices of the parties. Courts often protect reliance in the name of fairness, not in the name of implementing a private arrangement that the parties have assented to.

One particularly laments that Fuller decided to spend so little of his time writing about contract law. He founded what is today often called reliance theory. His work on the problems falling under the rubric "consideration and form" was seminal. He was almost alone in his discovery of a vast problem area that might, adapting a current idiom, be called "the mental element in contract." He differentiated contract and custom and explored their interrelations in illuminating ways. It is unfortunate that he published only one article on each of the first two topics, almost nothing on the third, and only part of an article on the fourth—the more so, since his other writings include numerous insights into contract that call for fuller development.

11

Lawyers, legal education, and legal theory

Fuller wrote far more on legal education than any other American theorist except Karl Llewellyn. During his lifetime, he published twelve articles on the subject and two books of teaching materials.[1] Several additional pieces appeared posthumously.[2] He also authored a 175-page (typewritten) report by the Harvard Law School Curriculum Committee, dated March 1, 1947. It is most unfortunate that this report has not been published, for it includes much of interest to curriculum planners today, nearly forty years after.

Fuller's writings on legal education are of special interest for several reasons. He had great respect for the work of American lawyers. Fuller, who was fond of quoting Mill's remark that Americans are especially good at self-government, private and public, believed that our lawyers have a central role in this governance ("the fundamental ordering of society"). Indeed, he even held that the legal profession is, or can be, one of the great creative and directive forces of modern society.[3] It is lawyers, after all, who must plan and draft the complex institutional arrangements required of the welfare state and the regulatory state. Of equal, if not greater, importance, lawyers in private practice have been the architects of countless sophisticated and highly varied arrangements that facilitate private ordering.

Fuller knew a great deal more about the education of American lawyers in his day than the usual professor of law, having taught as a regular faculty member at four rather different law schools. Moreover, in the early 1950's he did an elaborate field study of all the law schools in Pennsylvania. His published report on this study includes many perceptive observations, several on the decline of the "Socratic method" of teaching.[4]

By the time Fuller started writing about lawyers and legal education, he had himself both taught and practiced for several years. His period of practice, as we have seen, came after he had been a legal educator for over a dozen years. He was thus in a position to reflect in an unusually pointed fashion on educational issues, and he emerged from this period of practice with a number of ideas about the work of lawyers and the kind of education they should have.

As chairman of Harvard's curriculum committee just after the Second World War (a committee that functions only once every decade), Fuller was called on to assume an important leadership role in matters of curriculum design. As noted earlier, Dean Sacks remarked that the reforms Fuller's committee introduced "were among the most successful in recent times."[5] Partly in recognition of this, the American Bar Association called on him (and John Randall) to draft the influential report for a Joint Conference on Professional Responsibility, published in 1958.

Finally, Fuller's status as a scholar and theorist of jurisprudence equipped him specially here. He was conscious that the "influence of philosophy is particularly apt to be marked in legal education,"[6] and he knew that the legal theories that happen to prevail at any given time could profoundly influence educational practice.

Fuller was most concerned to develop a general conception of the lawyer's true responsibilities and tasks, and to secure reforms in legal education adequate to that conception. His account of the lawyer's main responsibilities and tasks is today almost entirely familiar. It was not always so. Most of his criticisms of legal education are similarly familiar today. Again, it was not always so, and at many law schools, much of what he criticized has yet to be remedied.

The main responsibilities and tasks of the lawyer

Some legal educators today hold that the training of practitioners is at most a secondary function of law schools. Rather, the primary function is to create and disseminate new knowledge and understanding about law. But to Fuller these two purposes "are so closely related that it is unrewarding to discuss which is primary and which is secondary."[7] Obviously, creative scholarship is a key part of legal education, but scholarship tends to take on an air of unreality if too divorced from the lawyer's practical concerns.

As Fuller also recognized, to train practitioners well, legal educators must have a general conception of the lawyer's responsibilities and tasks. But in setting himself to work out such a conception, he seems to have been motivated in part by a desire to combat common public misconceptions of lawyers. His efforts here provide inspiration for practitioners as well.

As members of a public profession, lawyers have certain special responsibilities to society at large, Fuller maintained. They should be ready to concern themselves with law reform, especially in the realm of "lawyer's law." By virtue of their training, they can and should seek to rescue public debate from any "unreality in which it is assumed that ends can be selected without any consideration of means."[8] Lawyers have a special duty to uphold equality in the administration of law.

They should strive to see that legal services are made available to the poor, and that the champions of unpopular causes are duly represented. Lawyers have special responsibility for the health of the rule of law, including "guardianship of due process." Thus, they should help foster wholesome public attitudes of concern and regard for the fairness of legal procedures. Fuller did not take it for granted that the public would understand, accept, and if need be, fight for fundamental rules embodying norms of orderly and decent government. Accordingly, he argued that "understanding must be vitalized by an appreciation of the reasons why these rules are necessary." Thus, a theory like positivism that grounded the authority of law in a monopoly of state force was not merely wrong, but dangerous:

> The prevention of indecencies in the use of governmental power must depend ultimately on the pressures of public opinion, particularly the opinion of the legal profession. This opinion can be effective only if it is informed by a sound philosophy. It cannot be so informed when it accepts a view that treats governmental power as a brute datum and refuses to examine the rational and moral grounds of its justification and acceptance.[9]

Alongside these general responsibilities, lawyers also have certain basic tasks for which they must be trained. Although Fuller never drew up a single comprehensive list of these tasks, one can be assembled from his writings.

Above all, it is the task of a lawyer to apply reason to the human relationships he confronts in his work. Thus he should see law practice as a purposive enterprise involving the rational analysis of problems and the rational adjustment of practical means to defensible ends. Fuller, always impatient with skepticism about the force of reason, believed "the basic problems of law and government can be solved by reason."[10] He loathed the "black-letter mind"—the mind that is neglectful of the purposes of legal precepts, content with mechanically applying the law, incapable of analyzing problems into their constituent elements, and unable to bring independent judgment to bear.

In private or public practice, the lawyer must participate regularly in the planning and creation of legal arrangements and forms of law. He does not merely apply what someone else has created. As a participant in this creative endeavor, he assumes some responsibility for the overall result. The lawyer, Fuller once said, is the "chief architect of our legal, political, and economic order, or at least so much of it as can be said to be the result of deliberate planning."[11] In forcing clients to think through their goals; in suggesting possible goals for clients to pursue; in ruling out goals as impractical, unworthy, or illegal; in arguing for the primacy of some goals over others, and in favor of some means over others; and in performing the art of draftsmanship, the lawyer contributes to the content of contracts, labor agreements, administrative or judicial decrees, regulations, statutes, institutional structures and procedures, and more.

Much of the lawyer's work consists of establishing frameworks for future human interaction. This work typically requires that the lawyer be able to foresee likely consequences of different alternatives, to identify and weigh both legal and nonlegal factors, to draw on and synthesize rules from different fields of law, and to draft. He is an "expert in structure," not someone "who stands to one side blinking legal 'Stop and Go' signs to laymen for whose destination he has no responsibility."[12]

The well-trained lawyer is also an "expert in process," capable of participating effectively in most of the public and private law-making and administering processes through which human relations are ordered. As a participant in adjudication he may contribute to the creation of new law as well as to the application of the old. In litigation over the meaning of a statute, lawyers not infrequently supply arguments that the judges adopt in their interpretations. In common law cases, lawyers, through their proofs and arguments, contribute even more directly to the evolution of law.

Still another task of lawyers is that of reconciling conflicting interests as negotiators or advocates.[13] An apparent deadlock of opposing interests can often be resolved by well-trained lawyers. They dig beneath slogans and facile catch phrases to narrow the range of real disagreement. They ferret out relevant facts, too, and thus enable the principals to understand their own interests more fully. They draw on their imagination to identify possible trade-offs. They employ their detachment to try to get each party to see the point of view of the other. They resort to their own powers of argument to bring the parties together. They absorb the shocks of adversarial confrontation, and seek themselves to use tact and diplomacy. That only a tiny fraction of serious disputes between private parties ever goes to final adjudication or arbitration in Anglo-American society is in some measure due to the efforts of lawyers.

One of the most important tasks of the lawyer is fact-finding. The good lawyer understands the primacy of fact in relation to law. The facts determine what rule of law is applicable, if any. Many rules of law are framed in terms of "equities" between the parties that are highly circumstance-bound and thus require close sensitivity to factual nuances in determining the equities. Facts necessarily figure in substantive reasons for decision that appeal directly to moral, economic, and social concerns. One cannot construct such reasons if relevant facts are not available, yet reasons of this kind influence the application of rules. Such reasoning is ordinarily determinative when there is no applicable law or when the law is being changed. The good lawyer is sensitive to the possible presence of issues of fact, and can effectively gather, sift, organize, and present facts. He is aware of the main sources of distortion in finding and stating facts (including the necessity of condensation). He also knows how to cope when doubts about the facts cannot be cleared up.

Frequently the lawyer's task is that of serving as a counselor. Indeed far more of a lawyer's time goes into counseling (and negotiation) than into litigation. It is a common fallacy that the purposes of the law are carried out mainly through some coercive mechanism of the state. Actually, as Fuller phrased it, "the most effective realization of *the law's aims* often takes place in the attorney's office" (emphasis supplied).[14]

When serving as counselor, negotiator, mediator, planner, draftsman, advocate, or legislator, the lawyer in private or governmental practice must often synthesize legal facts and considerations with other non-legal facts and considerations. These non-legal matters are diverse and may include the various goals of the client, business considerations, applicable government policy (not yet reduced to law), and relevant teachings of the social sciences. The well-trained lawyer will be capable of coping with all of these, either alone or with outside help.

Deficiencies in legal education: Curricular

Fuller was a vigorous curricular reformer, something for which he is not well known today. He sought to broaden legal education in a number of ways, and was especially emphatic that the various interrelations between the legal and the non-legal must become a more central part of the curriculum: "Only by bringing interrelations of this sort within the scope of legal education can we break the circle by which the problems arising from these interrelations are regarded as irrelevant in law school because they are so treated in practice, and are so treated in practice at least partly because lawyers and judges have learned in law school to regard them as irrelevant."[15]

In the late 1940's, Fuller emerged as a sharp critic of the law school curriculum and as a proponent of various remedies. As chairman of the Harvard curriculum committee, he criticized the failure of educators to stress the purposive and reason-laden character of law. He thought there was still too much formalism in the teaching of legal method and too much emphasis on law as a form of state fiat rather than as an effort to apply reason to human relations. Too many faculty members believed that reason could have something to say about means, but nothing about ends. "The core of our interest as teachers," he maintained, "should be the right solution of controversies and the right ordering of the rules by which men are expected to live together."[16] Lawyers ought to be educated to "articulate, define, and defend standards of rightness."

Legal educators were preoccupied with the breakdowns in socio-legal ordering—with disputes, litigation, and the like. Rather than focusing on the lawyer's role as an expert in structure, as a planner and architect of frameworks for human interaction, legal educators too often saw him as a troubleshooter, after the fact. The appellate case-method of teaching, with its focus on breakdowns, reinforced this myopia. The method inherently neglected the planning choices that lawyers and businessmen make, choices that typically involve no ultimate recourse to litigation:

> By the time the case is argued in the appellate court, most of the planning and strategy have been completed, and most of the lawyer's bridges have been burned behind him. His primary task now is to defend, or challenge, as persuasively as he can a position, or a series of positions, already taken. Because law school instruction is largely based on appellate decisions, its focus is inevitably upon this last phase of a controversy, and the student receives little direct training in the choices that have to be made before this final phase is reached.[17]

Appellate case materials actually exclude many of the non-legal factors that must enter into such choices. Yet, in Fuller's words, "it is virtually impossible to discuss a problem of legal planning without taking into account extra-legal considerations." In addition, appellate cases seldom involve enough "means-goal" thinking of the kind that planning calls for. The students must have materials that require them "to conceive a sound objective and then to direct effort consistently toward the attainment of that objective."

Further, the appellate case method can actually mislead the lawyer who must plan. "For example, the ability to draw the sharp distinctions essential for reconciling a series of decisions may be dangerous in legal planning unless tempered by a realization that, to preserve a margin of safety, the sharpness of distinctions taken must be accommodated to the level of the least perceptive of the tribunals that might have jurisdiction over the case."[18]

Again, partly because of the appellate case method, legal education was highly court-centered. This meant that students were exposed largely to adjudicative processes in civil cases. If they were to receive, as Fuller argued they should, a general education in process, they would have to study other processes too. In his writings on legal education, Fuller stressed the importance of introducing students much more fully to lawmaking processes, including the processes of private ordering through contract negotiation and drafting, as well as those of public ordering through legislative and administrative action. In his contracts casebook, he introduced problems on drafting, and in a later edition he inserted a lengthy text note putting contractual ordering in its place among the whole range of legal processes. He also stressed the importance of teaching students how our processes shape our values and patterns of thought and behavior: "The forms and restraints which make our living together possible are created by us, but they in turn help to make us what we are and to define what we should do toward one another."[19]

Another educational deficiency to which Fuller frequently called attention was the overemphasis on "legal" skills to the neglect of fact-finding skills. The appellate case method was partly to blame here as well. Cases include frozen facts rather than raw facts; they are poor tools for developing insights into the proof of facts or the ability to sift, organize, and transmit "intact a set of facts from one human head to another."[20] The case method also centers on "forensic facts," on the facts of a written record or the skeletally reported facts of an appellate opinion. But lawyers must often cope with "facts in the raw" and must even assume a managerial responsibility for ongoing facts—live facts. The task of the lawyer acting as planner, negotiator, or draftsman is to "gear his decision to a range of factual probability, and [he] must devise a plan that will anticipate, and absorb without disruption, future changes in the facts."[21]

Despite reams of programmatic writing in the 1930's about the need to integrate social science into legal education, this continued to be an unresolved problem after the war (and remains so today). Fuller agreed that something further should be done. He was certain that if, for example, there was no time for economics in the law school curriculum, there would be no time for it in a busy law practice either. But he faulted law professors for failing to help experts from other disciplines identify problems for study that would give direction and legal relevance to their expertise. And he stressed that the fusion of social science and law must not and need not be "forced." Problems should be selected for classroom use in which the fusion flows naturally.

The famous 1944 Association of American Law Schools Curriculum Committee Report (written by Llewellyn) presaged some of Fuller's criticisms.[22] Yet he articulately and authoritatively pointed up serious deficiencies, including several that this famous report neglected. And his emphasis on process was distinctive. He was relatively persuasive, and through the Harvard example, widely influential elsewhere. In my view, Fuller's 1947 Curriculum Committee Report is a much richer document than the AALS Report.

As we have seen, Fuller traced many of the deficiencies of legal education to the narrowness of the appellate case method. Yet he did not think this method should be abandoned in toto. Nor did he think that its narrowness at mid-century was an inherent problem. To a considerable degree, in fact, this narrowness was an accident of fate:

> It is a curious and in some ways unfortunate fact that the most invigorating reform in the history of American legal education should have occurred at a

> time when the limits of legal study were more closely drawn than they had ever been before, and that legal instruction through cases and problems should have begun when the law's function was most narrowly conceived. There are certainly few today who would agree with Langdell's famous dictum that the law is a science of which all the available materials are contained in printed books. Yet methods, particularly successful methods, are often more powerful than beliefs. The overwhelming success of the case method tended to crystallize and to carry into a later period a conception of the proper scope of legal study that was dominant when this method was receiving its first mold. If the case method could have originated in 1810 and have received its initial impress from the thinking of that period, it is a safe assumption that legal education would today have a much broader scope than it actually has.[23]

In the 1980's, law school curriculum reform is a hotly debated topic. It is of interest that Fuller anticipated a major theme of current criticism, namely, that legal education is both insufficiently theoretical and insufficiently practical.[24] He did not, however, seem willing to go as far in either direction as many curricular reformers would today. On the practical side, there is little evidence that he would have endorsed the widely favored clinical movement. For one thing, he did not believe that effective instruction in practical skills having genuine "transfer value" requires that students immerse themselves in the level of detail that characterizes so much modern clinical education. In his 1947 Curriculum Committee Report, Fuller suggested a number of concrete ways in which teaching materials (and methods) could be modified to teach fact skills, planning, and the like without introducing live clients or simulations. Overall, he believed that the rise of the professional law school was a major advance over "apprenticeship" education with all its inefficiencies and other drawbacks. Yet, at the same time, as we have seen, he urged that educators put far more emphasis than they had been wont to do on skills outside the realm of litigation.

One may lament that with all of his theoretical background and training, Fuller did not go farther in suggesting ways of making legal education more theoretical. Much more can be done on this front than merely introducing a list of "perspective courses" from which every graduate must elect one prior to graduation, which seems to have been Fuller's main proposal.

Deficiencies in legal education: Teaching method

By 1952 Fuller was disturbed to find instructors abandoning the Socratic method of teaching over the country as a whole. That method, he believed, had a vital role to play in the education of every law student, and he was much troubled both by its abandonment and by the failure of those who did use it to capitalize on its distinctive potential. When he visited classrooms in the early 1950's during his study of the Pennsylvania law schools, he found that many instructors were simply lecturing, serving as "quizmaster," or acting as moderators of round-table discussions. Even those who were not guilty of these faults often assigned far too many cases or proceeded in class at a pace far too rapid for Fuller's taste.[25]

The emphasis should not be on conveying the authoritative solutions of others, Fuller wrote—either of the lecturer or of judges, legislators, and other professional restaters of the law. Rather it should be on the cases as problems to be explored and thought through by the class. The case method combined with the Socratic method is at its best, he argued, when it generates free, lively, spontaneous, impersonal, and selfless absorption in concrete problems.[26] It can be used to sharpen the ability to frame issues. The student will not fully understand a problem until he has tried to define and solve it. The method can also be used to refine the sense of relevancy, to alert the mind to factual nuance, to prime the imaginative faculties (through hypothetical variations, and more), to develop the ability to draw distinctions, to nurture creative thinking, to provoke thought about the standards of rightness that should govern, and to foster maturity of judgment. Education in law does not consist essentially of items of information to be transferred from the teacher's head to the student's. It is a participatory process aimed at developing the student's ability to think. But for all this to work, the classroom pace must not be too rapid or the cases assigned too numerous. The instructor must take care not to place "too high a value on the answer that is quick and adequate as distinguished from one that may be slower in coming but more profound and searching when it arrives."[27] (Ultimately, Fuller came to stress another and different virtue of Socratic teaching: that of providing the student "with a vicarious experience in the task of conceiving, explaining, justifying and applying the rules by which society is enabled to function successfully."[28])

The casebooks, Fuller noted, include many hard problems, and instructors and students alike are sometimes tempted to deal with the easier ones. Facing up to the hard ones is not just a matter of marshaling and focusing brain power. It requires moral courage, all the more so when the problems are novel and call for creative thinking. The student must come to live with the inevitable pains of reasoning, and be able to cope with the frustrations of being wrong. The student who is learning these things is not merely improving his intellect; he is taking *moral* instruction and experiencing *moral* growth.[29] Fuller stressed, too, that the student must learn to control his instinct for self-assertion. "As long as we have that instinct, we are going to have people consciously or unconsciously twisting facts and distorting issues in order to obtain an arena where their special talents will show to best advantage."[30] Fuller even claimed that perhaps the "highest aim" of education is to "put this instinct under proper control and to make men aware of its dangers."[31] Of course, much of the opportunity to learn these things is lost if the student is not called on to participate in class.

One matter of method much discussed in American law schools today has to do with whether the number of students in a course should go beyond a given number. A related issue is whether law schools should provide "small sections," at least in the first year, where students can feel more comfortable than in the usual large classes. Law schools are currently spending thousands of dollars on such small sections. It is a safe guess that Fuller might have opposed this development:

> There are very real educational advantages in a large class, say, of at least eighty students. The work of such a class involves a public appearance for the instructor and student alike, and puts both on their mettle. The student who recites is addressing himself to a problem and an impersonal audience. In a smaller class he is likely to have his thinking about the problem hampered by a concern for what his classmate Jones will think about what he thinks. Finally, it should be recalled that law is not practiced in the atmosphere of a fire-side chat. Three years of easy-going, pipe-and-slippers discussion are scarcely the best preparation for modern law practice, however enjoyable they may be at the time.[32]

One may ask whether Fuller's preference for classes of eighty or so students is really consistent with his emphasis on broadening the scope of legal education to include training in such non-litigation skills as negotiation, fact gathering, planning, and drafting. Certainly there is no logical inconsistency. An instructor can teach about these matters to some degree even in classes of a thousand. But if students are to "learn by actually doing," a method now much more in vogue than in Fuller's day, eighty-student classes are plainly too large. Fuller almost certainly would not have agreed that learning by doing is the necessity that so many of today's educators seem to think it is. He pointed out, for example, that many American law students graduate well trained to write appellate opinions, yet none ever actually *do* such work while in law school. Similarly, one can learn a great deal about the art of contract drafting without ever actually drafting a contract.

More fundamentally, was Fuller inconsistent in stressing the deficiencies of the appellate case method while at the same time extolling the virtues of the Socratic method? I am sure he would have seen no inconsistency. As the philosophers taught us long ago, Socratic teaching does not require that the underlying materials consist of cases of any kind, let alone court cases. Moreover, there is a good deal of evidence that Fuller did not believe the Socratic method ought to be used in all courses.

A prominent theme in contemporary curricular discussions is that legal education has been and is dehumanizing. Law schools, it is said, teach law students to be insensitive, crassly competitive, and authoritarian and domineering in their lawyer roles. Fuller did not address these issues in a systematic way in his published writings. What he had to say about aspects of them in his Curriculum Committee Report suggests that he either did not consider these to be very serious problems, or, perhaps, saw them as beyond the powers of educators to remedy. Yet today many teachers would at least agree that Socratic teaching can and should be done in a fashion that exemplifies humanistic values.

The course in jurisprudence

The curriculum should not be without a course in jurisprudence, Fuller insisted. Its main purpose would be to foster an awareness of the law's deep problems rather than to inculcate a point of view. It should subject to critical scrutiny "the basic premises that underlie reasoning about legal problems."[33] It must stop short of ultimate issues of epistemology and metaphysics, yet go much farther in these directions than other courses in the curriculum. Fuller often opened his own course with the problem of justice and its relationship to law. He recommended that instructors explore whether justice is undefinable and therefore cannot be said to exist, or is merely a feeling and purely subjective. He believed objective reasons for decisions can be given in the name of justice.

Fuller, hardly a moral skeptic, believed that even the simplest problem of contract or tort raised basic issues of moral justification. A course in jurisprudence in a law school is an ideal setting in which to explore the general relations between law and morals. In the jurisprudence course I took from Fuller in 1957, he devoted many hours to this complex topic, displaying both a remarkable critical acuity (he was then engaged in debates with H. L. A. Hart and Ernest Nagel) and a deep faith in the power and force of reasoned justification in human affairs.

Today, when Fuller's view is more fashionable, his emphasis on justification may seem self-evident. In truth, many other leading thinkers of this century have voiced quite different views of the lawyer's role, views that imply deep and controversial theories about the nature of law. Those in the formalistic tradition of Langdell and Williston at Harvard saw the lawyer as essentially someone who is an expert in the necessary implications of certain basic legal concepts: for example, whether an offer to enter into a contract is "by its nature" revocable. Those in the court-centered and scientific tradition of Holmes and certain legal realists conceived of the lawyer essentially as a predictor of the incidence of state force—"which way judges will jump." Modern theorists interested in the "total power process" such as Harold Lasswell and Myres McDougal viewed the lawyer essentially as filling a power role in which he either makes public policy or influences the makers of public policy. Each of these conceptions implies a general theory about the nature of law: law as a system to be elaborated according to the internal logic of its concepts; law as predictable fiat of an identifiable sovereign; and law as a more or less open-ended process for making public policy in which competing power blocs participate. Fuller rejected each of these, and was especially eager to counter the view that law is mere state fiat and the lawyer merely one who predicts and seeks to influence which way a judge will jump. He conceded that lawyers must try to influence the holders of power, but stressed that they must usually bring some form of law and some form of reasoned persuasion to bear. Sometimes the justifications they construct will consist of reasoned appeals to existing law. Frequently they will consist of reasoned arguments about how state power ought to be exercised, or about what the law ought to be. In engaging in these efforts, the lawyer does not go beyond his calling. He answers to it.[34]

At Harvard during much of Fuller's tenure, second-year law students were required to elect as one "perspective" course jurisprudence, comparative law, legal process, or legal history. According to Fuller, the object of these courses was "taking the student outside the legal system and giving him some view of it as a whole, so that he might be led to reflect on the more general aims of law and government and the conditions that conduce to realization of those aims." The proposed requirement encountered some opposition from teachers of particular branches of substantive law, but the faculty adopted it. When Professor George K. Gardner then urged that his course in admiralty law be listed as a perspective course, Fuller and others succeeded in preventing this breach in the dike. As Fuller wrote Gardner: "In a sense, every course is one in perspective, but a workable line can be drawn between courses that are primarily aimed at perspective and those that aim primarily at an understanding of the legal problems of a particular field."[35]

Research

Fuller held strongly to controversial views on faculty research, and was several times embroiled in debates and imbroglios at Harvard on this complicated matter. For the sake of the record and because of their great contemporary relevance, his general views on three issues will be recorded here.

Although Fuller wanted to broaden legal education to include the social sciences, particularly economics, and although he favored the addition of social scientists to law faculties, it is safe to say that he was rather skeptical of much of the empirical social science research he thought he saw about him.[36] As we know, he flatly rejected the view of some legal realists that law's ends and means could be determined solely by resort to empirical research, holding that much in social life is relatively impervious to scientific method. He seems to have thought that much social science research was poorly done, and that it was peculiarly susceptible to political manipulation. Many social scientists, he felt, were hostile to the humanistic tradition. Merely because science yields no reliable findings, it hardly follows that we must fall back on arbitrary preference.

In the 1950's, Harvard Law School began to support several research projects that required either fieldwork or extensive recourse to materials not in the law library. In most instances, funds were obtained from outside sources; for example, the World Bank made a grant for a study of the regulation of electric power in Latin America. Fuller viewed these projects with growing concern. His views led Associate Dean David F. Cavers to prepare an extended report on these projects and similar studies previously sponsored by Harvard and other law schools, on the problems they posed, and on possible precautionary measures. In reply, Fuller submitted a draft memorandum to the faculty, vigorously objecting to "project" or "commissioned" research and stressing its incompatibility with freedom of scholarship. This exchange led to a lengthy discussion at two meetings of the law faculty in 1957–58. Not all of Fuller's colleagues shared his concern, and though the faculty recognized that there was a real and important problem in all this, no formal action was taken to establish a school policy on such research. In 1958, when Dean Cavers became president of the Walter A. Meyer Research Institute of Law and Harvard's representative on its board, he resigned as associate dean. The encouragement of school-sponsored research was not among the charges given his successor.

As for scholarly publication, Fuller held that this required a certain maturity of thought, and he frequently advised new appointees to the Harvard faculty not to publish anything for at least five years or so. Since he was a much esteemed faculty member, his advice tended to be influential. In this he probably saved some colleagues the embarrassment of publishing half-baked ideas, but he may also have deterred some from writing as much as they might have in the course of their careers.

In my view, Fuller rather plainly failed to give empirical social science its due and was probably excessively alarmed about the dangers of group or "project" research. One rather serious problem he seems to have neglected altogether: how far are law, legal education, and legal research relatively autonomous rather than essentially reducible to some other discipline, such as economics, or history, or philosophy? This broad issue (variously defined) is beginning to enter into current discussions,[37] and we can only regret that Fuller did not address it, for he was superbly qualified to do so.

Perennial obstacles

Most obstacles to the best kind of legal education stem from three sources: faculty, students, and the practicing bar! Though Fuller often assumed the role of critic and reformer, he was usually tolerant and gentle with faculty opposition. To those who said that sound legal education is merely a matter of recruiting good faculty and giving them their heads, he replied that the existing curricular scheme itself represents an effort at coherence and coordination, and that those who would preserve it should be called on to defend it. To those who proclaimed that the case method adequately serves all relevant goals, if not directly, then via its by-products, he pointed out serious omissions and distortions. To those who urged that legal educators should "stick to the law" because you "cannot teach the student to be a lawyer in three years," let alone teach him to be an "economist, psychologist, accountant, sociologist, and personnel manager," he retorted that the law school does not really try to teach students to be full-fledged lawyers on graduation, but merely takes them part of the way and lays the foundation for self-education. The young lawyer ignorant of all interrelations between law and economics, for example, lacks an important element in the foundation.

But, said Fuller, the student is also an obstacle to his own education. Take the student who views creative classroom experiences as beside the point, for example—who sees a hypothetical or even an actual case of first impression as merely an exceptional or aberrant affair. Such a student will often be "thinking about the bar examination," which will, of course, require vast knowledge of black-letter law. And classroom focus on creative tasks will certainly not touch the zealous chap who arrives in class, canned briefs in hand, eager to get down to truly important business.[38] Even a student who goes along with such teaching methods may go no more than halfway. Creative legal thinking, for example, may be seen as only a kind of game of wits, a puzzle with a single solution that can and will be fully "charted, mastered, and finally tucked away." Here, the student really wants contradictory things. "He wants the thrill of exploring a wilderness and he wants to know where he stands every foot of the way."[39]

Finally, Fuller was especially concerned that the legal community itself, through the bar examination, was deeply distorting the aims and methods of legal education. In 1961 he wrote that many law schools must unfortunately "struggle bravely under a shadow that reaches even into the first year."[40] Bar examinations often stressed mere "knowledge of the law" and a kind of mechanical ability to apply it, rather than the enlarged capabilities and conceptions for which Fuller fought, and which are not easily tested in a written examination.

12

Conclusion

Lon L. Fuller's position as a major figure in modern legal theory is secure. He is unquestionably the leading secular natural lawyer of the twentieth century in the English-speaking world. His work on legal processes and on the principles of legality qualify him as the greatest proceduralist in the history of legal theory. He was also one of the foremost theorists of means-end relations in legal ordering. He was a major critic not only of British and European legal positivism, but also of the crudities of the instrumentalist legal theory dominant in the United States in his day.

In the hope of shedding some further light on the man and his work, I want to conclude with some brief remarks, inevitably partly speculative, on Fuller's views, and on how he came to them. Fuller's contributions to secular natural law theory may be divided into two categories: those relating to the roles of reason, morals, and purpose in law, and those relating to the nature, varieties, uses, and limits of legal processes. For the moment, I will address only the first. From his earliest period as a teacher, beginning at the University of Oregon in the 1920's, Fuller seems to have read the classics of natural law thought. Partly as a result of this, he did not join in the robust skepticism about the force of reason or the objectivity of morals so fashionable among his "science-minded" contemporaries. He also read Jhering's work very early, and this helps explain his closely related emphasis on purpose in the law.

Even so, it is interesting to note that in the 1930's, Fuller at times seemed somewhat hesitant to embrace reason, morality, and purpose as wholeheartedly as he would later. This is most evident in two pieces he published in these years, his article "The Legal Mind," which appeared in the *Atlantic Monthly* in 1933, and his famous review of "Williston on Contracts," which was written in 1938.[1] By the time he published *The Law in Quest of Itself* (1940) and "Reason and Fiat in Case Law" (1946), however, this hesitancy had disappeared.[2] What explains this significant shift?

Doubtless several factors were at work. By 1940 Fuller had thought through a great many legal problems and had presumably concluded quite on his own that reason (as opposed to fiat) has much more room in the law than many of his contemporaries conceded. He was also reacting in part to the extremism of certain American theorists of the period, among them his former teacher Joseph W. Bingham. Bingham, a professor first at Cornell and then at Stanford, had so low a view of the force of reason that he believed we could, without loss, dispense with the judicial practice of setting forth justifications in the writing of opinions.[3] Probably a more important factor was Fuller's outspokenly critical attitude toward Hitler and the rise of fascism in Europe. This critical stance was itself reasoned. And if reason should be so powerful in the service of criticism, then why should it not be similarly powerful when affirmatively deployed to support one rather than another general position in legal theory? (It is ironic that the star of reason seems here to have risen more in this way rather than through the efforts of academics to refute academic skeptics.)

One likewise finds the first hint of Fuller's great work as a proceduralist in *The Law in Quest of Itself*, published on the eve of the Second World War,[4] though his sustained interest in legal processes almost certainly grew largely out of his practice at the Boston law firm of Ropes and Gray during the war. Here, too, his penchant for criticism surely spurred him. There were, it seems, many in the law who refused to believe there was even a subject for study here: all social reality was utterly plastic and manipulable; hence there could be no such thing as a legal process that conformed to "natural laws of social order." Or, as Myres McDougal put it in 1941: "Nature doesn't present us with anything. . . . We have to slice nature as we do cheese, in ways that suit our convenience and our specific practical purposes."[5] Fuller strongly disagreed with such views. He was also critical of what he perceived to be the overuse and misuse of legal forms, particularly adjudication, in his own country. (A few personal details may be of interest here. Each of the hobbies Fuller pursued through much of his life—cooking, carpentry, and music—involved activities with a distinctive and indisputable "inner order." Why should not much in the law be relevantly similar? It is interesting to note that cooking and music also show up in the pseudo Platonic dialogue *Minos*, a highly Fullerian work.[6])

By 1949, the forty-seven-year-old Fuller had outlined the beginnings of a general theory of legal processes; and by 1954, when he published his seminal article "American Legal Philosophy at Mid-Century," it is evident that he had formed a general conception of the subject.[7] Thereafter, though he did not write the book he had projected, he did produce a steady stream of contributions, ending with the "The Forms and Limits of Adjudication," published after his death.[8]

Fuller did not publish much on the other facet of his proceduralism—his principles of legality—until 1958, when he had his famous exchange with H. L. A. Hart. He was in fact sixty-two years old when he published *The Morality of Law*, his principal contribution in this department.[9] Fuller himself stressed that this pursuit had been triggered by an interest in seventeenth-century natural law writing.[10] But again a major impetus seems to have come from his reflections on events in the legal world and a compelling desire to demonstrate the errant ways of legal positivism. He observed the flagrant abuses of the principles of legality in Nazi Germany, and less flagrant but still worrisome abuses in the United States, as in the failure to make rules at all (e.g., the "public interest" standard in the Federal Communications Act). In seeking to show that the procedural "oughts" of the rule of law constitute an "internal morality of law," Fuller thought of himself as refuting the positivistic separation of law and morals. He demonstrated the moral significance of the "rule of law" and carried us far beyond the standard view that it is concerned mainly with securing legal certainty for practical purposes.

Fuller was one of the greatest "means-end" theorists in the history of legal theory, and very likely the leading one of this century. Of course, his proceduralism was part of this. But the category "legal means" includes more than basic legal processes and the principles of the rule of law. It includes techniques, sanctions, remedies, and various implementive devices. Moreover, means-end theorizing requires inquiry into the possible combinations of means and ends, their interdependence, and their interactions (among other things). Fuller was deeply interested in this kind of theorizing. His best essay on the subject, "Means and Ends," appeared only after his death,[11] but his published writings include many isolated insights and some sustained discussion of these matters. The earliest writings date from the late 1940's and early 1950's. Here, as much as anything, Fuller seems to have been motivated by dissatisfaction with the scholarly literature. He thought that much writing in philosophy and in political and moral theory on such basic social ends as freedom, equality, and justice was of little value. This work was far too abstract—far too divorced from social context and from all legal means and modes of implementation. In his own means-end theorizing he seems to have drawn heavily on the work of John Dewey and of sociologists like Georg Simmel. Fuller helped to roll back the frontiers so that today's theorists can see more clearly many large problems that await systematic effort.[12]

Fuller, unlike many able members of American law school faculties, was a true intellectual and a formidable scholar. Doubtless his wide reading did much to shape his legal theories, and in ways that cannot easily be traced. The evidence is that he drew general inspiration and many ideas from Aristotle, Aquinas, Hegel, Nietzsche, Bentham, Jhering, Weber, Geny, Simmel, Ehrlich, and Dewey, among others. My own view is that he was particularly influenced by Hegel and the German idealists, but that must await another essay.[13] As one might expect of an undergraduate in economics, he also drew importantly on the classical and neoclassical economists.

Given the magnitude of Fuller's contributions to legal theory, it may seem odd that he wrote very little about the nature of legal theory or about sound method in pursuing the subject. He did consider legal theory an eminently practical subject, aimed at giving "a profitable and satisfying direction to the application of human energies *in* the law" (emphasis supplied).[14] This viewpoint seems to explain a great deal, including his own skepticism with respect to "ultimate distinctions"—ones drawn by theorists without reference to any general or specific practical purposes. It may explain some of his impatience with abstract theorizing about "basic social ends" as well.

Fuller also held that prescriptive legal theory, even when unsound, and descriptive legal theory, even when inaccurate, nevertheless have the capacity, over time, to shape the prevailing law and legal method in a society. Unsound prescriptive legal theory can easily beget bad legal method. According to Fuller, the excessively literal and wooden approach of English judges to the interpretation of statutes during much of the present century could be attributed to their effort "to conform their practice to the pattern legal theory has been ascribing to it for more than a century."[15] Equally important, inaccurate descriptive theory can transform the reality it purports to describe. For example, legal theorists purporting only to describe might say that, in reality, when a judge must decide a case for which there is no governing rule, he is not bound by any standards at all and is therefore free to decide as he pleases regardless of the compulsions of substantive reason bearing on the case. Now, if this purported description (a favorite of certain realists in the 1930's) is adopted sufficiently widely, then the nature of the legal system in question will, in this vital respect, become as described. Thus, in matters of social reality, merely believing that things are so, or that they ought to be so, can *make* them so. As Fuller put it: "In human affairs [even] what men mistakenly accept as real tends, by the very act of their acceptance, to become real."[16] Ronald M. Dworkin has explicitly subscribed to a version of this view.[17] Though these matters are complex and call for further analysis, Fuller and Dworkin are surely right. And to the extent that they are, the implications are profound. For one thing, influential legal theorists had better be especially careful . . .

In light of Fuller's belief that legal theorists can shape the very legal reality they address, we can easily see how he could hold that "the problems of justice and right law furnish the driving force of jurisprudence."[18] For him, the improvement of a legal system might be brought about not only through specific procedural and substantive reforms, but also through the subtle and not so subtle influences of general legal theory.

We now come to a most explosive issue for academics concerned with law. Fuller clearly believed that legal theory as a subject has a kind of autonomy of its own. At least he did not think of it as a mere branch of philosophy, or as a mere applied social science, or simply as an exercise in the history of ideas. Though this matter, too, requires extended consideration, I now believe he was right. At the very least, those who do the subject should, in particular, be constantly mindful of the unusually large empirical element inevitably involved, and be wary of importing irrelevant or inapposite models and methods from other disciplines.

In this century, we have not been short of influential thinkers who have viewed legal theory merely or primarily as a branch of philosophy or as a type of social science. These thinkers have sometimes gone awry in ways attributable to their willingness to import foreign models and methods, and to their failure to respect what Fuller might have called the "autonomy" of the subject. I will cite two prominent examples. In my view, H. L. A. Hart, who views himself as a philosopher, proposed in 1958 a quite untenable non-purposive theory of interpretation of *legal* texts (so far as their "core" meaning is concerned), a theory based on a philosophy of language then influential at Oxford.[19] In my view, Karl N. Llewellyn, a social science–minded legal theorist subscribed, in his early period, to a quite untenable theory of the very nature of law as "official behavior patterns."[20] Many other examples might be cited. Much can be at stake here: truth in legal theory, soundness of law and legal method, basic orientations and attitudes of bench and bar, law school curriculum design, appointments to law faculties, the assignment of courses to be taught, the availability of grants for research, space in learned journals, and more. It is sobering to reflect that if certain professional philosophers and social scientists of today had been influential in the curricular and instructional affairs of the law faculties on which Fuller served, they might well have concluded that he did not have the "credentials" (a mere lawyer?) and have given him little opportunity, let alone encouragement, to pursue legal theory. I hope to have shown here how much the poorer this would have made us all.

References

Chapter 1: Introduction

1. For assistance on this biographical sketch, I am especially indebted to Professors Kenneth I. Winston and David F. Cavers.
2. Brock Fuller, professor of mathematics at the California Institute of Technology, and Cornelia Fuller Hopfield.
3. Note, "Adverse Possession," 7 OR. L. REV. 329 (1928).
4. These were later published, essentially unchanged, as a book: LEGAL FICTIONS (1967).
5. See, generally, R. SUMMERS, INSTRUMENTALISM AND AMERICAN LEGAL THEORY (1982).
6. It is no simple matter to identify and differentiate all the various issues involved. For one effort, see *id.* 136–58.
7. L. FULLER, THE PRINCIPLES OF SOCIAL ORDER 297 (K. Winston ed. 1981).
8. Fuller, "American Legal Realism," 82 U. PA. L. REV. 429 (1934).
9. Fuller (with Perdue), "The Reliance Interest in Contract Damages," 46 YALE L. J. 52, 373 (1936–37).
10. Harvard Law School Library, Lon L. Fuller Papers, R. Pound to Fuller, Jan. 10, 1938.
11. Williston also wrote an autobiography: LIFE AND LAW (1941).
12. Fuller, "Williston on Contracts," 18 N. CAR. L. REV. 1 (1939); Harvard Law School Library, Lon L. Fuller Papers, Fuller to C. Lowndes, Apr. 15, 1940.
13. Harvard Law School Library, Lon L. Fuller Papers, Fuller to H. C. Horack, Jan. 15, 1940.
14. *Id.*, Fuller to C. Lowndes, Apr. 15, 1940.
15. *Id.*, Fuller to K. Llewellyn, May 13, 1940.
16. *Id.*, Fuller to D. Cavers, Feb. 28, 1940.
17. L. FULLER, THE LAW IN QUEST OF ITSELF 10 (1940).
18. Harvard Law School Library, Lon L. Fuller Papers, Fuller to K. Llewellyn, Jan. 14, 1942.
19. *Id.*, May 13, 1940.
20. Fuller, "Consideration and Form," 41 COLUM. L. REV. 799 (1941).
21. Fuller, "Reason and Fiat in Case Law," 59 HARV. L. REV. 376 (1946).
22. This is confirmed by correspondence and other materials in the Lon L. Fuller Papers in the Harvard Law School Library.
23. "The Case of the Speluncean Explorers," 62 HARV. L. REV. 616 (1949).
24. L. FULLER, THE MORALITY OF LAW Chap. 5 (rev. ed. 1969).

25. Harvard Law School Library, Lon L. Fuller Papers, W. V. Quine to Fuller, Nov. 26, 1953.

26. Fuller, "Human Purpose and Natural Law," 53 J. PHIL. 697 (1956); Nagel, "On the Fusion of Fact and Value: A Reply to Professor Fuller," 3 NAT. L. FOR. 77 (1958); Fuller, "A Rejoinder to Professor Nagel," *id.* 83; Nagel, "Fact, Value, and Human Purpose," 4 NAT. L. FOR. 26 (1959).

27. Harvard Law School Library, Lon L. Fuller Papers, Fuller to C. Galvin, Nov. 29, 1957.

28. H. L. A. Hart, "Positivism and the Separation of Law and Morals," 71 HARV. L. REV. 593 (1958); Fuller, "Positivism and Fidelity to Law—A Reply to Professor Hart," *id.* 630.

29. Harvard Law School Library, Lon L. Fuller Papers, L. Strauss to Fuller, Mar. 19, 1958.

30. *Id.*, Fuller to H. L. A. Hart, Dec. 17, 1957.

31. Fuller, "The Forms and Limits of Adjudication," 92 HARV. L. REV. 353 (1978).

32. "Freedom—A Suggested Analysis," 68 HARV. L. REV. 1305 (1955).

33. In addition to *ibid.*, see Fuller, "Freedom as a Problem of Allocating Choice," 112 PRO. AM. PHIL. SOC. 101 (1968).

34. See, generally, Chap. 6, below, and references.

35. Harvard Law School Library, Lon L. Fuller Papers, Fuller to E. Rostow, Sept. 29, 1960.

36. *Id.*, R. Nixon to Fuller, Nov. 8, 1961.

37. Harvard Law School Library, "An Unsolicited Report on Poland, with an Appendix on West Germany and Berlin and a Second Appendix Containing Some Reflections on Our Policy Toward Communism," Cambridge, Mass., 1963, 43 pp.

38. HARVARD LAW SCHOOL ALUMNI BULLETIN 11 (Fall 1978).

39. FULLER, THE ANATOMY OF LAW 63–119 (Penguin ed. 1968).

40. Harvard Law School Library, Lon L. Fuller Papers, Fuller to R. Nixon, June 1, 1965.

41. Fuller, "Some Presuppositions Shaping the Concept of 'Socialization,'" in LAW, JUSTICE AND THE INDIVIDUAL (J. Tapp and F. Levine eds. 1977).

42. H. M. HART and A. SACKS, THE LEGAL PROCESS (temp. ed. 1958).

43. See, generally, R. DWORKIN, TAKING RIGHTS SERIOUSLY (1978).

44. See, e.g., Selznick, Book Review, 83 HARV. L. REV. 1474 (1970).

45. See, generally, Hudec, "Restating the Reliance Interest," 67 CORNELL L. REV. 704 (1982).

46. P. ATIYAH, THE RISE AND FALL OF FREEDOM OF CONTRACT (1979).

47. Sacks, "Lon Luvois Fuller," 92 HARV. L. REV. 349, 350 (1978).

48. See, generally, Chap. 11 on legal education.

49. Griswold, "Lon Luvois Fuller," 92 HARV. L. REV. 351, 352 (1978).

Chapter 2: The purposive and value-laden nature of law

1. See generally, Fuller, "American Legal Philosophy at Mid-Century," 6 J. LEG. ED. 457 (1954); Fuller, "Human Purpose and Natural Law," 53 J. PHIL. 697 (1956); Fuller, "A Rejoinder to Professor Nagel," 3 NAT. L. FOR. 83 (1958).

2. Indeed, later Fuller preferred not to use the language of value for quite special reasons that do not militate against its use here. See, for example, L. FULLER, THE PRINCIPLES OF SOCIAL ORDER 57, 285 (K. Winston ed. 1981).

3. See, for example, L. FULLER, THE MORALITY OF LAW 145–46 (rev. ed. 1969); L. FULLER, THE LAW IN QUEST OF ITSELF 55–59 (1940); L. FULLER, ANATOMY OF THE LAW 160–67 (Penguin ed. 1968); and Fuller, "Afterword: Science and the Judicial Process," 79 HARV. L. REV. 1604 (1966).

4. FULLER, ANATOMY 161.

5. H. KELSEN, GENERAL THEORY OF LAW AND STATE 30–37 (1945).

6. H. L. A. HART, THE CONCEPT OF LAW Chap. 6 (1961).

7. See, for example, Llewellyn, "A Realistic Jurisprudence—The Next Step," 30 COLUM. L. REV. 431 (1930).

8. H. L. A. Hart, "Positivism and the Separation of Law and Morals," 71 HARV. L. REV. 593 (1958).

9. See, generally, R. SUMMERS, INSTRUMENTALISM AND AMERICAN LEGAL THEORY (1982).

10. FULLER, ANATOMY 64.

11. Fuller, "American Legal Philosophy" 470.

12. Fuller, "Positivism and Fidelity to Law—A Reply to Professor Hart," 71 HARV. L. REV. 630, 661–69 (1958).

13. FULLER, QUEST 114–15.

14. On these various views, see Chap. 4, below.

15. FULLER, SOCIAL ORDER 236.

16. Harvard Law School Library, Lon L. Fuller Papers, Fuller to I. Jenkins, Mar. 5, 1959.

17. *Id.*, Fuller to F. Olafson, Mar. 22, 1960.

18. Fuller, "American Legal Philosophy" 462–67.

19. *Id.* 463.

20. *Id.* 464.

21. FULLER, QUEST 11.

22. Fuller sometimes used almost identical terminology, as when he wrote Karl Llewellyn that in social reality, "What is and what ought to be come to us blended." Harvard Law School Library, Lon L. Fuller Papers, Fuller to Llewellyn, Aug. 9, 1940.

23. *Id.*, Fuller to K. Llewellyn, Jan. 14, 1942.

24. J. AUSTIN, THE PROVINCE OF JURISPRUDENCE DETERMINED 184–85 (Lib. Ideas ed. 1954).

25. J. C. GRAY, THE NATURE AND SOURCES OF THE LAW 94 (1921).

26. H. KELSEN, GENERAL THEORY 29–50, 123–62.

27. H. L. A. Hart, "Positivism and the Separation of Law and Morals," 71 HARV. L. REV. 593 (1958).

28. Nagel, "On the Fusion of Fact and Value: A Reply to Professor Fuller," 3 NAT. L. FOR. 77 (1958).

29. FULLER, MORALITY 106.

30. *Id.* 93, 97, 202, 206. There has been some controversy about whether Fuller attributed the eight procedural purposes to the system as a whole rather than merely to legislation.

31. *Id.* 212.

32. Fuller, "American Legal Philosophy" 468.

33. FULLER, MORALITY 91; FULLER, ANATOMY 59.
34. Fuller, "What the Law Schools Can Contribute to the Making of Lawyers," 1 J. LEG. ED. 204 (1948); Fuller, "A Reply to Professors Cohen and Dworkin," 10 VILL. L. REV. 655 (1965).
35. FULLER, MORALITY 39, 122–23.
36. Fuller, "The Forms and Limits of Adjudication," 92 HARV. L. REV. 353 (1978); FULLER, SOCIAL ORDER 87–124 (1981).
37. Fuller, "Some Unexplored Social Dimensions of the Law" in THE PATH OF THE LAW FROM 1967, p. 60 (A. Sutherland ed. 1968).
38. Fuller and Randall, "Professional Responsibility: Report of the Joint Conference," 44 A.B.A. J. 1159, 1161 (1958).

Chapter 3: The morality and immorality of law

1. 59 HARV. L. REV. 376 (1946).
2. *Ibid.*
3. L. FULLER, THE LAW IN QUEST OF ITSELF 11–16 (1940).
4. Fuller, Book Review, 87 U. PA. L. REV. 626 (1939).
5. FULLER, QUEST. See also Harvard Law School Library, Lon L. Fuller Papers, Fuller to K. Llewellyn, Jan. 14, 1942.
6. Harvard Law School Library, Lon L. Fuller Papers, Fuller to W. Friedmann, Oct. 9, 1959.
7. L. FULLER, THE MORALITY OF LAW 157–59 (rev. ed. 1969).
8. See, for example, Fuller, "Positivism and Fidelity to Law—A Reply to Professor Hart," 71 HARV. L. REV. 630, 648 (1958).
9. See, generally, H. L. A. HART, LAW, LIBERTY AND MORALITY 17–24 (1963).
10. See, for example, H. L. A. Hart, "Positivism and the Separation of Law and Morals," 71 HARV. L. REV. 607 (1958).
11. Fuller, "Fidelity to Law" 637.
12. *Id.* 631.
13. FULLER, QUEST 88–95.
14. L. FULLER, THE MORALITY OF LAW Chap. 2 (rev. ed. 1969).
15. Cohen, "Law, Morality and Purpose," 10 VILL. L. REV. 640 (1965).
16. Harvard Law School Library, Lon L. Fuller Papers, Fuller to W. Friedmann, Jan. 18, 1966.
17. FULLER, MORALITY 40–41, 202–3.
18. *Id.* 200–224.
19. *Id.* 39. For a similar yet ultimately different line of thought, see D. Lyons, "The Internal Morality of Law," 71 PRO. ARIST. SOC. 105–19 (1970–71).
20. FULLER, MORALITY Chaps. 2, 5.
21. *Id.* 216–17.
22. *Id.* 159.
23. *Id.* 155–57.
24. *Id.* 159.
25. Fuller, "Jurisprudence," in 13 ENCY. BRITANNICA 149 (14 ed. 1965).
26. See Chaps. 6–8, below.
27. See L. FULLER, THE PROBLEMS OF JURISPRUDENCE Chap. 6 (temp. ed. 1949).

28. Fuller, "Some Unexplored Social Dimensions of Law," in Tı THE LAW FROM 1967, pp. 60–61 (A. Sutherland ed. 1968).
29. *Ibid.* See also FULLER, THE PROBLEMS OF JURISPRUDENCE 70

Chapter 4: The differentiation of law from non-law

1. For Fuller's main writings on the topics of this chapter, see especially THE LAW IN QUEST OF ITSELF (1940); THE MORALITY OF LAW (rev. ed. 1969); ANATOMY OF THE LAW (Penguin ed. 1968); and "Positivism and Fidelity to Law—A Reply to Professor Hart," 71 HARV. L. REV. 630 (1958).
2. See, generally, R. DWORKIN, TAKING RIGHTS SERIOUSLY, especially Chaps. 2, 3 (1978).
3. H. L. A. HART, THE CONCEPT OF LAW 92 (1961).
4. FULLER, QUEST, *passim*; Fuller, "Fidelity to Law" 641.
5. See, generally, R. SUMMERS, INSTRUMENTALISM AND AMERICAN LEGAL THEORY, Chaps. 4, 7 (1982).
6. FULLER, MORALITY 140.
7. Fuller, "Fidelity to Law" 641.
8. FULLER, ANATOMY 61–157.
9. *Id.* 67–68.
10. *Id.* 120–57. For what Fuller meant by intrinsic or rational appeal, see his examples in the section on objective reason in Chap. 5, below.
11. DWORKIN, SERIOUSLY Chap. 2.
12. FULLER, QUEST 28.
13. H. KELSEN, GENERAL THEORY OF LAW AND STATE 13 (1945).
14. FULLER, QUEST 84 n.35.
15. Fuller, "Fidelity to Law" 637.
16. FULLER, QUEST 90–91.
17. See, generally, FULLER, QUEST; Fuller, "Fidelity to Law" 648 and *passim*; FULLER, MORALITY Chap. 2; and FULLER, ANATOMY 161–62.
18. See, for example, FULLER, ANATOMY 87–99; and Fuller, "Fidelity to Law" 641.
19. FULLER, QUEST 55–56.
20. *Id.* 9.
21. *Id.* Chap. 2.
22. Holmes, "The Path of the Law," 10 HARV. L. REV. 457 (1897).
23. See, specifically, his Harvard Law Review article "Positivism and Fidelity to Law."
24. For references, see H. L. A. Hart, "Positivism and the Separation of Law and Morals," 71 HARV. L. REV. 593, 595–98 (1958).
25. FULLER, QUEST 90–91.
26. Fuller, "Fidelity to Law" 632.
27. FULLER, QUEST 103.
28. Fuller, "Fidelity to Law" 637.
29. FULLER, QUEST 4–6.
30. Fuller, "Fidelity to Law" 636.
31. This is largely a reconstruction of Fuller, "Fidelity to Law" 636–38.

Chapter 5: Natural law and the role of reason

1. Fuller, "Reason and Fiat in Case Law," 59 HARV. L. REV. 379 (1946). This was first given as a lecture, in 1942.
2. For Fuller's own brief yet suggestive effort at such a model, see ANATOMY OF THE LAW 162–63 (Penguin ed. 1968).
3. See, generally, Fuller, "American Legal Philosophy at Mid-Century," 6 J. LEG. ED. 457 (1954).
4. See, generally, A. P. D'ENTREVES, NATURAL LAW (2d ed. 1970); and J. FINNIS, NATURAL LAW AND NATURAL RIGHTS (1980).
5. FULLER, ANATOMY 163.
6. Cited in L. FULLER, THE PRINCIPLES OF SOCIAL ORDER 86 (K. Winston ed. 1981).
7. L. FULLER, THE LAW IN QUEST OF ITSELF 110 (1940).
8. FULLER, ANATOMY 163–64.
9. See, generally, Fuller, "American Legal Philosophy" 472–73; and L. FULLER, THE MORALITY OF LAW 184–86 (rev. ed. 1969).
10. FULLER, MORALITY 186.
11. See, generally, D'ENTREVES, NATURAL LAW; and FINNIS, NATURAL LAW.
12. H. L. A. HART, THE CONCEPT OF LAW 189–95 (1961).
13. Hume, however, denied that there could be such matters of fact. See D. HUME, TREATISE OF HUMAN NATURE III, i, 1 (1739). This "scientific" approach is not the only alternative, of course, but a discussion of this old and thorny issue is beyond the compass of this book.
14. H. KELSEN, GENERAL THEORY OF LAW AND STATE 13 (1945).
15. Fuller, "American Legal Philosophy" 472.
16. Fuller, "Reason and Fiat" 378.
17. Fuller, "The Place and Uses of Jurisprudence in the Law School Curriculum," 1 J. LEG. ED. 499 (1949).
18. L. FULLER, THE PROBLEMS OF JURISPRUDENCE 694–95 (temp. ed. 1949).
19. *Southern Pacific Co.* v. *Jensen*, 244 U.S. 205, 222 (1917) (Holmes, *J.*, dissenting).
20. Fuller, "Reason and Fiat" 378–79.
21. Fuller, "Human Purpose and Natural Law," 3 NAT. L. FOR. 72 (1958).
22. Fuller, Book Review, 9 U. CHI. L. REV. 760 (1949).
23. See, generally, W. HUDSON, THE IS-OUGHT CONTROVERSY (1959).
24. See, generally, FINNIS, NATURAL LAW 33–34.
25. FULLER, QUEST 5–6.
26. *Id.* 6.
27. See, generally, FINNIS, NATURAL LAW 26.
28. A. P. D'ENTREVES, AQUINAS: SELECTED POLITICAL WRITINGS 65 (1959).
29. Harvard Law School Library, Lon L. Fuller Papers, Fuller to S. I. Shuman, Feb. 28, 1958.
30. D'ENTREVES, AQUINAS 90.
31. J. BENTHAM, "A Fragment on Government," in 1 WORKS, 221, 230 (J. Bowring ed. 1843).
32. FULLER, MORALITY 123.
33. Fuller, "American Legal Philosophy" 476.

Chapter 6: Law's means and ends: A "processual" theory

1. Fuller, "Freedom—A Suggested Analysis," 68 HARV. L. REV. 1305 (1955). See also Fuller, "Freedom as a Problem of Allocating Choice," 112 PROC. AM. PHIL. SOC. 101 (1968).
2. Fuller, "American Legal Philosophy at Mid-Century," 6 J. LEG. ED. 457, 477 (1954).
3. *Id.* 477–78.
4. J. S. MILL, UTILITARIANISM, LIBERTY, AND REPRESENTATIVE GOVERNMENT 2 (A. Lindsay intro. 1910); I. BERLIN, TWO CONCEPTS OF LIBERTY 3 (1958).
5. L. FULLER, THE PRINCIPLES OF SOCIAL ORDER 47–64 (K. Winston ed. 1981).
6. M. Oakeshott, "Political Education," in PHILOSOPHY, POLITICS, AND SOCIETY 10 (P. Laslett ed. 1956).
7. FULLER, SOCIAL ORDER 55.
8. See, for example, L. FULLER, THE MORALITY OF LAW 39 (rev. ed. 1969).
9. See generally, on customary law, FULLER, SOCIAL ORDER 212–24; FULLER, MORALITY 221–24, 233–36; L. FULLER, ANATOMY OF THE LAW 64–75, 101–20 (Penguin ed. 1968); and L. FULLER, THE LAW IN QUEST OF ITSELF 110–14 (1940).
10. FULLER, ANATOMY 105.
11. FULLER, SOCIAL ORDER 219–20.
12. *Id.* 221.
13. *Id.* 227.
14. FULLER, ANATOMY 65.
15. FULLER, SOCIAL ORDER 241.
16. FULLER, ANATOMY 106.
17. FULLER, SOCIAL ORDER 241.
18. FULLER, ANATOMY 119.
19. H. L. A. HART, PUNISHMENT AND RESPONSIBILITY 10 (1968).
20. See, generally, on contract law, FULLER, SOCIAL ORDER 169–87, 211–46; FULLER, ANATOMY 101–20; and L. FULLER, THE PROBLEMS OF JURISPRUDENCE 708–14, 729–34 (temp. ed. 1949).
21. FULLER, ANATOMY 108.
22. FULLER, JURISPRUDENCE 732.
23. 14 AMER. J. JURISPRUDENCE 1 (1968). See, generally, on enacted law, FULLER, SOCIAL ORDER 230–37; FULLER, ANATOMY 64, 126–58; FULLER, MORALITY Chaps. 2, 5; Fuller, "Law as an Instrument of Social Control and Law as a Facilitation of Human Interaction," 1975 B.Y.U. L. REV. 89; and Fuller, "Jurisprudence," in 13 ENCY. BRITANNICA 149 (14 ed. 1965).
24. FULLER, MORALITY 169–70.
25. *Id.* Chaps. 2, 5.
26. *Id.* 216–24.
27. FULLER, SOCIAL ORDER 230–37.
28. FULLER, PROBLEMS OF JURISPRUDENCE 703–5.
29. Fuller, "Jurisprudence" 152.
30. FULLER, ANATOMY 127.
31. FULLER, SOCIAL ORDER 243.
32. FULLER, PROBLEMS OF JURISPRUDENCE Chap. 6.
33. See also K. Winston, in FULLER, SOCIAL ORDER 37–40.
34. See, generally, on managerial direction, FULLER, SOCIAL ORDER 116–21, 178–80, 189–210, 234; and FULLER, MORALITY Chap. 5.

35. FULLER, MORALITY 207–12.
36. M. POLANYI, THE LOGIC OF LIBERTY: REFLECTIONS AND REJOINDERS 171 (1951).
37. FULLER, MORALITY 171–75.
38. *Id.* Chap. 5.

Chapter 7: Law's means and ends: Civil adjudication

1. See, generally, on adjudication, L. FULLER, THE PRINCIPLES OF SOCIAL ORDER 86–124 (K. Winston ed. 1981); Fuller, "The Forms and Limits of Adjudication," 92 HARV. L. REV. 353 (1978); L. FULLER, ANATOMY OF THE LAW 121–58 (Penguin ed. 1968); Fuller, "Collective Bargaining and the Arbitrator," 1963 WIS. L. REV. 3; Fuller, "Adjudication and the Rule of Law," 54 PROC. AM. SOC. INT. L. 1 (1960); L. FULLER, THE PROBLEMS OF JURISPRUDENCE 705–8, 712–14, 727–29 (temp. ed. 1949); Fuller, "The Adversary System," in TALKS ON AMERICAN LAW (H. Berman ed. 1961); Fuller and Randall, "Professional Responsibility: Report of the Joint Conference," 44 A.B.A. J. 1159, 1216 (1958).
2. FULLER, SOCIAL ORDER 96; Fuller, "Adjudication" 369.
3. See, especially, Fuller, "Adversary System."
4. FULLER, SOCIAL ORDER 92–98.
5. Eisenberg, "Participation, Responsiveness, and the Consultative Process: An Essay for Lon Fuller," 92 HARV. L. REV. 410 (1978).
6. FULLER, JURISPRUDENCE 706–7.
7. See, especially, FULLER, ANATOMY 120–57.
8. Fuller, "Adjudication" 357–62, 375–77.
9. See, for example, Fuller, "Adversary System"; Fuller and Randall, "Professional Responsibility"; FULLER, ANATOMY 152–57; and L. FULLER, THE MORALITY OF LAW 171–75, 177–81 (rev. ed. 1969).
10. FULLER, MORALITY 172.
11. FULLER, SOCIAL ORDER 112.
12. *Id.* 115.
13. These examples are scattered through Fuller's writings. See, for example, FULLER, ANATOMY 155.

Chapter 8: Law's means and ends: General assessment

1. L. FULLER, THE PROBLEMS OF JURISPRUDENCE 715 (temp. ed. 1949).
2. L. FULLER, THE PRINCIPLES OF SOCIAL ORDER 47–64 (K. Winston ed. 1981).
3. Fuller, "The Forms and Limits of Adjudication," 92 HARV. L. REV. 353 (1978); Fuller, "Some Unexplored Social Dimensions of the Law," in THE PATH OF THE LAW FROM 1967 (A. Sutherland ed. 1968).
4. L. FULLER, THE MORALITY OF LAW 180 (rev. ed. 1969).
5. During a discussion on May 16, 1982, in Berlin.
6. FULLER, JURISPRUDENCE 739.
7. FULLER, SOCIAL ORDER 298–300.
8. Fuller, "American Legal Philosophy at Mid-Century," 6 J. LEG. ED. 457, 476 (1954).

9. Fuller, "Unexplored Social Dimensions" 68.
10. FULLER, MORALITY 153–67.
11. FULLER, JURISPRUDENCE 740.
12. Fuller, "Memorandum," in ON THE TEACHING OF LAW IN THE LIBERAL ARTS CURRICULUM 37–43 (H. Berman ed. 1956).
13. R. SUMMERS, INSTRUMENTALISM AND AMERICAN LEGAL THEORY Chaps. 8, 9 (1982).
14. See, generally, Summers, "The Technique Element in Law," 59 CALIF. L. REV. 733 (1971).
15. See further R. SUMMERS, COLLECTIVE BARGAINING AND PUBLIC BENEFIT CONFERRAL: A JURISPRUDENTIAL CRITIQUE (1976).
16. For the beginnings of such a theory, see Summers, "Evaluating and Improving Legal Processes—A Plea for Process Values," 60 CORNELL L. REV. 1 (1974).
17. Chayes, "The Role of the Judge in Public Law Litigation," 89 HARV. L. REV. 1281 (1976); Chayes, "The Supreme Court 1981 Term Foreword: Public Law Litigation and the Burger Court," 96 HARV. L. REV. 4 (1982).
18. Fiss, "The Supreme Court 1978 Term Foreword: The Forms of Justice," 93 HARV. L. REV. 1 (1979).

Chapter 9: Legal method

1. See, generally, on common law method, L. FULLER, ANATOMY OF THE LAW 120–57 (Penguin ed. 1968); Fuller, "Reason and Fiat in Case Law," 59 HARV. L. REV. 376 (1946); and L. FULLER, THE LAW IN QUEST OF ITSELF *passim* (1940).
2. Fuller, "Oliver Wendell Holmes, Jr.," in AN AMERICAN PRIMER 591–92 (D. Boorstin ed. 1966).
3. C. C. LANGDELL, A SUMMARY OF THE LAW OF CONTRACTS Sec. 178 (2d ed. 1880).
4. Fuller, "Williston on Contracts," 18 N. CAR. L. REV. 4 n.5. (1939).
5. The complexities of formalism and what prompted it are beyond the compass of this book. For a detailed account, see R. SUMMERS, INSTRUMENTALISM AND AMERICAN LEGAL THEORY Chap. 6 (1982).
6. *Id.* General Introduction. See also Chaps. 3–6 of the same work.
7. Fuller, "Williston" 8–11.
8. *Id.* 3–4 n5.
9. Fuller, "The Reliance Interest in Contract Damages" (with Perdue), 46 YALE L. J. 52, 373 (1936–37).
10. Fuller, "Introduction," THE JURISPRUDENCE OF INTERESTS xx (M. Schoch ed. 1948).
11. Fuller, "Williston" 12.
12. FULLER, ANATOMY 130.
13. *Id.* 129.
14. FULLER, QUEST 9.
15. Fuller, "Reason and Fiat."
16. *Id.* 380.
17. "An Enquiry Concerning the Principles of Morals," in D. HUME, ENQUIRIES CONCERNING THE HUMAN UNDERSTANDING AND CONCERNING THE PRINCIPLES OF MORALS 195–96 (1902).
18. Fuller, "Williston" 12.
19. FULLER, ANATOMY 134.

20. For a start, see Summers, "Two Types of Substantive Reasons: The Core of a Theory of Common-Law Justification," 63 CORNELL L. REV. 707–88 (1978).

21. FULLER, ANATOMY 133–34.

22. FULLER, QUEST 132.

23. FULLER, ANATOMY 131.

24. FULLER, QUEST 133.

25. FULLER, ANATOMY 120–57.

26. FULLER, QUEST 136.

27. Fuller, "Reason and Fiat" 379.

28. Holmes, "The Path of the Law," 10 HARV. L. REV. 457 (1897).

29. FULLER, QUEST 137–38.

30. L. FULLER, LEGAL FICTIONS 51 n6 (1967).

31. See, generally, on statutory interpretation, FULLER, ANATOMY 14–18, 38–39, 56–59, 82–86, 95; L. FULLER, THE MORALITY OF LAW 81–91, 224–32 (rev. ed. 1969); Fuller, "Positivism and Fidelity to Law—A Reply to Professor Hart," 71 HARV. L. REV. 630, 661–69 (1958); and FULLER, QUEST 89.

32. FULLER, MORALITY 91.

33. H. L. A. Hart, "Positivism and the Separation of Law and Morals," 71 HARV. L. REV. 607 (1958). Hart did turn to purposes in borderline cases.

34. Fuller, "Fidelity to Law" 663.

35. *Id.* 664–65.

36. FULLER, ANATOMY 83.

37. Fuller, "Introduction," JURISPRUDENCE xxiii.

38. Harvard Law School Library, Lon L. Fuller Papers, Fuller to E. W. Patterson, Jan. 6, 1941.

39. FULLER, MORALITY 84.

40. Fuller, "Fidelity to Law" 667.

41. FULLER, ANATOMY 57–58.

42. *Id.* 85–86.

43. H. M. HART and A. SACKS, THE LEGAL PROCESS 1225 (1958).

44. FULLER, MORALITY 159.

45. Fuller, "Fidelity to Law" 669–72.

46. Fuller, "American Legal Philosophy at Mid-Century," 6 LEG. ED. 470 (1954).

47. FULLER, MORALITY 88.

Chapter 10: Contract jurisprudence

1. Fuller, "American Legal Realism," 82 U. PA. L. REV. 429, 443 (1934).

2. See, generally, on contract jurisprudence, L. FULLER, THE PRINCIPLES OF SOCIAL ORDER 169–87, 264–70 (K. Winston ed., 1981); Fuller, "The Reliance Interest in Contract Damages" (with Perdue), 46 YALE L. J. 52, 373 (1936–37); Fuller, "Williston on Contracts," 18 N. CAR. L. REV. 1 (1939); Fuller, "Consideration and Form," 41 COLUM. L. REV. 799 (1941); Fuller, "Special Nature of the Wage-Earner's Life Insurance Problem," 2 LAW AND CONT. PROBS. 10 (1935); and L. FULLER and M. EISENBERG, BASIC CONTRACT LAW (3d ed. 1972).

3. Fuller, "Consideration" 824.

4. *Id.* 812.

5. *Id.* 821.

6. *Id.* 811.

7. Fuller, "Reliance Interest" 57.

8. Fuller, "Consideration" 800–803.

9. J. AUSTIN, "Fragments on Contracts," in II LECTURES ON JURISPRUDENCE 940 (4th ed. 1873).

10. Fuller, "Consideration" 813.
11. *Id.* 819.
12. *Id.* 821.
13. Fuller, "Reliance Interest" 57.
14. *Id.* 53–56.
15. *Id.* 60–63.
16. *Id.* 91–92.
17. *Id.* 64, 401–6.
18. *Id.* 420.
19. Hudec, "Restating the Reliance Interest," 67 CORNELL L. REV. 704 (1982).
20. Harvard Law School Library, Lon L. Fuller Papers, Fuller to K. Llewellyn, Dec. 8, 1938.
21. FULLER and EISENBERG, BASIC CONTRACT LAW 276–77, 804–8.
22. See, for example, RESTATEMENT (SECOND) OF CONTRACTS, Chap. 11 (1981).
23. For discussion of Holmes's view, see R. SUMMERS, INSTRUMENTALISM AND AMERICAN LEGAL THEORY 130 (1982).
24. Atiyah, Book Review, DUKE L. J. 669 (1983).
25. Compare C. FRIED, CONTRACT AS PROMISE (1981).

Chapter 11: Lawyers, legal education, and legal theory

1. In the preparation of this chapter, I am indebted to Professor Roger Cramton of the Cornell Law School for valuable advice. Fuller's major writings on legal education include "Objectives of Legal Education," 2 ASSOC. BAR CITY OF NEW YORK: RECORDS 120 (1947); Preliminary Statement of the Committee on Legal Education of the Harvard Law School, Harvard Law Library, 1947 (hereafter called Curriculum Committee Report); "What the Law Schools Can Contribute to the Making of Lawyers," 1 J. LEG. ED. 189 (1948); "The Place and Uses of Jurisprudence in the Law School Curriculum," 1 J. LEG. ED. 495 (1948); "On Teaching Law," 3 STAN. L. REV. 35 (1950); "What Is the Bar Examination Intended to Test?," 20 BAR EXAMINER 111 (1951); "Legal Education and Admissions to the Bar in Pennsylvania," 25 TEMP. L. Q. 249 (1952); "Professional Responsibility: Report on the Joint Conference" (co-authored with Randall), 44 A.B.A. J. 1159 (1958); and "The Academic Lawyer's House of Intellect," 14 J. LEG. ED. 153 (1961).
2. L. FULLER, THE PRINCIPLES OF SOCIAL ORDER 272–81, 282–90, 293–303 (K. Winston ed. 1981).
3. Fuller and Randall, "Professional Responsibility" 1159.
4. Fuller, "Legal Education in Pennsylvania" 265–68.
5. Sacks, "Lon Luvois Fuller," 92 HARV. L. REV. 349, 350 (1978).
6. Fuller, "What Is a Lawyer?," unpublished manuscript, Harvard Law School Library, Lon L. Fuller Papers.
7. Fuller, Curriculum Committee Report 4.
8. Fuller, "Professional Responsibility" 1218.
9. Fuller, "American Legal Philosophy at Mid-Century," 6 J. LEG. ED. 465 (1954).
10. Fuller, Curriculum Committee Report 94.
11. Fuller, "On Teaching Law" 37.
12. Fuller, Curriculum Committee Report 59–60.
13. FULLER, SOCIAL ORDER 283–90.

14. Fuller and Randall, "Professional Responsibility" 1161.
15. Fuller, Curriculum Committee Report 122.
16. Fuller, "On Teaching Law" 45.
17. Fuller, Curriculum Committee Report 36.
18. *Id.* 40.
19. Fuller, "The Philosophy of Codes of Ethics," 74 ELEC. ENG. 917 (1955).
20. Fuller, "What the Law Schools Can Contribute" 193.
21. *Id.* 195.
22. Llewellyn and committee, "The Place of Skills in Legal Education," 45 COLUM. L. REV. 345 (1945).
23. Fuller, Curriculum Committee Report 95.
24. See, generally, Cramton, "The Current State of the Law Curriculum," 32 J. LEG. ED. 321 (1982).
25. Fuller, "Legal Education in Pennsylvania" 258–68.
26. Fuller, "On Teaching Law" 38–41.
27. Fuller, "Legal Education in Pennsylvania" 261.
28. L. FULLER and M. EISENBERG, BASIC CONTRACT LAW xiii (3d ed. 1972).
29. Fuller, "What Law Schools Can Contribute" 191.
30. Fuller, "On Teaching Law" 40.
31. *Ibid.*
32. Fuller, Curriculum Committee Report 164.
33. Fuller, "The Place and Uses of Jurisprudence" 495.
34. FULLER, SOCIAL ORDER 272–81.
35. Harvard Law School Library, Lon L. Fuller Papers, Fuller to G. K. Gardner, Sept. 30, 1953.
36. See, generally, Fuller, "American Legal Realism," 82 U. PENN. L. REV. 429 (1934); and Fuller, "An Afterword: Science and the Judicial Process," 79 HARV. L. REV. 1604 (1966). See also Summers, "Professor Fuller's Jurisprudence and America's Dominant Philosophy of Law," 92 HARV. L. REV. 433 (1978).
37. See, generally, Summers, "The Future of Economics in Legal Education: Limits and Constraints," 33 J. LEG. ED. 337 (1983).
38. Fuller, "On Teaching Law" 41.
39. *Id.* 42.
40. Fuller, "The Academic Lawyer's House of Intellect" 157.

Chapter 12: Conclusion

1. Fuller, "The Legal Mind," 152 ATL. MONTHLY 85 (1933); Fuller, "Williston on Contracts," 18 N. CAR. L. REV. 1 (1939).
2. L. FULLER, THE LAW IN QUEST OF ITSELF (1940); Fuller, "Reason and Fiat in Case Law," 59 HARV. L. REV. 376 (1946).
3. Bingham, "My Philosophy of Law," in MY PHILOSOPHY OF LAW: CREDOS OF SIXTEEN AMERICAN SCHOLARS 13 (Rosenthal Foundation ed. 1941).
4. FULLER, QUEST 79.
5. McDougal, "Fuller v. the American Legal Realists: An Intervention," 50 YALE L. J. 832 (1941).
6. PLATO, MINOS 403, 407 (12 Loeb Classical Lib. 1927).

7. L. FULLER, THE PROBLEMS OF JURISPRUDENCE Chap. 6 (temp. ed. 1949); Fuller, "American Legal Philosophy at Mid-Century," 6 J. LEG. ED. 457 (1954).

8. "The Forms and Limits of Adjudication," 92 HARV. L. REV. 353 (1978).

9. "Positivism and Fidelity to Law—A Reply to Professor Hart," 71 HARV. L. REV. 630 (1958); L. FULLER, THE MORALITY OF LAW (rev. ed. 1969).

10. FULLER, MORALITY 99–101.

11. L. FULLER, THE PRINCIPLES OF SOCIAL ORDER 47 (K. Winston ed. 1981).

12. For an inventory of the problems that await further study, see R. SUMMERS, INSTRUMENTALISM AND AMERICAN LEGAL THEORY 278–80 (1982).

13. R. Summers, "Lon L. Fuller's Jurisprudence and the Possibility It Was Much Influenced by G. W. F. Hegel," 10 CORNELL L. FOR. 9 (1983).

14. FULLER, QUEST 2.

15. FULLER, PRINCIPLES 236.

16. Fuller, "Fidelity to Law" 631.

17. Dworkin, "Judicial Discretion," 60 J. PHIL. 624, 638 (1963).

18. Fuller, Book Review, 87 U. PA. L. REV. 626 (1939).

19. H. L. A. Hart, "Positivism and the Separation of Law and Morals," 71 HARV. L. REV. 606–15 (1958); Fuller, "Fidelity to Law" 661–62.

20. Llewellyn, "A Realistic Jurisprudence—The Next Step," 30 COLUM. L. REV. 431 (1930); Llewellyn, "Legal Tradition and Social Science Method—A Realist's Critique," in ESSAYS ON RESEARCH IN THE SOCIAL SCIENCES 94–108 (Brookings Institution ed. 1931).

Index